Reluctant Intimacies

RELUCTANT INTIMACIES
Japanese Eldercare in Indonesian Hands

By Beata Świtek

berghahn
NEW YORK · OXFORD
www.berghahnbooks.com

Published by
Berghahn Books
www.berghahnbooks.com

© 2016 Beata Świtek

Library of Congress Cataloging-in-Publication Data
A C.I.P. cataloging record is available from the Library of Congress

British Library Cataloguing in Publication Data
A catalogue record for this book is available from the British Library

ISBN 978-1-78533-269-2 (hardback)
ISBN 978-1-78533-270-8 (ebook)

Dla Rodziców

For My Parents

 # Contents

List of Illustrations

Figures

Acknowledgements

As in any ethnographic piece of research the centrality of those whose lives and experiences became the basis for the researcher's analysis is a testimony to their indispensability for the project. They are all the more important if they choose to welcome and support the researcher who out of individual professional interest probes into their most private affairs, asks to live with them, and shadows their steps. My first and foremost words of gratitude are therefore directed towards those who were my informants and friends in Japan. These were, of course, the young Indonesian workers who so readily became my hosts and teachers and put up with my presence, sometimes around the clock, in their lives. Their hospitality, humour and patience made this project possible.

A thank-you goes also to the Japanese members of staff, who had far less say in whether they wanted me around or not, but who also showed much goodwill and shared their views with me. The residents of the care homes, as well, often surprised at my presence and confused as to what the purpose of my hanging around might be, did not choose to be a part of my investigations. It is therefore the more appreciated that, on the whole, they showed so much support for me and were willing to share personal stories and jokes with me. Their company was a soothing element in the often-daunting task of research in a care home. It would have been impossible for me to even have met the Japanese staff and the residents if it were not for the receptiveness of the employers and the managers in the institutions I visited. I appreciate the leap of faith they made in allowing a stranger like me to wander around among the residents for whose health and well-being they were responsible. Their interest in my research, their willingness to share their concerns and opinions with me, and the time they put into organising my visits are all deeply appreciated. Although I do not use the real names of my Indonesian informants, the Japanese members of staff, the residents, or the employers, I am particularly grateful to the individuals who incognito appear on the pages of this book. It was the conversations and the experiences we shared that not only provided the most valuable insights but also made conducting this research enjoyable. It is a shame that not all the stories we shared could make it to the pages of this book.

I also received crucial support from a range of individuals from outside the accepting institutions. At the beginning of my research journey, Professor Glenda Roberts from Waseda University agreed to be my local supervisor in Japan, and it was also she who, at her own initiative, triggered the network of personal relationships that ultimately opened a way for me to meet my future informants. Professor Roberts's thoughtful and encouraging replies to the informal reports on my progress offered a springboard to continue or to change a line of inquiry when sometimes I found myself at a crossroads. I am grateful for her continuous support and help, which extended beyond the field stage of this research. When I first met my Indonesian informants-to-be at a training centre where they were studying the Japanese language, I wrote in my research diary that it finally felt like I was inside an ethnographic situation. This experience was possible thanks to the staff members at the training centre who did more than just let me stay in one of the centre's rooms. They actively introduced me to the workings of the centre and to the activities they organised for their Indonesian students.

As the research progressed, I experienced friendship and disinterested support from an ever-expanding number of people: the reporter who introduced me to one of the Indonesian embassy employers, the Japanese language teachers who let me participate in their classes, the employee at the Japan International Corporation of Welfare Services (JICWELS) who repeatedly welcomed me in his office and who went out of his way to organise my access to the Indonesian workers arriving in Japan in 2009, a year after my main informants' arrival, and many others. Among them was Professor Matsuno Akihisa who introduced me to one of the support groups and invited me to join him during a visit to the University of Indonesia, where we discussed the issues affecting Indonesian migration to Japan. The Indonesian Embassy employer, who preferred to remain unnamed, showed a great deal of human warmth and personal interest in my project. It was he who made my trip to Indonesia in 2009 worthwhile by not only arranging formal and informal introductions to secure my access to people within the Indonesian administrative apparatus, but also looking into accommodation for my husband and me during our journey. The list of contacts and more practical information he provided proved invaluable. Similarly, I am indebted to the family who hosted my husband and me during our time in Bandung and who readily included us in the festivities marking the end of the fasting month of Ramadan. Back in Japan, the members of the support organisation that appears in the book anonymously consistently treated me as a full member and included me in their debates and the events they organised. It is impossible to account for everyone whose help and support I received during research, but nevertheless, even if they are not mentioned here, I am equally grateful for their help.

Behind each individual there are always a number of others who in more or less direct ways affect the individual's actions. In the context of doctoral research on which this book is based, these are of course the student's supervisors. Dr Ruth Mandel and Dr Allen Abramson have offered their comments on what admittedly was never complete enough to comment on. I greatly appreciate their time invested in my work and me, and their commitment to turn me into an anthropologist. Perhaps less obviously, Professor Alfred Majewicz from the University of Poznań and Professor Charles Husband from Bradford University have also made my research project possible through their support and encouragement when I sought to enter a doctoral course, and played a crucial role in my introduction to the British educational system, where I settled for nearly a decade. My examiners, Dr Ratna Saptari and Professor Roger Goodman, offered invaluable critical commentaries on the original text this book builds on and gave me the confidence to publish it. Similarly, the two anonymous reviewers who commented on the first draft, as well as Professor Gabriele Vogt who offered her opinion on my earlier writing, have all supported my work.

I also would not have been able to conduct this research if it were not for my Indonesian teachers in London and in Yogyakarta. In particular, Lanny (whose name I use as a pseudonym in the book) has become more than a teacher, but a friend as well, who taught me a lot about the realities of life in Indonesia. Similarly, my Japanese friends from years ago played a crucial part in my acquisition of the Japanese language, but they also made me want to return to Japan and then welcomed me back. My particular thanks are owed to Hirokazu and Tomoya who acted as my psychological valve in Tokyo, and to Matsu, my linguistic advisor and a critic, and his family who hosted me when I was travelling to the more distant research sites. I also appreciate the patience of my family who have been waiting with their fingers crossed for me to stop being a student and then for this book to finally appear. I thank my father in particular, who after years of dealing with PhD students as a supervisor and examiner was perhaps even too relaxed about his own daughter taking her time to write the thesis that became the basis for this book, and later offered his time and skill to help to produce it.

The venture called doctoral studies would not have been possible without the generous funding I received from two sources. In the first instance I became a Bonnart Trust (formerly known as The Frederick Bonnart-Braunthal Trust) scholar, a funded position that made my studies at University College London possible. Secondly, The Japan Foundation provided resources for me to conduct the field research on which this book is based. Without this financial support neither my studies nor this work would have been possible.

Finally, the person on whom the production of this research must have taken the greatest toll is my husband. From making it financially possible for me to even consider entering a doctoral course with all the savings he had at the time, through accompanying me to Indonesia and Japan at the expense of his own career and social life, committing hours to correcting my English, and dealing with the ups and downs that come in the process of book production, to making sure that I had something to eat, his support has been fundamental. For all this and more, thank you.

Note on Language

In the text I indicate words and phrases translated into English by a subsequent qualification 'Jpn.' or 'Ind.', and the original in parentheses, when the translation is being used as a part of a sentence. When the original is used instead, the translation is provided in parentheses, with 'Jpn.' or 'Ind.' to indicate the language. I omit these qualifying elements when the original language is evident from the context.

All Japanese words are romanised according to the modified Hepburn system. Long vowels are indicated with macrons, apart from in words commonly used in English – for example, geographical names such as Tokyo. Japanese names are presented according to the standard ordering in Japan, with the surname followed by the given name. The names of the main informants are pseudonyms. I only use real names in referring to people whose opinions as presented here have been made public elsewhere by the individuals in question.

I use the terms 'foreigner', 'migrant' and 'immigrant' fairly liberally and sometimes interchangeably. To an extent, this reflects the meaning conflation of the terms used in Japan. On the other hand, the ubiquity of the two latter terms in this book is not reflective of the popular expressions used in Japan, where representation of Japan as a 'country of immigration' is still nascent.

All translations in the text are mine. Any errors, either factual or linguistic, are solely my responsibility.

List of Abbreviations

AHP	Asia Human Power Networks
ASEAN	Association of Southeast Asian Nations
COMPAS	Centre on Migration, Policy and Society
EPA	Economic Partnership Agreement
FTA	Free Trade Agreement
JICWELS	Japan International Corporation of Welfare Services
JITCO	Japan International Training and Cooperation Organisation
LTCI	Long-Term Care Insurance
METI	Ministry of Economy, Trade and Industry
MHLW	Ministry of Health, Labour and Welfare
MoFA	Ministry of Foreign Affairs
MoJ	Ministry of Justice
NHK	Japan Broadcasting Corporation
STIKes	Sekolah Tinggi Ilmu Kesehatan

Map 1: Distribution of Indonesian caregiver candidates who arrived in Japan in 2008. Cartography by Jerzy Świtek.

Map 2: Distribution of Indonesian caregiver and nurse candidates who arrived in Japan in 2008. Cartography by Jerzy Świtek.

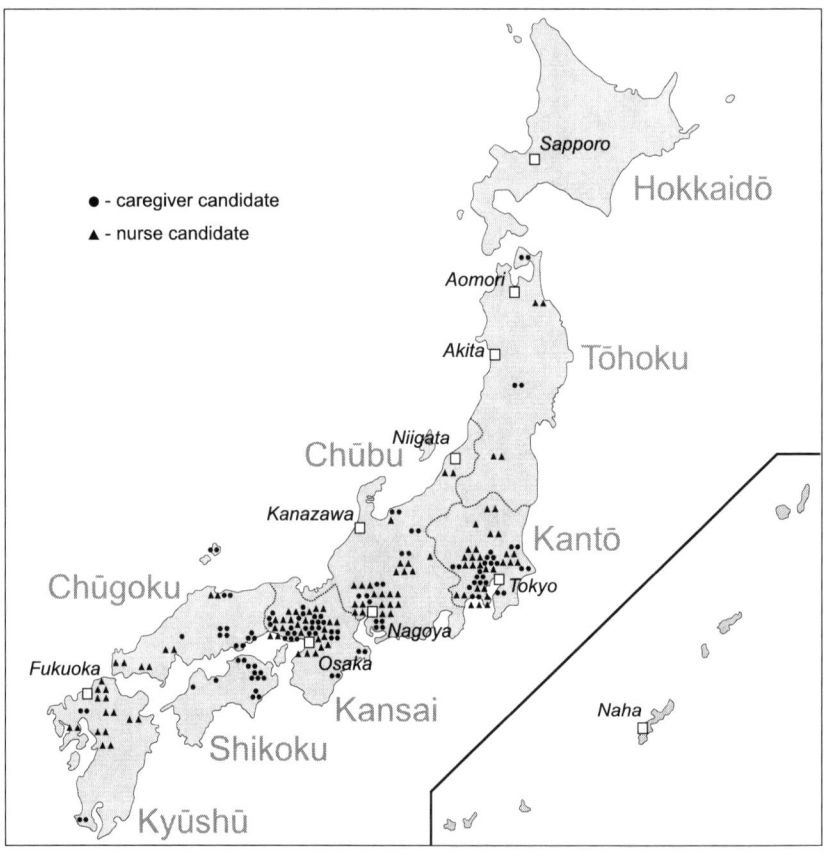

Introduction

In the summer of 2009, on a hot August night that promised to offer a spectacle of shooting stars, Jasir and I were standing on a top-floor terrace of an external staircase in the building where Jasir shared a flat with two other young Indonesian men. We were looking up at the dark sky over this town in rural Japan in hope of spotting the fleeting line of light made visible to us by a dying meteor. As the display was markedly scant we filled the time talking about Jasir's work.

Twenty-three years old at the time, Jasir had arrived in Japan almost exactly a year earlier, in August 2008, as one of the 208 Indonesians who were selected to train in Japan under an Economic Partnership Agreement (EPA) signed between Indonesia and Japan. Half of this group were nurse candidates, and half were caregiver candidates (*kōhosha*; Jpn.) in a total of ninety-nine institutions spread across the country (Fukushi Shinbun 2008). On paper at least, the candidates were able to stay and work in Japan indefinitely as long as they passed a relevant Japanese national examination within a timeframe set under the agreement for each profession. Although qualified in Indonesia as a nurse, Jasir was now a caregiver candidate (*kaigofukushishi kōhosha*; Jpn.) because he lacked the minimum two years of practical experience required under the EPA scheme as a condition to train in Japan as a nurse. Alongside two other Indonesian men, he was now working in a facility offering residential and day care services to elderly Japanese.

A year into his stay in Japan, Jasir had formed an opinion on the experience. *Manusia mau rasa berarti* (Ind.), a human being wants to feel that he means something, and not *seperti tidak dibutuh* (Ind.), as if he was unneeded.[1] Jasir was referring to his disillusion with the situation at the eldercare institution where he worked. He recalled an instance when he had noticed an elderly woman fall out of her bed and experience faecal incontinence just as he was changing bedding in the room she shared with two other residents. Jasir knew that he was not allowed to help the woman autonomously. Instead, he had to summon other members of staff, who had to abandon whatever task they were involved in and rush to lift the woman off the floor and clean her up. Jasir's role was limited to passive observation even though he felt perfectly capable of dealing with the situation, particularly given his nursing background. Such a manner of dealing with emergencies (and indeed most other tasks involving direct contact with or action on the bodies of the elderly) made Jasir feel irrelevant. To his mind, these feelings were not what a human being should be experiencing.

Another evening, a few months into his employment, when discussing the day's events while cycling through the rice fields on the way home, Amir told me about the frustration over his inability to acquire an independent standing at work. He, too, had arrived in Japan in 2008 and was now working as a caregiver candidate at the same rural eldercare institution as Jasir, but on a different ward. At the age of twenty-five, and qualified as a nurse in Indonesia, Amir found himself on a plane to Japan only a few days after his own wedding. As a married man he was now hoping that his wife would become pregnant when he goes to visit her in Indonesia; and by working in Japan he felt he was attending to his family's material future. A hopeful father and the family's breadwinner in Indonesia, in Japan Amir resented being treated as a child (*seperti anak anak*; Ind.). Confined to tasks such as setting up the tables for meals, preparing elderly residents' toothbrushes for easy use after they had finished eating, wiping the tables, changing bedding, and so on, Amir was not allowed to perform any duties involving handling of the elderly. Moreover, apart from having no freedom to act independently at work, he was not even allowed to leave the town without first notifying somebody from the employing institution about the destination and the anticipated return time. Amir saw these limitations as unjust and based on prejudiced perceptions of his practical and mental capabilities, which seemed to be simply 'unreliable, undependable, not to be trusted' (*tidak dipercaya*; Ind.). He explained that he had come to Japan aware of the fact that he would not be working in his learnt profession (i.e. as a nurse), and did not expect, or plan for that matter, a fast-track or bright career in Japan's eldercare sector. He did, however, expect to be treated on equal terms with the other employees, and was hoping for recognition as a reasoning adult, or as 'an adult person who can think for themselves, a person who has their own brain/with a brain of their own' (*orang dewasa yang bisa berpikir diri sendiri*, [*orang yang*] *punya otak sendiri*; Ind.).

I met Jasir and Amir for the first time on 4 January 2009 during a residential language course they were undertaking after arrival in Japan under the EPA scheme. Along with another fifty-four caregiver candidates assigned to the same training centre, Jasir and Amir spent six months there attending classes devoted primarily to language acquisition, but also focused on the introduction to the eldercare system in Japan. Once the training was over, candidates were scattered across Japan to work and train towards obtaining a Japanese caregiver qualification. The EPA that brought the Indonesians to Japan was primarily an economic treaty concerned with regulation of tariffs. However, it also opened an unprecedented possibility for non-Japanese workers to find employment and remain in Japan permanently. Moreover, for the first time in Japan's history it stipulated that a government-led programme should bring workers into eldercare provision from outside of the country's national borders. Although almost negligible in numbers (208 people in 2008), the arrival of the Indonesian workers became a topic very widely publicised by the Japanese media. Often discussed in light of the progressing ageing of Japanese society, the Indonesians' arrival has become a pivot for the Japanese reckoning with the national imagination that has been reluctant to open up the country to outside influences, but is now forced to do so due to the ongoing demographic changes.

Ideas behind the Research

In this book I concentrate on the early period of the EPA Indonesians' presence in Japan when they were still discovering the nature of the work they had signed up to perform, and when they only began to negotiate their relationship within the workspaces and beyond. The arrival of this new group in a sector that at the time had not seen many foreign workers in Japan was a promising field of investigation into the formation of mutual imaginations and into the negotiation of newly forming relations. Before conducting the research described in this book, my main question was whether it mattered that the Indonesian workers would be providing direct, that is bodily, care to the Japanese elderly. Would their immediate and unalienable positioning in direct proximity to the Japanese bodies influence the mutual imagining and the experiences of the Indonesians and the Japanese? Would the physically intimate nature of their work matter, and if so, how? Also, would it have any bearing on their mutual perceptions and experiences that the arrival of the Indonesian workers was organised and strictly controlled by the Japanese government in cooperation with the accepting institutions? After two months in Japan a further question proved impossible to ignore: why was it that the Indonesians, despite almost negligible numbers, received such extensive and, more importantly, positive media attention? Was it to do with the kind of work they came to perform in Japan? If so, why would it matter? Why, I also started asking after a few months, were the Indonesians receiving rather exceptional treatment from their employers? Was it again about the nature of their work in Japan, or did it have something to do with the way the acceptance programme was organised, or both? Thinking through these questions, I was looking at a broader issue of which the EPA acceptance was but one incarnation. I was looking at how Japan's demographic shifts engendered small-scale sites of 'multicultural coexistence' within the accepting institutions, which, although unique, could not be understood without reference to a broader system of values, beliefs and practices. The reactions, relationships, experiences and discourses represented the anxieties of coming to terms with the abrupt change of the social landscape of the institutions, and the Japanese society by extension, caused by the demographic processes and their global political, social and economic embeddedness.

Through the prism of the Indonesian eldercare workers' experiences in Japan, this book explores the day-to-day practices, national imaginations and public discourses to track their potential for constructing, recognising and denying the viability of certain kinds of person. The ability to imagine oneself, another individual or a group as a viable option for a partner at work, a neighbour, or in this particular instance, a care provider, care receiver or a member of the same society, is at the basis of a migratory encounter. It shapes the experiences of the migrants and the host society alike. Using ethnographic descriptions of the Indonesian workers' lives at work and beyond in Japan, as well as already existing materials on Japanese constructions of foreignness, I rewrite the mechanisms of constructing national imaginations in the language of intimacy to trace the connections between the ideas of the national, interpersonal and bodily intimacies. The choice of care provision as the setting for observation of national imaginations rendered making this connection unavoidable. Therefore, the book revolves around the idea of 'intimate imagination', a cluster of processes by which the intimate spheres inform the way we position (imagine) ourselves in relation to others, and by which the imagination defines and redefines the reach of the intimate on a personal and cultural (national) level, and acknowledges the viability of some people as friends, colleagues, employees, co-residents or co-nationals while denying it to others. The exercise in thinking about migration in terms of negotiations based on intimate imagination aims to suggest that the notion of intimacy can be a useful operating tool in understanding resultant interactions. The notion's composite nature allows for more flexibility than such ideas as otherness or difference. In fact, intimacy allows us to foreground what experiencing the other and its differences is actually about. The notion of intimacy, which in this book is expanded to emerge beyond the romantic or eroticised relationships, although not always explicitly mentioned by my informants, appeared as a composite idea encompassing the themes, which regularly made their way into our conversations, which marked their presence in the media coverage of the EPA acceptance, and which appeared in the relationships between the Indonesian workers and those Japanese with whom they met directly. Admittedly, some of the themes were direct opposites of what intimacy would imply. However, I took them to point towards intimacy by negating it, such as with the case of discomfort or distrust, which I describe in Chapter 2. As a term that is relatively easy to define, yet not so rigid as to disallow its transplantation between contexts and scales of observation, I found intimacy to be a handy tool in bringing together data that at first glance had little to do with each other. In the process, I also highlight the need to acknowledge and track (rather than deconstruct) the processes of stereotypisation and their role in shaping the migratory experience understood as encompassing both those who arrived and those who 'were arrived to' as a result of a migratory movement. The essentialising stereotypical imaginations were recounted and sometimes produced anew to define the reach of the intimate imagination, allowing it to construct incarnations of viable friends, co-workers or co-citizens. Finally, the Indonesian experiences in Japan have also something to tell us about the way the Japanese nation, and the individuals that form it, imagine themselves in light of the ongoing demographic transformations.

Japan-Indonesia Partnership Agreement (EPA) Background

At the outset, it is important to situate the acceptance of Indonesian caregiver candidates within the wider context of international interdependencies which lay behind their arrival in Japan in 2008. This will enable the drawing of connections between the experiences of the Indonesians in Japan and the broader processes affecting Indonesia and Japan alike. Equally, such contextualisation makes it possible to see how the experiences were structured by the political–economic mechanisms beyond the immediate lives of the workers and beyond the operations of the accepting sites. A brief look at the genealogy of the programme that brought the Indonesian eldercare workers to Japan shows why certain discourses about Japan's ideas of nationhood, which are discussed in later parts of this volume, emerged in response to this particular instance of labour migration.

For Japan, the bilateral EPA with Indonesia that brought Amir and Jasir to Japan was part of a bid to maintain the country's position as one of the world's leading economies, a matter of economic necessity. This, at least, was the case according to such political stakeholders as the Japanese Ministry of Foreign Affairs (MoFA), the Japanese Ministry of Economy, Trade and Industry (METI), and the Keidanren, the Japan Business Federation. Finalising the agreement with Indonesia meant securing access to Indonesia's ample deposits of natural resources and attending to Japan's position within the Asian trade market, particularly vis-à-vis the growing competition from the United States, South Korea and China. A similar motivation was behind most other EPAs concluded by the Japanese government, which through such deals counteracted Japan's decreasing share in international trade as Japanese goods were losing to the more preferentially tariffed products of other countries that had already entered into multiple bilateral relations. Not surprisingly, then, while conducting talks with Indonesia, Japanese representatives were almost simultaneously engaged in group negotiations with the Association of Southeast Asian Nations (ASEAN), as well as in bilateral talks with the Philippines, Thailand and Vietnam. According to the information provided by the Japanese MoFA, by March 2011 Japan had signed fifteen EPA/FTAs,[2] primarily with South East and East Asian countries, but also with Mexico, Chile, India and Switzerland.[3]

The reduction or complete abandonment of tariffs on goods exported to the partner country, opening new and wider venues for Japanese investment in Indonesia, and the clauses on 'capacity building' (albeit not unconditional) in Indonesia, to name just a few areas covered, were expected to boost bilateral trade, benefiting the economies of both countries. However, from the perspective of Indonesian commentators, the potential economic benefits of the agreement for their country were more debatable. The agreement opened the door for Japanese investors to locate their resources in Indonesia, but by no means obliged them to select Indonesia as the destination of choice for their investment. Indonesian commentators pointed to the need for Indonesia to lower its costs and simplify its regulations before the potential of Japanese and other foreign investment could be realised and be of sizable benefit to the Indonesian economy.[4] 'Japan got to expand their production in Indonesia for some bananas', commented an employee at the Indonesian embassy in Tokyo during our first meeting in early 2009. This was a reference to the free access to raw materials granted to the Japanese firms operating in Indonesia under the EPA on the one hand, and to the relaxation of the import tariff on Indonesian tropical fruit on the other. The employee felt that the profitability of the agreement's provisions for the two countries was of completely different, incomparable scales, where Japanese companies would benefit greatly, while, for example, Indonesian fruit exporters would still be unable to export significant amounts, not least due to powerful non-economic barriers posed by the internal Japanese market, such as customer choice and stringent quality control regulations.[5] This relative positioning was presented as having resulted in the EPA's clause on the acceptance of Indonesian nurse and caregiver candidates into Japan.

Although primarily concerned with the revision of trade and tariffs regulations, Japan agreed to accept a thousand nurses and caregiver trainees (officially known as 'candidates') within two years of the date of implementation of the EPA. The same provision was earlier included in a similar treaty between the Philippines and Japan, but due to delays in ratifying the agreement by the Philippine senate, it was from Indonesia that the first-ever group of foreign workers to be employed in the care and health sector – and under a government-led scheme at that – arrived in Japan in August 2008.[6] The Philippine government was the first to demand that a number of its workers, nurses and care workers be allowed to take up employment in Japan. The negotiations were taking place at the time when a United Nations report on trafficking in people criticised the Japanese government for not taking sufficient steps to curb the practice in their country. At the time, the majority of trafficked victims were brought to Japan on 'entertainer' visas from the Philippines. Although not all Filipina women who came to Japan as entertainers fell victim to human traffickers, the stricter regime for receiving a visa resulted in a significant decline in the number of Filipina women finding work in Japan. Through the EPA scheme, the Philippine government established a new route for their nationals to seek employment in Japan. Once the negotiations had been concluded, however, the ratification of the Japan–Philippines EPA had to be postponed, as the Philippine Senate was divided over the issue. The opposition to the agreement in the Philippines stemmed from the popular perception that under its provisions the Japanese side acquired undue privileges, such as being able to dispose of nuclear waste in Philippine territory. As a result of these Philippine internal debates, it was not until 2009 that the agreement was finalised. In the meantime, the Indonesian nego-tiators, knowing of the provision contained in the Japan–Philippines EPA, also requested that Japan accept its nurses and carers.

The decision to grant the request to accept foreign workers under the EPA was not made unanimously by the Japanese side. In line with the arguments coming from the nurses' and caregivers' professional associations, the Ministry of Health, Labour and Welfare (MHLW) was adamant in its position that there were enough native Japanese work-ers to fill the existing labour shortages, and that the priority should be placed on improving working conditions to attract Japanese employ-ees rather than importing people from abroad. Therefore, the EPA ac-ceptance was not to be a means of addressing the internal problems of the Japanese labour market but rather a skill-transfer scheme. On the other hand, both the METI and the MoFA also engaged in the ne-gotiations on the EPA, as long-standing proponents of an opening of the Japanese labour market to people from a wider range of occupa-tions were in favour of the proposed acceptance. Gabriele Vogt (2006: 11) observed that the MoFA saw EPAs such as the one signed with Indonesia as a means to avoid the lengthy legal proceedings required for an introduction of new immigration policies. Instead, by signing bilateral agreements with selected states, the MoFA de facto shaped these policies by removing them from under the direct jurisdiction of the Ministry of Justice (MoJ), an authority regulating immigration to Japan. Seemingly, as a result of a compromise in the interdepartmen-tal talks, and perhaps as a relatively minor concession in an already profitable deal for Japan, the conditions of the EPA acceptance were settled. The Indonesian candidates themselves suggested that, given the incongruities of the system, which I highlight later on in this book, there was an ulterior, hidden motive (*sesuatu di belakang*; Ind.) for their being sent to Japan under the EPA. The sense of being a trade off in an economic deal was amplified by the experiences such as those talked about by Amir and Jasir. What was the point (*tujuan apa*; Ind.) of their presence in the eldercare homes, asked Amir, if they were to be per-ceived as unviable members of staff, unrecognised as individuals able to contribute knowledge or personal qualities to the construction of the care homes as working and living spaces? Symbolically, this lack of recognition was inscribed in the conditions of the acceptance that stipulated that the Indonesian candidates would not be included in the institutional employee count. Their work was thus rendered invis-ible in official duty rotas that might have contained the Indonesians' names, but still had to include enough Japanese employees to meet the legally required ratio of staff to cared-for residents, as if the Indonesian workers were in fact not there at all. Thus, the candidates themselves believed that they were simply used to buy a good deal for Japan in an agreement that was primarily aimed at economic co-operation. The divergent stances on the issue of accepting Indonesian workers within the Japanese central administration were later reflected in the conditions of the acceptance, which, in turn, triggered debates over Japan's overall position on welcoming foreign workers.

Objectives of the Accepting Eldercare Institutions

In contrast to the officially promoted objective of the EPA acceptance scheme, the majority of the accepting eldercare homes decided to join the programme in order to 'examine [the possibility of hiring foreigners] as a means to tackle future labour shortage' in the sector.[7] This was according to a questionnaire survey conducted in autumn 2009 by one of the support groups that emerged in response to the acceptance. A similar picture emerged from an analogous investigation carried out by the MHLW in March 2010. Here, out of thirty-seven respondents, who incorporated care home as well as hospital representatives, thirty-three said they treated the EPA acceptance as a test case for future acceptance of foreign workers, thirty saw it as an opportunity for 'international contribution' (*kokusai kōken*; Jpn.), and twenty-nine hoped that the EPA workers would revitalise the workplace (MHLW 2010). Thus, contrary to the official discourse in line with the argumentation of the Japanese MHLW, the accepting eldercare homes were treating the scheme as a way to supplement the insufficient number of workers available to work in eldercare within the internal Japanese labour market. This was particularly so in light of Japan's changing demographics whereby one of the main considerations was an ever higher number of older people in need of care expected to be supported by an ever lower number of people in the active workforce. The proportion of working-age people to non-working elderly was expected to drop significantly. While in 2010, there were, on average, two workers supporting one elderly person, by 2060 this ratio was predicted to drop to 1.3 or even 1.0 (IPSS 2012). Such demographic trends were expected to aggravate not only the domestic eldercare labour market, which has already been wrought by shortages and high turnover of personnel (often explained as an outcome of unsatisfactory working conditions in terms of pay and the physical strenuousness of providing eldercare), but also affect the wider economy of the country, which would have to operate on a diminished tax base. Frequent discussions in the main mass media saw reporters in their thirties ponder about just how large contributions in taxes they would have to make in the future, who would look after them and who would pay for their future care given the low birth rates and the apparent unwillingness of many Japanese to engage in care work. The already long waiting lists for admission to an eldercare institution offered an indication of the difficulties the country might face in securing an adequate eldercare provision system based on sufficient labour force within its own borders in the coming decades. In joining the EPA scheme in order to stave off the current or expected shortage of people to work, the eldercare institutions were also foreseeing the time when a foreign care worker would be a viable option, and one coming with a degree of necessity as a means to tackle Japanese labour shortages. Not unlike in other industrialised nations, the changing demographics combined with the increasing participation of women in the labour market and a decrease in the incidence of multigenerational households has complicated the arrangements needed to' support family members in their old age. Across the globe, eldercare has come to be more commonly outsourced to non-family members, with hiring a domestic worker being one solution. Increasingly, it has also become an accepted, albeit not unproblematic, practice to place the elderly (or to choose to be placed in one's old age) in an external facility dedicated to providing round-the-clock professional care and support. In Japan in 2009, the hiring of a live-in person to look after the elderly's needs had not yet taken root. Instead, it was the external care facilities that were gaining popularity as a viable option to ensure adequate eldercare. It was to these kinds of institution, laden with the ideal of familial eldercare, that the Indonesian workers first arrived.

Ambivalent Goals of the EPA Acceptance

While granting the requests of the partner governments to accept their workers and responding to the Japanese MoFA's and METI's influences, the EPA programme contained several important restrictions. Firstly, the accepted foreigners were not to be considered workers but trainees, or literally candidates, until they passed the Japanese national examination. This examination was required to be taken in Japanese in the candidates' respective target professions within a specified period of time: three years for the nurse candidates, and four years for the caregiver candidates. In the event of failure, they were required to leave Japan. Secondly, the candidates were to be remunerated according to the standards applied to Japanese nationals performing the same tasks, but as trainees were not to be counted in the minimum staff to resident ratio of 1:3 until they obtained the Japanese qualifications.[8] Also, until they became certified caregivers or nurses, they were not allowed to change employers, although they could report any problems to a helpline established by the Japan International Corporation of Welfare Services (JICWELS) overseeing the EPA acceptance on behalf of the Japanese MHLW. Importantly, however, if the candidates passed the Japanese national examination, they were to be able to remain and work in Japan indefinitely.

This latter provision was without precedent in Japan in that it opened a path for a group of foreign workers to permanent residence in Japan. On the other hand, however, the national examination, which required a high degree of literacy in Sino-Japanese characters, was widely perceived as a particularly 'high hurdle' (*hādoru ga takai*; Jpn.), practically precluding the Indonesians from ever obtaining the right to work and remain in Japan. Passing the examination required knowledge covering not only medical and practical areas, but Japan-specific laws and regulations as well. Combined with the lack of a structured, uniform language and professional training programme, it was widely believed that the majority of the candidates would fail the exam and would have to return to Indonesia. These predictions were based on the pass rate among Japanese, which over the years had oscillated around 50 per cent, and the zero pass rate of Indonesians in a mock examination. If the candidates were to fail the examination, not only would the accepting institutions be unsuccessful in securing additional members of staff, but it would also mean a lost financial investment. However, according to some institutions, the certainty of having someone remaining in employment for the period of four years was already a bonus and worth the investment in light of the high turnover rates of the Japanese staff.

Such terms of acceptance of foreign nurses and care workers, which on the one hand offered a possibility of settling in Japan and on the other made it nearly impossible to use this path, sent an ambivalent message about the official intentions of the acceptance. This apparent ambivalence of the programme was picked up by various observers and so, given the unprecedented concessions granted the EPA workers, the acceptance came to represent Japan's stance on accepting foreign workers, and foreigners in general. It was posed to represent the unwillingness of the Japanese government to deal with this politically delicate but increasingly pressing issue and, as I will show in the penultimate chapter of this book, was consequently connected to the ideas of Japanese nationhood.

Contemporary Migration and National Imagination

Thinking about contemporary migration is almost impossible without linking it to the idea of a nation or nation-state. One of the primary distinctions made when talking about migration is that between international and internal – that is, movements within nation-state borders. In fact, if left unqualified, migration will likely be assumed to be international. It is at this level of nation (or nation-state) that migration becomes a contentious issue that flares up into discourses on security, rights and obligations, and cultural differences. It is also almost impossible to think about migration without reference to culture. Not without reason, migrant communities have been at the centre of discussions about assimilation, integration, and multiculturalism, which more often than not debate the (in)congruities between the migrants' and the accepting nations' cultures. This is because contemporary nations are still imagined as fairly bounded entities that at one level or another share in what is imagined to be a fairly homogeneous culture. It is in reference to this culture that many a difference is represented, although what popularly counts as national culture varies. I am using the term 'culture' here as a kind of representative for the imagined shared ideas and ideals that are meant to guide actions and interactions of co-nationals in similar ways. I will return to discuss this issue in more detail later in the book. Various processes of reification of these imaginations distinguish between who is seen as culturally 'ours' and 'theirs', as typically national or alien. These broad, rigid but at the same time mouldable and often elusive generalisations and stereotypical categorisations come with certain assumptions about individuals. People are expected to act in certain ways and not know certain things if they have or belong to a different culture. The identification of nations with given cultures suggests a degree of incongruity between the national 'us' and 'them'. In Japan, too, there exist powerful ideas distinguishing Japanese from non-Japanese.

The Japanese Nationality Law (Art. 2–5)[9] states that a person is of Japanese nationality if born to parents of whom at least one was a Japanese national at the time of the child's birth. Provided that one fulfils certain conditions of residency and 'upright conduct', it is also possible to become a 'naturalized' Japanese national. Such civic inclusion in a nation does not, however, necessarily convey the recognition of shared sociality or cultural engagement. Representation of national belonging in terms of descent, as codified in the Japanese Nationality Law, suggests the importance of the idiom of blood in establishing one's Japaneseness. The validity of relatedness through blood and its causative role in determining an individual's cultural or social familiarity is contained in the idea of race, which has been shown to converge with notions of ethnicity, culture and nation in Japan (Yoshino 1992; Weiner 1997; Lie 2001: 130–36; see also Oguma 2002). The history of the representation and social and legal position of people of Japanese descent, the *Nikkeijin*, the permanent residents of predominantly Korean and Chinese origins and children of returnees or of 'mixed' background in Japan, illustrates how such convergence works to construct individuals and groups as either similar and therefore sharing in cultural commonalities, or different and unfamiliar. The arrival of the EPA Indonesians in Japan, their experiences and representations described in this book, need to be seen against the background of such historically sanctioned Japanese national imaginations.

Descent without Culture

In 1990 the Japanese government amended the Immigration Control and Refugee Recognition Act, commonly known as the Immigration Act, with the intention of opening the Japanese labour market to a selected group of foreign workers. The Japanese economic boom of the late 1980s had created a surplus of work opportunities, which were not being filled by the native workers. Prior to 1990, foreign workers, some of them undocumented, were arriving from South Asian countries – such as Pakistan and Iran (with both of which Japan had signed a visa exemption agreement) and Bangladesh – and from countries closer to Japan, such as China, Taiwan and Thailand. After the visa agreement with Pakistan had been rescinded and the issuing of visas for nationals of other sending countries had been severely restricted in 1989, the 1990 amendment opened the Japanese door to workers able to replace the halted groups (Linger 2001: 278 after Yamanaka 1996: 76–77). According to the Immigration Act, any person of Japanese descent down to the third generation, *Nikkeijin*, could arrive in Japan and take up employment virtually without any restrictions. The legislation was primarily aimed at the largest population of Japanese living outside of Japan, in Brazil, whose first cohorts arrived there at the beginning of the twentieth century to supply Brazil's plantation labour force.

The effective abolition of labour migration of people not of Japanese descent and their substitution with overseas 'Japanese by birth', the *Nikkeijin*, reflected the preference for consanguineous people. The Sino-Japanese character *kei* in *Nikkeijin*, also used in the compound *kakei*, a lineage, or *kakeizu*, a family tree, conveys the idea of commonality of origin between the Japanese Brazilians and the Japanese from Japan who together come from the same Japanese family – evoked by the *nichi* (*ni*) character of the compound, symbolising Japan. It was expected that thanks to their Japanese origins and therefore presumed similarities, the *Nikkeijin* would easily assimilate into Japanese society. The Japanese essence endowed on the *Nikkeijin* by the blood of their ancestors was to pass on cultural competency as well.

However, much like in the case of Russian German *Aussiedler* who failed to 'integrate' into German society (Mandel 2008: 67–71, 159), the reality of the *Nikkeijin* acceptance did not fulfil expectations either. Even if able to speak the Japanese language, common especially among the first and second generations, or appearing Japanese, they were not perceived as such by the majority of Japanese born and bred in Japan. *Nikkeijin* stood out with their different clothing style, non-Japanese work ethic, different food, and alien forms of entertainment (Tsuda 2003a). Despite the common origins and, often, bodily similarity, they were no longer Japanese; absence from Japan had made them lose their Japaneseness, which was expressed through their comportment.

Nineteen years on since the introduction of the Immigration Act, the ultimate sign that *Nikkeijin* did not become members of the Japanese nation came with the dawn of the global economic crisis in 2008. With more and more factories and companies scaling down or going out of business, a growing number of people were made redundant. A significant proportion of these newly unemployed were the *Nikkeijin*, the majority of whom occupied manual positions in the manufacturing industry. In March 2009 the Japanese MHLW issued a news release concerning the Japanese Brazilians who found themselves out of work. The release presented a scheme under which *Nikkeijin* persons could opt for funding to return to their motherland (*bokoku*; Jpn.), together with their family. The only condition to be eligible for the scheme, apart from being a *Nikkeijin*, was to renounce the right to return to Japan on the basis of the 1990 Immigration Act until the employment situation in Japan had improved. Not only the reference to the *Nikkeijin*'s other country as their 'motherland', a country of origin, but also the suggestion in the text that they might have lost their jobs due to a lack of familiarity with 'our country's' (*wa ga kuni*; Jpn.) labour market (which, given that many of the Japanese Brazilians had lived and worked in Japan for more than ten years, seemed to have little grounds), excluded the *Nikkeijin* from participation not only in the Japanese labour market, but also in the origins which were previously seen as shared, and therefore the implied Japaneseness allowing membership in the ethnically and culturally defined Japanese nation.[10]

A similar losing of Japaneseness by absence from Japan was implied for the children of Japanese expatriates, the so-called *kikokushijo*, who before their return to Japan had taken part of their education outside of the country. Until the 1980s they were considered to be problem children. They were thought to be too Westernised and therefore in need of reintegration into Japanese society. These children would suffer bullying at school, while their progress to higher education was impeded by structural obstacles. The *kikokushijo* were not considered to be full Japanese due to their long-term exposure to a foreign environment in their formative days (Goodman 1990: 58–59).[11] Therefore, one not only needed to be of Japanese descent, but it was also a prerequisite for one to live in Japan, in order to maintain Japaneseness.

Foreign by Descent

The immersion in and spatial proximity to Japanese society that the *Nikkeijin* and *kikokushijo* lacked are characteristic of a large proportion of the nearly four hundred thousand *Zainichi* Korean residents in Japan.[12] After the Second World War, there were some two million Koreans settled in Japan. According to international law, as former colonial subjects they were Japanese nationals at the time. However, when in 1946 Japan was readying itself for general elections they were not given the right to participate. Such a distinction was made possible thanks to a family register in which Japanese subjects were assigned to one of two categories. A family could belong to the *naichi* (inner land) or *gaichi* (outer land, i.e. the Japanese colonies), which was equated with a divide between ethnic and non-ethnic Japanese, respectively (Kang 2003: 3). In the following year an Alien Registration Ordinance imposed on the *gaichi* (i.e. non-ethnic Japanese) a requirement to carry identity cards at all times. Their situation changed even more drastically when, with the implementation of the 1952 San Francisco Peace Treaty ending American occupation, the Japanese authorities declared all former colonial subjects to be aliens. They were not given any official status; nor were they guaranteed re-entry permission if they decided to leave Japan temporarily (Morris-Suzuki 2006). Their de facto stateless status was not resolved until 1965, when

Japan and South Korea signed a treaty regulating relations between the two countries. Under the terms of the agreement, Japan offered the colonial-Koreans the more secure status of 'Treaty Permanent Residents'. It protected them from deportation and allowed leaving and re-entering Japan without fear of not being accepted on their return. However, the terms of the treaty did not apply to those Koreans who identified themselves with North Korea or who chose to define themselves as nationals of Korea as a whole rather that just South Korea (ibid.).[13] From 1955 the *Zainichi* were required to renew their alien registration cards every three years and to submit their fingerprints on each occasion (Chapman 2008: 73–74). This requirement was ultimately abolished in 1993.

The descendants of the disenfranchised former colonial subjects were eventually granted a unique residence category of 'Special Permanent Residents'. This status conveyed on them the right to continuous residence, and economic, social and labour rights, but did not award them full political rights. Relatively recently, some local governments have decided to make efforts towards granting, albeit still limited and of a probationary nature, voting rights in local-level elections to their special permanent residents (Tegtmeyer Pak 2000: 252–53). However, the *Zainichi* still do not have the right to vote in the general elections, they have limited possibilities to achieve professional positions of power, and they continue to face various other, non-systemic forms of discrimination. In the statistical records, unless they naturalise, they remain classified as *gaikokujin*, 'foreigners'.

The Japanese term *gaikokujin* literally means 'a person from (or of) an external country', not of Japan. The compound is formed by a sequence of three Sino-Japanese characters, which in their order of appearance mean 'external, outside', 'country' and 'person'. *Koku* and its Japanese reading *kuni* in wider usage may mean a country, region, province, or home country, which, unless qualified, would usually refer to a place within Japan, or Japan itself. The initial, default or 'normal' meaning is therefore Japan, or Japanese, and that which is not Japanese comes somehow marked by an additional description. *Kuni* can also be used as a reference to the state, or the state administration, the state decision makers. Sometimes the term incorporates all these notions, as in the expression *wa ga kuni*, which should be understood as 'our [Japanese] country' in the broadest sense of the land, the people and the ruling apparatus together forming one entity. What is from or of the outside of such *kuni* – *koku* is therefore excluded from all the spheres the term designates.

Although the special permanent resident status de facto recognised the particularity of the *Zainichi* position in Japan – that is, that they were unlike other foreigners since they were to stay in Japan permanently – they remained aliens of non-Japanese descent. The lack of common origins differentiated them from the Japanese, despite the fact that, as in the majority of cases today, they had been born in Japan, had lived there their whole lives, spoke only Japanese as a native language, knew only Japanese culture, and were in Japan to stay. Sharing in all other qualities, but not Japanese by birth, they confused the categories of belonging to the Japanese nation, and as such, the *Zainichi* needed to be excluded from, or denied, Japaneseness. Already not of Japanese ethnicity (*minzoku*), and excluded from civil participation, the *Zainichi* were therefore denied membership in the political-administrative category of the Japanese nation (*kokumin*) as well. The conflation of the idea of biological descent with that of individual cultural traits excluded the *Zainichi* from the shared recognition of belonging and from the imagined commonality of culturally defined sociality.

Halves and Doubles

Similarly, whether or not a person of Japanese nationality born of parents of whom only one was Japanese is popularly recognised as being Japanese highlights the discursive interconnectedness of culture and descent as well. *Hāfu*, a Japanese pronunciation of the English word 'half', is used in reference to a child of 'mixed' parentage, suggesting that the person is somehow incomplete, only partially Japanese. The usual lack of an attribute qualifying what the other half is leaves that part void of any content, as if suggesting that it does not really matter what it is. What is seemingly the more important statement, one that indicates being only half Japanese, is already made and does not need further qualification. Another expression used to describe children of mixed parentage is *konketsu*, literally meaning mixed blood or mixed breed, indicating that the person is not purely Japanese, again based on the presumption that it is Japanese blood mixed with another, unspecified, kind of blood. Such linguistic silencing of the non-Japanese essences in a person is also apparent in the virtual absence of a Japanese term equivalent to an English-language expression used in such countries as the United Kingdom and the United States, namely 'British/American of such-and-such descent' or simply Japanese American, for example.[14] In Japan, naturalised persons, regardless of where they originally hailed from, are registered as Japanese without any information about their previous national affiliation. Their ethnic or national origins are formally erased, allowing Japan to represent the Japanese nation as being composed only of Japanese (without multiple or ambiguous ethnicities) with the support of statistical data.[15] Jeffry Hester (2008) notes, however, within the Korean circles in Japan, the propositions of a possible 'hyphenated' (2008: 139) identity representing the *Zainichi* as Japanese of Korean origins – that is, *Kankoku-kei Nihonjin* or *Korian-kei Nihonjin* (ibid.: 145–46). Predominantly, however, when the 'mixing of blood' is recognised on the linguistic level, such as in the case of the descendants of the Japanese migrants to South America who arrived in Japan in large numbers after 1990, the term *Nikkeijin* suggests somebody of Japanese origin, not a Japanese of foreign origin. The partiality and mixing metaphors are used to differentiate individuals who do not conform to the standard ideal of a Japanese, which, along with full or pure Japanese descent, presupposes a range of characteristics and qualities as typical of any and all Japanese, but not of others. The extent of discursive familiarity and therefore predictability of social relations is therefore again predicated on the convergence of descent and a geographically bound Japanese culture.

However, this is not to say that such representations and convergences have been static. In fact, it has already been argued and shown that ideological representations of nationhood have to be flexible in order to adjust to the changing realities brought about not least by globalising or internationalising processes (for example, Ko 2009: 30).[16] Along with Japan's engagement with foreign countries and the growing importance of the English language, or bilingualism in general, the *hāfu*, thanks to their assumed linguistic abilities and despite their 'mixed' origins, have come to be represented in a more inclusive way. This shift has been marked by the appearance of a new term, namely *dāburu*, a Japanese-language rendition of the English world 'double' to signal the affinity of the 'mixed children' with the Japanese. Although it still essentialises the national or ethnic qualities, and denies the individuals the possibility of self-definition, the new term signals an opening of the notion of Japaneseness to acquiring new definitions. Similarly, the *kikokushijo*, not least thanks to the actions of their influential parents (Goodman 1990: 204–5), have come to represent a new ideal of the Japanese competent in – that is to say, familiar with – cultures other than Japanese in times of internationalisation (*kokusaika*).

Homogeneity, Demographic Change and Internationalisation

Usually translated into Japanese as *jinshu*, race is closely intertwined with the ideas of a Japanese ethnos or ethnic group–ethnicity (*nihon minzoku* – *minzoku-sei*), Japanese nation–nationality (*nihon kokumin* – *kokumin-sei*), and Japanese culture (*nihon bunka*) to the extent that the notions are often used interchangeably. Such nearly total conflation of the terms is epitomised in the expression *Yamato minzoku*, usually translated as 'Japanese race', where *Yamato* refers to the ancient province associated with the origins of the Japanese nation and the unique, indomitable Japanese spirit (as in the expression *Yamoto damashi*, bearing nationalistic associations). Much like the German *Volk*, the Japanese *minzoku* is constituted not only through descent, but also encompasses language, history and religion associated with ethnicity (Yoshino 1992: 26–27).[17] Full Japaneseness is therefore possible only when descent, culture and nationality can be simultaneously attributed to a person. Although in view of an increasing number of people not fitting such ethnicised definitions, the need for dissociation of *nihon minzoku* ('Japanese ethnic group') from *nihon kokumin* ('Japanese nation[al]') has been argued (Yamawaki, Kashiwazaki and Kondō 2002; Gotlieb 2012: 2–3), the association remains powerful. It finds its expression in the ideal of homogeneity working as a dominant folk theory (Gelman and Legare 2011; see also Yoshino 1992; Weiner 1997; Lie 2000, 2001; Befu 2001).

The ideal of homogeneity gained prominence in Japanese self-representations via a rich body of post–Second World War literature devoted to the 'discussions' or 'discourses' of Japaneseness, collectively known as *nihonjinron*. Japanese society in this ideological frame is ideally composed of similar individuals fitting the ethnicised image of a Japanese person, and is bound by culture, language, history and tradition intrinsic to the Japanese, and only to them. Stringent immigration regulations reflect and perpetuate these national imaginations. In 2008 people registered as foreigners accounted for 1.7 per cent – that is, around 2 million – of the total population of 127 million. Such a relatively small portion of non-Japanese has contributed to the common (mis)perception that there has been no immigration to Japan at all (Douglass and Roberts 2000: 11), supporting the popular image of Japan as relatively homogeneous and unique in its ways of social organization and interpersonal interactions. This image reinforces differentiation between who is, or can be, considered 'a Japanese', who can or should belong to the Japanese nation and/or society. Such considerations underlie the debates about whether Japan should allow more foreigners to settle within its borders.

These debates have become particularly salient in view of the profound demographic transformations that Japanese society has been experiencing in recent decades. As the most aged society in the world today, Japan is at the forefront of the demographic change expected to affect populations across the globe. As of 2013, no less than 32.3 per cent of the Japanese population were over the age of sixty, a proportion predicted to further rise to 42.7 per cent by 2050 and then drop only slightly to 41.1 per cent by 2100 (United Nations 2013: 24). Simultaneously, Japan's population is poised to shrink. It is predicted that having reached its peak of 127.75 million in 2005, it will decline to just above 100 million by 2050, and possibly to 64 million by 2100 (Kono 2011: 42). The challenges posed by such demographic changes – including an ever higher number of older people in need of care[18] – have brought about considerations about viable ways of organizing the society in the forthcoming decades.

In Japan, two visions of the future have emerged. According to the 'Small Option' (Sakanaka 2005) the future Japan is less numerous but self-sufficient. It operates on a downsized economy and possibly utilizes robots to fill positions that lack manpower due to the smaller size of the working age cohorts (Mori and Scearce 2010). The 'Big Option', sometimes denying feasibility of the former, presents a Japanese future as unavoidably open to significant numbers of migrants in order to sustain the country's existence (Sakanaka 2005). Consequently, one of the main questions has been whether to opt for a country that should limit the number of non-Japanese residents as much as possible, or whether Japan should intentionally become home to more foreigners. Both propositions rely on a different image of what Japanese society should or could become. Both, however, are a reflection of the dominant portrait commonly serving as either the ideal or current representation of Japanese society. In this context, neither the objective validity of either of the propositions nor their respective advantages and disadvantages are an issue.[19] Instead, what is central here are the implications these discourses may have for the Japanese national imagination, since both solutions present different cultural visions of Japan. It is these visions that will ultimately shape Japan's future, and they are the factors that inform experiences of such people as Amir, Jasir and the remaining 206 Indonesian caregiver and nurse candidates who arrived in Japan in 2008. Given its focus on care, and eldercare in particular, the EPA scheme fed directly into the deliberations over the prevailing image of Japanese national homogeneity in light of the demographic and concomitant economic and social transformations.

The arrival of the Indonesian workers in Japan in 2008 has been framed in Japan in terms of *kokusaika* and *tabunka kyōsei*, often translated as 'internationalisation' and 'multicultural coexistence' (or multiculturalism), respectively. Such interpretation of this new migratory flow relied on the utopian image of Japan as homogeneous, despite the efforts by both scholars and various activists to replace it with a more nuanced representation of Japanese society. Up until the 1990s, the tendency was to focus on Japan's minorities, who were defined as either indigenous to the isles, or foreign. The first group was represented by the Ainu, Okinawans and Buraku (for example, Vos and Wagatsuma 1967; Higler 1971). The latter referred to the Korean and Chinese residents who were brought to Japan by force during the Second World War and their descendants, and to the more recent migrant workers from Asia. While providing vivid examples of cultural plurality in Japan, these accounts focused on the groups' marginality within Japanese society. As such, they further contributed to the dominant representations of 'the Japanese' as homogeneous. The arrival of the so-called newcomers – that is, the postwar groups of refugees from Indochina and the female entertainers from Asia in the 1970s, the male migrants from South and South East Asia in the 1980s, and, in particular, the *Nikkeijin*, that is, people of Japanese descent since the 1990s – has propelled an additional challenge to the ideal of homogeneity (Burgess 2008: 63). Analytical efforts turned to examine how the understanding of 'the Japanese' was shaped by the plethora of 'historical engagements' within Japan and between Japan and other countries (Morris-Suzuki 1998 in Graburn and Ertl 2008: 5; also Goodman et al. 2003; Goodman 2008: 331).

About the same time, in the late 1990s, the notion of internationalisation, or *kokusaika*, had emerged in the Japanese policy discourse in response to the growing number of sojourners settling in Japan. This internationalisation has been said to have happened in Japan in two ways. At first, it involved familiarising the Japanese travelling abroad with local cultures and spreading knowledge about Japan rather than accepting foreign elements within the Japanese milieu. However, as Japan's engagements on the global scene continued and multiplied, and the number of foreign workers finding employment in Japan was on the increase, Nelson Graburn and John Ertl (2008: 7) argued that 'parts of the nation have been "internationalized" through migration'. Hence came the second, 'domestic' incarnation of internationalisation: the *uchinaru kokusaika* or *kokunai kokusaika*, internal or domestic internationalisation

(Morris-Suzuki 1998: 194 in Graburn and Ertl 2008: 7) that posed a challenge to the notion of a homogeneous Japanese society.

Along with the internationalisation there emerged in the popular discourse the notion of 'multicultural coexistence', or *tabunka kyōsei*, often translated as 'multiculturalism'. The term has been deployed to account for the progressing acknowledgement of the changing face of Japanese society, including now not only the Japanese but also those old and new arrivals settled, or at least residing, in the country. On a discursive level, *tabunka kyōsei* has become one of the ideals for the future shape of Japanese society. Such discursive commitment may have suggested critical engagement with the diversifying Japanese reality. However, it has been criticised for being a merely discursive policy tool that has not only rectified the difference between the Japanese and the Other, but with its focus on foreigners has also obliterated any differences among the Japanese (such as those related to disability or class status) and among those external Others (Flowers 2012).[20] The emergence of the multicultural ideal did not mean that immigration and the growing (visible) presence of foreigners in Japan, or the future prospects of accepting even more foreign workers to mitigate the effects of Japan's population ageing, would not be contested. Particularly in popular media discourses, the presence of migrants has often been seen as disruptive to the national fabric of Japanese society. For example, although the authors of articles in scholarly compilations – such as those edited by Douglass and Roberts 2000, Goodman et al. 2003, Graburn and Ertl 2008, Willis and Murphy-Shigematsu 2008 and Vogt and Roberts 2011 – discuss a plethora of cases exemplifying the undergoing changes and the formation of new constellations of (multicultural?) meanings in Japan, they also point to the still powerful national sentiments that resist but also shape these processes. The current book aims to contribute to this literature by focusing on these tensions, but also on alliances within a workplace that until recently has been outside the arena of 'internationalisation' – that is, eldercare institutions.

Looking at the EPA acceptance as a case study of migratory movements bringing about 'multicultural coexistence' suggests the importance of paying attention to the ways the structural conditions not only regulate the very flow of people, but also influence the perceptions, motivations, expectations and embedding of the migrant workers in the countries of destination. This can happen, for example, through promoting or precluding the formation of relationships between the migrants, through the way those allowed into the country are selected, through the way their sojourn is organised, and indeed through the way it comes to be imagined. Immigration regulations and the acceptance criteria select individuals of certain characteristics, which, in turn, affect the image of the country and people's orientation towards the migratory experience. The mode of opening the labour market to foreign workers can also affect the local discourses surrounding immigration. As I show in later parts of this book, a combination of these factors and the migrant workers' orientation towards their own experiences had a profound effect on the way the encounters were imagined and interpreted.

Care Workers' Migration, Ethnographies of Eldercare Institutions and Multicultural Coexistence

The changing family structure and the increased participation of women in the labour market has had a great influence on the nature of contemporary migratory flows. Domestic work and care for family members, traditionally performed by women who have now left the home to enter various paid jobs, have had to be outsourced to hired workers. Across the globe, the tendency has been increasingly to meet the demand for care personnel by accepting migrant workers (Huang, Yeoh and Toyota 2012). Not surprisingly, then, since the late 1990s, there has been a growing scholarly interest in international migration to perform care and domestic work as creating new sites of international or multicultural encounter. In these studies, care provided by migrant workers has commonly been represented as an additional service provided to the employer, often outside of what the work of the migrant in question was defined to be. Therefore, the emphasis has been on the exploitative nature of the relationships between the migrant workers and their employers (for example, Parreñas 2001; Lutz 2008). There have emerged discussions on the boundaries between work and care, or formal and informal care (Ungerson 2004; Litwin and Attias-Donfut 2009; Lyon 2010), and on the reconceptualisation of care coming with its marketisation (Finch and Groves 1983; Graham 1991; Tronto 1993; Lee-Treweek 1996; Qureshi 1996; Folbre and Nelson 2000; Zelizer 2000, 2005; Williams 2001; Simoni and Trifiletti 2004; Fine and Glendinning 2005). Furthermore, stressing the double role of migrant women as (traditional) caregivers to their own families and to their employers, the ideas often underlying the accounts of domestic work have been reflected in such concepts as 'global care chains' (Hochschild 2001; Parreñas 2001; but see also Yeates 2004), 'care drain' (Bettio, Simonazzi and Villa 2006), or 'the international division of reproductive labour' (Parreñas 2001; see also Glenn 1992). Also, given that the majority of migrant care workers have been women, research focused on their experiences has contributed immensely to the discussion of changing gender roles in modern societies (for example, Parreñas 2001; Liebelt 2011), and the power structures within the domestic sphere and within the wider context of economic disparities between sending and receiving countries (for example, Sassen 1984; Glenn 1992; Phizacklea and Anderson 1997; Momsen 1999; Ehrenreich and Hochschild 2002).

Through the ethnographic prism of the accepting sites, this study looks at Japan entering the international stage as a country receiving migrants to provide care for its citizens, rather than to work on its assembly lines. As such, it too focuses on a new configuration of personal and structural factors giving shape to the zones of encounters (Faier 2009). Issues highlighted in the domestic work context, such as the workers' ethnicisation – that is, the use of essentialised stereotypes based on ethnicity, nationality or gender as a means of constructing hierarchies between workers affecting their employability (Lovebond 2003)[21] – featured in the experiences of the EPA Indonesian care workers as well, but they played out in different ways. This was partly because of the way the acceptance was organised, as I will show in the following chapters. Importantly, the current research was based in eldercare institutions rather than in private homes. In this context, the employer was not the one cared for, and the carers worked alongside and together with other workers looking after not one but many elderly. In this study there is, therefore, less emphasis on the boundary between work and non-work. I pay more attention to the nature of the work the Indonesians performed, what meanings they attached to it, and how it affected their relationships with the elderly, the Japanese staff, and the employers. Also, because the vast majority of the EPA care worker candidates were not caregivers to their own families at the time of their arrival in Japan, rather than looking at the 'care chains' caused by the Indonesians' relocation, I emphasise their private goals as young, educated individuals and the ways their move to Japan featured in their respective life projects.

While studies of domestic migrant workers have emphasised migrants' experiences, in the scholarship on the care provided in institutionalised settings the emphasis has been divided between the experiences of those cared for and the care providers. The earlier ethnographies of institutionalised eldercare focused on the plight of the elderly, usually presented in terms of diminished quality of life and the adverse effects of institutionalisation (Henry 1963; Laird 1979; Vesperi 1987; Shield 1988; Kayser-Jones 1990). Those studies that incorporated workers' experiences initially limited the accounts to the higher-level staff who provide specialised care. For example, Joel Savishinsky (1991) concentrates on the health professionals, such as physical therapists and social workers, and only mentions in passing the caregivers who provide direct care to the elderly. Savishinsky's predecessors, too, such as Jaber Gubrium (1975: 124–42) and Roger Clough (1981: 89–90), only briefly pause on the 'bed-and-body work' in order to discuss some of the tactics the staff deployed to mitigate its unpleasantness. These studies lack information about the relationships among the floor staff and the managerial staff, or about more nuanced understandings that the front-line staff ascribed to their jobs. While the elderly 'clientele' are represented as forming a network of relationships, the members of staff are discussed as a group of individuals whose social connections remain unaccounted for (see also Somera 1995).

More attention to the sociality of an eldercare home as a workplace is paid by Nancy Foner in her *Caregiving Dilemma*. Foner stresses the 'pressures for rapprochement' and the 'strong ethic of cooperation' (Foner 1994: 142) among the staff despite the various tensions and personal dislikes. Foner was also the first to pay closer attention to the ethnic (racial) identifications of the staff and the elderly. She concludes that although 'racial differences magnify the opposition with patients … race had little, if any, effect on actual patient care in individual cases [and] … racial and ethnic similarity between patients and aides did not lead to better relations with patients or more sympathetic care' (ibid.: 45). A turn towards the conceptualisation of experiences of direct care by the care providers is visible in the writings of scholars concentrating on 'bodywork' in care provision. This research focused on the embodied and emotional nature of care work (Diamond 1992; Lee-Treweek 1996, 1997), bodywork's ability to break privacies (Twigg 2000a, 2000b), the stigma of the 'dirty work' (Jervis 2001; see also Lawler 1991), and the gendered meanings and perceptions of bodywork (Isaksen 2002, 2005; Dahle 2005).

In the Japanese context, looking from the perspective of institutionalisation, ethnographic works in institutions for the elderly have predominantly focused on the lives of the elderly. Framing the residents' lives in the context of the Japanese cultural norm of familial co-residence, and eldercare provided by family members, Diana Lynn Bethel (1992a) shows how the elderly residents overcome the stigma of institutionalisation and recreate a thriving community around the structures provided by the institutionalisation of their lives. The elderly in Bethel's account reconstruct a community along the Japanese norms of interaction, as well as through introducing new norms in defiance of those accepted in the wider society – for example, in relation to the cohabitation of men and women. In Bethel's work (Bethel 1992a, 1992b) the focus is on the elderly, but she also signals the different relationships between the elderly and the staff of the institution, depending on the latter's apparent degree of willingness to bend the institutional rules. All the members of staff presented by Bethel are Japanese, and encounters with the new or the unknown are limited to the newness of institutional life and to encounters with Japanese strangers with whom the residents need to form neighbourly relationships. This was also the case in the institution visited by Yongmei Wu (2004). Wu, too, concentrates on the 'quality of life' dimension of institutionalised life, but unlike Bethel, she pays more attention to the experiences of the staff. The staff voices she presents in her book consider the position of the elderly within the institution from the perspective of the people who look after them. They touch on such themes as professional satisfaction in terms of the ability to provide personalised care and the rewards of being able to help people in need, and discuss their motivations for working with the elderly. Overall, however, Wu's ethnography is structured to show how the idea of Japanese eldercare is based on the notion of dependency, and the experiences of the care providers fulfil only a supportive function towards this end.

The current study builds on the body of work presented above in several ways. Although institutionalisation is not my subject of investigation I pay attention to the discourses of the elderly residents' welfare in relation to the arrival of foreign carers at the institutions. However, I particularly draw in this book on the line of thought combining the bodily and emotional aspects of care work with the sociality of the workplace, showing their interplay with the ideas of national or cultural difference. I also draw a link between the structure of the acceptance and the embodied nature of care work. Attending to the complexities and discourses surrounding care provision, both in terms of direct contact with the bodies of the cared-for Japanese elderly and in terms of its impact on interpersonal relations among the staff, I pose the experiences of the EPA Indonesian workers and the discourses surrounding their arrival as a case study in multicultural coexistence (*tabunka kyōsei*; Jpn.). This has something to tell us about contemporary Japanese ideas of nationhood and the ways one can imagine the other as a viable co-resident, co-worker, neighbour or friend.

Three existing monographs have taken on a similar task to that pursued by this book. In different settings they too explore the micro-level, interpersonal experiences against the background of macro processes shaping migratory flows. In *Intimate Encounters*, Lieba Faier delves into the interpersonal negotiations between the Filipina women employed in hostess bars in Japan, the Japanese male customers turned husbands, and their respective families. Faier uses the notion of cultural encounters to 'consider the messy, interactive, and sometimes surprising ways that people create cultural meanings and identities through everyday relationships with others' (Faier 2009: 5). She investigates what social and economic conditions contributed to the production of specific imaginations and desires held by both the Filipina women and the Japanese men. In doing so, she traces the link between the interpersonal relationships and the macro processes shaping them. However, despite the indication in the title, the book does not elaborate on the very idea of intimacy or how exactly it features in the experiences of both the migrant Filipina women and the Japanese members of the accepting rural community. The intimacy of encounters is equated with the formation of romantic and/or marital unions, and is therefore considered only implicitly. Moreover, by focusing on the social and economic forces affecting the lives of the people she studies, Faier does not analyse the minute mores of interactions that constitute the basis of any relationship. In addition, in this otherwise rich ethnography, there is little attention paid to the relationships between migrant and non-migrant co-workers. While globally romantic relationships between migrant and non-migrant individuals are ubiquitous, the majority of interactions are still taking place outside of the familial realm, often in the workplace. The current book introduces intimacy as a wider concept reaching beyond the romantic and sexualised encounters, and looks at how it transforms relationships between strangers who come in close contact through work.

Among ethnographic monographs dealing with eldercare provided by international migrants, Claudia Liebelt's *Caring for the 'Holy Land'* focuses most explicitly on the intimacy of relationships between the carers and the cared-for elderly. Against the background of a restrictive immigration regime in Israel and the national ideology of preserving the country's 'Jewishness' (not unlike the homogeneity ideal in Japan), Liebelt explores how the Filipina migrants in Tel Aviv transcend their representations as disempowered domestic workers. Liebelt's important contribution is showing how 'as female "working class cosmopolitans" … [the Filipina workers] embody subjectivities beyond the (theoretical) divide between parochial migrants and bourgeois cosmopolitans' (Liebelt 2011: 187). Within this framework, Liebelt discusses the relationships between the typically elderly employers and the Filipina carers. She shows the complexity and ambivalence of the structurally unequal relationships that have become complicated by the formation of intimate ties and feelings of attachment. In Liebelt's account these ties not only hold the potential to transform the day-to-day practices within the households employing Filipina women, but also have been the basis for public debate over the (legitimate) position of the Filipina domestic workers within the Israeli nation and state. In presenting the subjective experiences of the Filipina women as tightly connected to their interpersonal relationships with their cared-for employers, Liebelt discusses the notion of citizenship as a form of belonging. However, she does not explicitly make the connection between the intimacy of care and the representations of the Filipina on the national level. Nor does she explain how exactly the interpersonal bonds were formed, despite presenting emotional closeness between the carers and the cared-for employers. Liebelt mentions physical proximity stemming from living together, but does not elaborate on the actual processes or experiences within this context that would explain how and why such affective relationships should emerge, or how they could challenge the conventional understanding of citizenship in Israel. The current book makes this connection explicit through an array of ethnographic examples and a theoretical elaboration of the concept of intimacy. Moreover, it situates the debates over national representations within the context of the dramatic demographic change underway in Japan, where already nearly a quarter of the population is over the age of sixty-five. As such, this study addresses the broader issues affecting much of the world populations, and contributes to the debates over how to address the current demographic and ideological challenges without losing sight of the most immediate experiences of the individuals who are at the centre of these global changes.

Finally, David McConnell's *Importing Diversity* explores the practical implementation of the internationalisation ideas during the first decade since the realisation of the Japan Exchange and Teaching (JET) Programme began in 1987. Under the programme's provisions, schools across Japan accepted young graduates from primarily English-speaking countries to assist Japanese English teachers. The stated goal of the programme was to promote internationalisation in Japan. Within this context, McConnell recounts how various kinds of problems were conceptualised, approached and tackled. In doing so, he skilfully uncovers the cognitive frameworks (McConnell 2000: 3 and 167) of the individuals involved, and shows how much of the tension in the relationships between the foreign teachers and the Japanese engaged in the implementation of the programme at different levels of administration arose from the divergent understanding of what internationalisation actually means. While for the JET participants it meant dismantling differences between societies, for the Japanese it was seen as a means to improve communication between inherently and permanently different societies. While McConnell's detailed account provides an excellent window into the intersection between the ideology and practice, primarily at the institutional level, two areas are left out of his scope of investigation. The book does not expose the impact the JET programme had on its foreign participants, nor does it delve into the particular processes that led to the development of cordial relationships between the foreign English language teachers, their Japanese counterparts, other members of the teaching body and students, despite the tensions on which the author focuses. It therefore does not provide any insights into how the two different ideas of internationalisation informed each other, or how the direct interaction was situated vis-à-vis the dominant cultural representations. The current study deals exactly with these issues. In contrast to McConnell's work, by foregrounding the minute enactments of ideologies on a personal level this book exposes the intricate relationship between the structure and agency – that is, between the dominant cultural representations and individual experiences shaping mutual representations, and ultimately reflecting back on the structure.

Research Process

The research presented here spans the final weeks of linguistic training undertaken by the first batch of Indonesian workers prior to their employment, and a reunion a year later. In 2008, when this research began, there were 104 caregiver candidates and 104 nurse candidates accepted from Indonesia who took up positions in a total of ninety-nine Japanese institutions (fifty-two care homes and forty-seven hospitals).

In the months that followed the six-month language training, I stayed in regular contact with nine young Indonesian caregiver candidates. There were, however, a number of others, both Indonesian and Japanese, whom I met less regularly, but whose stories also feature in this book. In order to disguise the identities of those real-life protagonists, and my main informants in particular, most of the characters appearing on these pages are avatars. Their actions and experiences are amalgamations of what really happened to a greater number of real-life caregivers. Similarly, I have relocated some of the stories to further camouflage the individual identities, and those of the accepting institutions. Apart from Jasir and Amir, in this book we also follow Lazim and Daris, and three women, Iffah, Irdina and Lanny, whom I introduce in more detail in the following chapter.

A great part of the material used in this book comes from my first-hand experiences and observations within and without the accepting eldercare institutions, and the conversations I had with either the Indonesian candidates or Japanese individuals in one way or another linked to the EPA acceptance programme between December 2008 and March 2010. However, I also use information, such as from media reports, various booklets produced in relation to the EPA programme and statistical data, that originated outside of this time frame, but which is relevant to the story told in this book. In places I also weave in my own experiences in Japan that, I feel, reflect the ideas I am discussing here.

Once the language training was over, the seven friends who we will be following on these pages dispersed to work in six separate institutions. I gained regular access to three of them, and visited the others more sporadically. Obtaining access to the three institutions proved to be a lengthy process as it had to follow first a fairly unforced development of my relationships with the Indonesian candidates, and then a period of negotiations with representatives of the institutions. Hence, for example, while I spent my first night at Iffah's apartment at the beginning of February 2009, it was not until April that I managed to have a first official conversation with her deputy manager, which then resulted in my first period of observation in the institution beginning in early June 2009. Arranging access to Amir's and Jasir's workplace took only a month and I began my observation there in mid April 2009. Finally, I started my research alongside Lazim in July 2009 after a series of meetings with a number of administrative staff from the institution where he worked. The final arrangements with the three institutions were such that I would pay week-long visits to all of them on a rotation basis. This amounted to a total of roughly sixteen weeks spent inside the institutions. During each week I usually lived with the Indonesian candidates and went to work with them. The situation varied from institution to institution, from ward to ward, and across time, but in general I was free to move around the institutions and mingle with the elderly as well as with the members of staff. I usually followed the Indonesians and sometimes helped them in their tasks, but occasionally I talked with the elderly or with the Japanese members of staff regardless of whether my Indonesian friends were around or not. Between the visits I spent a lot of time researching and helping the candidates to buy bus or plane tickets, laptops and mobile phones, to set up new bank accounts, to look for possible alternative flats to move into, to translate presentations into Japanese, and so on. Also, once my routine visits were established, I tried to enlarge the number of institutions I could visit, but these attempts resulted only in shorter, often one-off visits, which sometimes were limited to interviews supplemented by a short tour of the facilities. These conversations and fleeting encounters did, nevertheless, help to supplement the information I gathered during the visits to my main three sites of participant observation.

In order to move observation beyond the micro level of quotidian occurrences, I participated in numerous meetings of various support groups that had emerged in Japan in response to the EPA acceptance, attended conferences and workshops related to the subject, and visited religious centres frequented by my informants as well as other Indonesians living, working or studying in Japan. In addition, I travelled to Indonesia to follow some of my friends during their home visits, but also to visit eldercare institutions in Indonesia as well as migrant worker training centres near Jakarta, and to interview Indonesian officials involved in the organisation of the EPA acceptance. I also conducted questionnaire surveys among selected employers, supervisors and co-workers of Indonesians who arrived under the EPA programme in the first batch in 2008, and among the Indonesian and Philippine caregiver candidates present in Japan at the beginning of 2010.

I extended my research focus beyond the immediate sites of contact because, although anthropological methods more comfortably fit the analysis at the micro and meso levels of the selected group – that is, the level of the individual and the family, or community – the experiences of people I worked with were very directly shaped by the larger-scale economic and political negotiations between Japan and Indonesia. Such macro-level analyses have become part and parcel of anthropological discussions of migration since, as Caroline Brettell (2003: 2) has put it, to account for how the migratory flows and experiences are shaped, we need to 'recognise … how global capitalism has fostered the often exploitative relationships that exist between developing and labour-supplying countries and developed labour-receiving countries' (see also Massey et al. 1993). I will be referring to these relationships both as they were played out in the interpretations of the day-to-day experiences as well as at the level of relationships between the two countries.

In Chapter 4, in particular, I refer to the content of the media coverage of the EPA programme. I am using the term 'media' here to refer collectively to what is known as 'mass media' – that is, printed newspapers, television and radio programmes, and the content available on the internet. Between January 2004 and December 2010 the three major Japanese newspapers, *Asahi Shinbun*, *Yomiuri Shinbun* and *Nihon Keizai Shinbun*,[22] published 312 articles referring to the Indonesian EPA care workers that I analysed.[23] A second type of source is radio and television programmes, and I added several of these to the collection. In addition, I collected forty-six Japanese texts published on the internet, which total 139 pages. The earliest text in this group is a blog post dated 22 May 2008, and the latest is a news feature from 22 October 2010 that reports on a symposium about the acceptance of the EPA Indonesian care workers.

In my search I also included several printed professional magazines and books which may not have as wide a readership as, for example, the most popular national newspapers, but are available for anyone who wishes to purchase and/or reference. Similarly, when searching the vast content of the internet, apart from pieces produced by journalists in their professional capacity, I decided to include examples of blogs and internet-based discussion as well. I did this for two main reasons. Firstly, I felt that it would have been detrimental to the present report to exclude some of the first-hand quotes I came across in the commentaries produced by unaffiliated individuals, which in my mind exemplified and supplemented very well the themes emerging from the stories published by the institutionalised media channels. Secondly, these voices represented the spread of interest in and concern about the EPA programme among Japanese who may not have been directly involved in it, and they were voices that I did not have chance to concentrate on to any great extent during my research among the Indonesians. Hence, I collected any piece of publicly available information that I came across, either as a result of a purposive search, or purely by chance.[24]

When analysing articles published in the three main newspapers, I first listed the titles and subtitles and coded them in search of the key themes emerging from the titles only. I was motivated to do this by my belief that the titles work as catchphrases and are often the only parts of articles read at all (Dijk 2006). The next step was to code the articles' content, and finally to choose specific articles that represented the emerged themes and served as a source for quotations and references. The material obtained from the online resources was coded in the same way as one would code field notes to produce a pool of themes or key terms around which the stories told by the texts revolve. I did not specifically concentrate on the titles of these texts (and some of them were without such) since, due to the nature of their means of publication (perhaps less omnipresent and opinion-shaping than those of major newspapers), I did not consider the titles to be considerably more influential than the contents of the full text. Finally, my intention was not to assess the ideological stance of the individual newspapers. Rather, the goal was to extract the general flavour of the publicity the EPA acceptance and the Indonesian candidates received during the period that marked the peak of public discussion on the topic and what this may tell us about Japanese national imagination vis-à-vis the incoming Indonesian eldercare workers.

Circulatory Ethnography

The circulatory nature of visits to the workplaces employing my main informants had its advantages and disadvantages. Although dictated by practical limitations (I was restricted by the length of time the employers were willing to let me shadow the Indonesians at any one time), it allowed me to observe the development of the relationships between the Indonesians and their Japanese colleagues, supervisors and employers almost simultaneously in three different settings. Importantly, it meant that I was getting to know a larger number of people at the same time. Were I to have committed myself to observation in only one care home at a time, it would have limited my contact to only one, two or three Indonesian candidates. Due to the nature of the EPA acceptance, which spread the candidates across Japan, in order to study their experiences as a group I had to study the 'local ecology of their activities' (Hannerz 2003) rather than the entirety of the institutional social milieus in which they were immersed. This meant that I needed to be 'there … and there … and there' (ibid.), a stance that also applied to my visiting Indonesia and participating in events outside of the eldercare homes.

Moreover, the comings and goings, the welcomes and goodbyes accompanying my travelling between the institutions seemed to ultimately speed up the development of close relationships between my informants and me. My periods of being away from any of the institutions introduced intervals to my otherwise almost constant interactions with the informants. Although we stayed in touch by email and mobile phone between my visits, upon my next arrival we felt we had so much to say to each other that these first-night conversations were almost as full of information as all the much shorter exchanges, which we would have over the coming week, taken together. The temporary detachment was not, as Matei Candea (2010) argues, a negation of engagement, but helped as if the periods of separation were used to skip the gradual familiarisation which would have been necessary if I had lived and worked together with my informants without intermission. Thanks to the possibility of building on the somewhat romanticised memories of previous encounters, my Indonesian friends and I were able to be 'up and running' with our relationships from the very first visit, which was preceded only by one short encounter at the language training centre.

On the other hand, unlike continuous relationships between a researcher and members of the group on which the research focuses, my truncated presence in the care homes and in the flats and lives of my Indonesian friends meant that I was unable to take part in or observe many of their experiences. Undoubtedly I missed a plethora of observations. Therefore, I had to rely on my informants' subjective accounts, and reconstruct the events from any reverberations (if such were detectable at all) I encountered during a following visit or a meeting outside of the workplace. In this sense, parts of the material used in this book are based on the narratives of my informants. As narratives they should not be understood as providing an objective record of events, but as expressing the subjective interpretations of the events and experiences the Indonesians had during my absence from the given site.[25]

Another important downside of the intermittent nature of visits to the three care homes was that my relations with the Japanese members of staff were not as extensive as I would have wished. During the short visits I spent most of my time with the Indonesians, and I returned home with them as well. During working hours I participated in or witnessed the interactions between the Indonesians and the Japanese, but it was more common for me to later have a discussion about the day's events with the Indonesians than with the Japanese. On various occasions I had an opportunity to have one-to-one conversations with the Japanese staff, such as during lunch or when there was a moment to pause and chat, but these discussions were far less numerous than those I had with the Indonesians. The gaps between my visits also meant that on return I would not necessarily meet the same members of staff, who might have been on leave or on different shifts to the Indonesians, or, as it happened, might have quit the job altogether. Therefore, I am able to discuss Japanese motivations and interpretations of the events presented here primarily through inference from the Indonesians' experiences. A similar limitation, although to a lesser degree, applies to my relationships with the elderly. Although, contrary to my concerns, those elderly with whom I talked did not forget me during my absence, the limited time we spent together affected the type and amount of information I was able to gain. However, as with the Indonesian candidates, so too with the Japanese staff members and the elderly, my circulating between the institutions created the impression that our knowing each other had a history due to the memories of my previous visits. This historicising effect helped to maintain, if not deepen, the intimacy of our relationships, and paved a path to meaningful exchanges.

Access to People and Ethics of Research

Securing access to the institutions did not necessarily mean warranting access to people. In the case of my main Indonesian informants, our relationships were already initiated prior to my arrival at the care homes. When I was not able to meet the second batch candidates without the mediation of their employers, I decided to approach the accepting institutions directly and ask them for an opportunity to talk to the Indonesian candidates they had accepted. I was aware that such an approach left virtually no choice to the Indonesians but to accept the proposition of meeting me. My attempts at mitigating the coercive nature of the circumstances involved certain linguistic choices.

The ability to speak both the Japanese and Indonesian was, unsurprisingly, the key to forming relations with people I encountered. Being able to communicate was the obvious issue, but equally important was a degree of familiarity, commitment and interest in the culture or the country, of which the linguistic ability was seen as a proof. Even if neither my Japanese nor Indonesian skill was that of a native speaker, but at a level I usually describe as fluent and conversational, respectively, my familiarity with the languages was recognised as indicative of my greater familiarity, and perhaps sympathy, with the issues pertinent to both countries. At the same time, my being Polish, which is to say foreign to Japan as well as to Indonesia, placed me in a neutral position of sympathiser with both and member of neither. Not partaking in the intimate workings of the two national and cultural communities of people whose experiences I was researching, and therefore not bearing the responsibility for whatever either of the groups could be resented for, I was able to balance, and sometimes manipulate, my perceived allegiance to either or neither side. Such fusion, of being an affiliate and an outsider at the same time, made it possible for me in conversations with the Japanese supervisors of the Indonesian candidates to align myself with their concerns over the Indonesians' ability to communicate sufficiently with the cared-for elderly or discuss certain Indonesian 'cultural traits' as observed by the Japanese. On the other hand, I shared in some of the experiences and frustrations of my Indonesian friends who, like me, were foreign to Japan. On other occasions, I was able to take a detached stance and comment on both, or on the interactions between them, from an outsider's point of view.

Being able to switch between the languages helped me to mitigate the somewhat coercive nature of the interviews I conducted with the Indonesian candidates who arrived as the second batch. Our conversations were often held in the presence of their Japanese supervisor, which was potentially another factor (alongside the lack of choice on the Indonesians' side about whether to meet with me or not) to affect the responses of the candidates. On such occasions, however, I asked the Japanese person for permission to speak with the Indonesians in the Indonesian language, justifying my request by the Indonesians' beginner's level of Japanese at the time. I would then explain to them in Indonesian that they were not obliged in any way to talk to me, or to give any information they were not comfortable giving. The possibility of sharing their experiences in a native language, and perhaps the oddity of a Polish person talking to them in Indonesian in Japan, made our encounters very amicable and the Indonesian workers seemed eager to share whatever observations and experiences they had. The linguistic connection and the mutual interest helped to create a more intimate relationship between the Indonesians and me. But it was also the joy of being able to talk in private, despite the Japanese supervisors' physical presence in the room – the inversion of roles whereby the Indonesians were conveying information of interest to the Japanese but in a language unfamiliar to them – that made our encounters feel very relaxed and open. There was no spite in these conversations, however, but a cheerful enjoyment of temporary control over the situation which seemed to make the interviewees particularly sincere and bold at times, as when the candidates openly complained about certain arrangements at work.

The mitigation of my researching imposition on the Japanese members of staff and the elderly, and informing them about my position, took on different forms. At Iffah's and Lazim's institutions I was officially introduced to the members of staff and I had a chance to say a few words explaining my presence there as well. Those present at the time of my introduction also had an opportunity to ask me questions. This seemed to break the ice and the encounters that followed built on these initial exchanges. Thanks to such introductions it was also possible for the staff members whom I had met to introduce me to those who had not been present at the time. Such a chain of introductions greatly facilitated my later interactions with the staff and allowed for more detailed explanations regarding the purpose of my presence and the staff's right to opt out from being included in the research outcomes. This was not, however, the case in the institution where Jasir and Amir were employed. There, at the beginning of my first visit, I was taken directly to the staff changing room, asked to change into my 'working clothes', and left to myself to follow the Indonesian workers. There was no official introduction that day. As I walked in to the ward nearest the changing room it was already breakfast time and every member of staff was busy either assisting the residents with eating, preparing tea or toothbrushes, or wheeling back to their rooms those residents who had finished eating. It was not a good moment for personal introductions. As it turned out, I could only use staff lunch breaks to explain what I was doing in the institution. Since I was not allowed to help in this particular institution, I was not actively engaged in any of the tasks the staff performed and therefore could not use this as an excuse for starting up conversations. Several times I tried to ask for explanations of different aspects of their work, such as what the various symbols on charts meant, or what the powder was that they were adding to some of the residents' tea.[26] I hoped that once a conversation was started we would be able to continue beyond the immediate answer, but this was rarely the case. The problem was exacerbated by the division of the institution into wards, with different staff (and a different Indonesian) working on each. I found it impossible to explain who I was to everyone. When I asked for a more official introduction, the deputy manager referred to me as a *kenshūsei*, a trainee, during a morning staff briefing. This created further confusion, as a *kenshūsei* entering the institution would usually be someone aiming to become a care worker and therefore expected to actively engage in the caring tasks. I was just walking around the institution. During my third visit to this particular institution, at lunch when only two of us were left in the break room, I had a short conversation with one of the male employees. It turned out that he thought I was the Indonesian workers' instructor. Such confusion and lack of opportunities for direct interaction resulted in my forming close relations with only a handful of the Japanese staff in this institution. Thus, in this book I focus primarily on those encounters that involved individuals I had a degree of rapport with and who I believed had a fairly good understanding of my role.

Collecting information from the elderly was limited by the poor mental state of the majority of the residents living on the wards where the Indonesian candidates worked. My contacts were therefore limited to those who were still able and willing to share their thoughts and impressions with me. This meant that on Iffah's ward I could not acquire much information from the elderly point of view because none of the residents were lucid any more. However, every week and sometimes twice a week, Iffah was sent to another ward on a floor above her own to help during the bathing of those residents who were in a better physical and mental state. There I would wait outside and help the elderly with their activities before and after bathing. Sitting in front of the bathroom together with the elderly waiting for their turn to get inside, then offering water as they left the hot bathroom, and being one-to-one during drying and combing hair, drying feet and putting on socks and shoes, provided opportunities for me to chat with them, as well as with the member of staff whom I was sometimes assisting. In the wards where Lazim and Amir worked there were more elderly who had no problems engaging in conversation, even if sometimes this was obstructed by various physical impairments making verbal communication difficult. I managed to develop close relations with four elderly on Amir's ward, and with three on Lazim's. They were all very accommodating of my presence in the care homes and offered their impressions about life in the institution, about the Indonesian workers, and, at times, a useful piece of advice as to how I should go about my engagement with other, less accommodating elderly. Jasir, who was based in the same institution as Amir, was assigned to a ward where it was impossible to communicate extensively with the majority of the elderly. Those who were physically able to speak were in advanced stages of dementia, and our (rare) conversations were confined to comments on food or repetitive fragments of stories from the past. These elderly, if they noticed my presence, did not seem to remember me when I arrived for a following visit and were often unwilling to interact with me. I therefore resigned myself to observing from a distance on these wards in order to minimise any possible anxiety that my presence might have been causing those elderly. I also refrained from observing bathing activities to respect the elderly's privacy, and only twice assisted during changing of diapers when explicitly asked to help. Those of the elderly who had no way of telling me that they would rather be excluded from my research record are mentioned here only sporadically as anonymous individuals. Instead, I draw mostly on the interactions with those who were actively supporting my work.

Eldercare Homes as Research Sites

Entering an eldercare home can be a bewildering experience. For Lynn Mason (1995: 73), who based her writing on a three-year experience as a volunteer in two nursing homes in Denver, Colorado, US, it was a 'culture shock' (see also Tisdale 1987). Maria Vesperi (1995: 7) compared her impressions of life inside an eldercare institution to the sense of a parallel world existing alongside the bustling of everyday life. This sense of eldercare homes as being somehow different to what one may experience in everyday life originates from two of their attributes. Firstly, they are total institutions in the sense elaborated by Erving Goffman (1961), where the lives and work of people are subjected to regulatory forces in the name of the institution's lasting command over individuals (see also Vesperi 1995). In fact, as mentioned earlier, the vast majority of ethnographies based in eldercare homes, especially the early ones, focused on the experiences of the elderly seen as shaped by their institutionalisation in one way or another. In the American context these were the works by Henry (1963), Shield (1988), Kayser-Jones (1990), and Savishinsky (1991); and there were Clough (1981) in Great Britain and Bethel (1992a, 1992b) and Wu (2004) in Japan. The majority of people lead most of their lives outside of such confined environments and therefore eldercare institutions present themselves as unfamiliar.

The other characteristic of eldercare institutions that makes them appear alien to researchers is the rather obvious fact that the majority of people one encounters in them are elderly. With the exception of Carobeth Laird (1979), who was admitted to a nursing home as a resident, all ethnographies have been produced by people significantly younger than the residents. Mine is no exception here. Ageing and 'elderhood', although unavoidable for most, represents a state unknown to younger people and has been an object of investigation in its own right. Asking about meanings of ageing in different societies are care home–based works compiled by Jay Sokolovsky (1987) and Rene Somera (1995). The age difference in itself does not, however, make the elderly appear unfamiliar. That is the result of the deterioration of bodily and mental functions, disabling conditions, and loss of independence that might come with age. Lynn Mason (1995: 74) expressed her consternation in encounters with the elderly in the following way: 'How does one begin conversations with those strapped in wheelchairs in the hallway dozing or gazing into space and seemingly oblivious to everyone and everything around them?' For Mason, the elderly's unfamiliar ways of being, both in terms of their physical comportment as well as their apparent (in)action, were a source of confusion about how to interact with them on the premise that these interactions would be based on a different set of rules from those to which she was accustomed.

Although I cannot claim that I am more familiar with institutional life or ageing than others, my experiences of the care homes I entered to conduct research were not as striking to me. Personally, I was never immersed in any of the institutions to the extent of any of the workers or elderly. This was due to the fact that I travelled between three care homes, visiting all of them only temporarily, as I discussed above. The institutionalisation of work as well as lives in the care homes did shape the experiences of my Indonesian informants. In fact, their becoming a part of the institutions was the very reason why they remained in close proximity to both the Japanese members of staff and the elderly. However, my investigative focus was on the interpersonal relationships and not on a quality of life, the latter of which would have brought the 'totalism' of the institutions more to the fore, both in my own experiences as well as in the analysis of the data collected. With regard to entering an environment of elderly 'strapped in wheelchairs in the hallway dozing or gazing into space', I believe I was prepared for it thanks to my work experience in the year prior to the fieldwork. As a first year PhD student I took up a part-time position of personal assistant, or, as my contract stated, travel body to the head of a policy department in one of the disability charities in the United Kingdom. My employer needed support since, born without legs, he relied on assistance in getting in and out of vehicles, sitting down and getting up, and so on. As the head of the policy department and in connection to his other public roles, my employer travelled around the country attending conferences and meetings, but also visiting various facilities for people with disabilities and for the elderly. I accompanied him. During these travels I often had the chance to help others who were hard of hearing, blind, or unable to verbally communicate as a condition linked to cerebral palsy. That year I moved in and out of a world where age or disability were not marked, although, of course, there was awareness that the very formation of this world was predicated on the markedness of the disabling differences in a wider society. When I entered the care homes in which I was to base my research in Japan for the first time, they felt familiar. I did not feel any inhibition in talking to the elderly, perhaps sometimes appearing too eager to do so. I still did not know the details of each elderly person's condition, or the proper way of reacting to or dealing with individuals with far-advanced dementia; nor was I aware of the specific working patterns on a given ward. This caused anxiety. The smells were also different. A discomforting mix of excreta, chemicals and medicine odours was not unknown but new in its preponderance over the 'usual' daily smells. All in all, my anxiety and discomfort upon arrival at the care homes were built on the details of the inside world, rather than on the distinctness of the entirety of this world.

Husband in the Field

One other intimate relationship I was engaged in during field research was with my husband. For a year beginning in February 2009 I was accompanied by him. When he arrived in Japan we were still an un-married couple, but decided to get married in April that year in order to secure a dependent visa allowing him to stay in Japan for as long as my research lasted since his dual British–New Zealand citizenship only al-lowed up to six months of residence in any twelve-month period. Being accompanied in the field, of course, had its consequences, but it did not affect the data I collected in any substantial way. This was thanks to the fact that my research sites were separate from where I lived with my husband. When I went away on research visits, to conduct interviews, or to participate in events related to my research I was never accompa-nied by him. My informants knew about his arrival in Japan and our later marriage, but they did not meet him until several months into the research. In some ways, being in a relationship proved helpful in finding commonalities with my informants. Before my husband-to-be joined me in Japan, I could share in the experiences of separation from loved ones with those of my informants who had left their partners in Indonesia. Although the length of separation was incomparable be-tween us, the similarity of experience became a starting point of several conversations when we met for the first time. Similarly, when we got to know each other better, the teasing of the two male informants at whose place I was a returning guest, about staying with two men while having a husband waiting in a different city, often allowed me to probe into similarly intimate aspects of their own relationships with their fe-male partners.

Representations

Before moving on, one note is due on the representation of persons in this book. As mentioned earlier, when relaying individual actions and interactions of the people I encountered during research, I use avatars sharing the characteristics and experiences of the people I met. I also substitute names with pseudonyms and sometimes transpose events into a different setting in order to preclude the possibility of identifi-cation of those involved. I report real names only of those individu-als whose opinions to which I refer have already been made publicly available. When referring to those Indonesians who arrived under the EPA programme, I interchangeably use such collective terms as 'the EPA Indonesians', 'the EPA candidates', 'the caregiver candidates', or 'the Indonesian workers'. Although each of these expressions may en-compass a different group of people, I use them all to refer to those Indonesians who arrived in Japan under the EPA scheme to train towards obtaining a Japanese caregiver qualification. Whether this refers to the particular individuals whose stories I am relaying or to the entire group can be extrapolated from the context. Whenever I refer to a different group, this is clearly indicated in the text as well. It should also be remembered that although the above expressions serve to distinguish the group of my informants from other Indonesian workers or residents in Japan, and although they shared many conditions of life and work in Japan, each of them experienced the sojourn in his or her own individual way. The abbreviation 'EPA' and any other collective term should not, therefore, be taken to stand for a set of inherent characteristics that the Indonesian workers shared, but merely as an indication of their formal status in Japan.

Finally, I also refer to the Indonesian candidates as my 'informants', although I remember my non-anthropologist friend recoiling at this term when, in an attempt to explain what my research was about, I used it to refer to the people I studied. The uncomfortable connotation of shadowy collaborators made the word sound too impersonal for people I claimed to have created intimate relationships with, and suggested their complicity in some illicit plan. Perhaps due to my being accustomed to the term I did not feel this discomfort. An informant could be a friend, and a friend could be an informant – that is, a person who simply offers information. There is, of course, a need to recognise a difference in practice when one is dealing with a non-informant friend compared to a friend whose knowledge or narratives one plans to use for research purposes. With this in mind, and in acknowledgement of the double role the Indonesian candidates fulfilled in my research experience, I refer to them interchangeably as friends and as informants.

***

When a Polish friend visited me in Japan during my field research, I asked him to bring a few boxes of various Polish sweets. I wanted to use them as a treat for the range of individuals involved in my project in the care homes for the elderly, my main research sites. In one of the institutions I opened a box of *ptasie mleczko*, marshmallow-like sweets covered in chocolate, and placed it on a table in a nurse station where everyone usually gathered for briefings and to eat their lunch. Towards the end of my lunch break, I offered one of the sweets to a Japanese female member of staff who had just entered the room. As soon as she bit into a piece, she commented that it 'tastes like a foreigner' (*gaijin no aji o shiteru*; Jpn.) in a manner that made me think she found the sweet barely palatable. Although a matter of an individual taste, appreciation of different flavours is a question of familiarity as well. Being 'familiar with' implies being able to predict the sensation one is to experience when exposed to that which is familiar. When the outcome is not what was expected, the sensation may be undesirable, coming with discomfort, confusion, uncertainty, or simply an unappreciated taste in the mouth, as seemed to be the case for the young Japanese woman who tasted her first Polish sweets. It may, on the other hand, offer quite a pleasant surprise and a new experience that can take us on a trajectory so far unknown. It may further still become an acquired taste that needs to be cultivated and may require persistence. This book tells a story of such a new life flavour experienced by the Indonesians and the Japanese alike, who all approached it in their own ways. In recounting those individual experiences and tracing their embedding in the wider discourses, this book explores what constitutes migratory encounters with the new and unknown, and what gives these encounters a direction in which to develop.[27]

Notes

1. I use a masculine pronoun because as much as Jasir was making a general statement, here he was primarily referring to his own experiences.
2. An EPA was essentially a Free Trade Agreement (FTA), but the difference in name given to this and other similar deals proposed by Japan was said to reflect the wider spectrum of issues covered. In the case of the agreement with Indonesia, apart from the usual customs relaxation clauses, the EPA included an agreement on the movement of people and capital.
3. Japanese Ministry of Foreign Affairs. Available from: http://www.mofa. go.jp/mofaj/gaiko/fta/ [10 March 2011].
4. See, for example, Haswidi 2007; Stott 2008.
5. This perception of the EPA as being potentially not as beneficial to the Indonesian economy as could have been hoped, seems to be behind the request to revise the agreement's conditions by the Indonesian government, issued in early 2015 (Yulisman 2015).
6. For more details, see Vogt 2007.
7. In a survey focused on hospitals with more than 300 beds conducted by scholars at the Kyushu University Research Centre before the EPA acceptance began, around 50 per cent of the hospitals responded that they would want to accept foreign nurse candidates as a countermeasure to the shortage of nurses (Kawaguchi et al. 2008 in Vogt 2011).
8. The ratio varies slightly depending on the type of care facility.
9. Japanese Ministry of Justice. Available from: http://www.moj.go.jp/ ENGLISH/information/tnl-01.html [7 September 2006].
10. Japanese Ministry of Health, Labour and Welfare. Available from: http:// www.mhlw.go.jp/houdou/2009/03/h0331-10.html [30 January 2012].
11. Goodman deals with this and related issues throughout his book.

12. This number excludes those who have taken Japanese nationality.
13. The vast majority of Koreans who came to Japan in the colonial period or immediately after the end of the Second World War came from a Korea that was not yet divided into two separate political entities. It was only after the Korean War (1950–53) that they faced the need to specify their affiliation with one state or the other.
14. I have never heard the term in use during my fieldwork, but an internet search for the expressions *Amerika kei Nihonjin*, that is, 'Japanese of American (ethnic) origin', and *Burajiru kei Nihonjin*, 'Japanese of Brazilian (ethnic) origin', suggested that such expressions are being proposed as valid and may be coming into use. For example, an article 'I am "Japanese of American Origins"' (from Jpn.: *Watashi wa Amerika kei Nihonjin*) by Shigeharu Higashi, published in 2010 on the website 'Discover Nikkei – Japanese Migrants and their Descendants', proposes the term as more adequate than 'American of Japanese origins'. There was also a discussion on an internet forum about the question 'Why do we not say: Japanese of … origins?' (*Naze … kei Nihonjin tte Iwanai no deshō ka? Kankoku kei Nihonjin toka Burajiru kei Nihonjin toka*; Jpn.). Available from: http://www.discovernikkei.org/en/journal/2010/10/5/watashi-ha-amerikakei-nihonjin/ [5 November 2010]; http://detail.chiebukuro.yahoo.co.jp/qa/question_detail/q1335111028 [5 November 2010].
15. See Wetherall 2008: 264–81 for other ways of formal construction of what he calls 'a raceless nationality' in Japan.
16. See Ko's Chapter 1 on the changing content of the discourses on Japaneseness, pp. 11–31.
17. See Mandel 2008 for discussion of the German case, e.g. p. 207.
18. Between 2000 and 2003 – i.e. in the first three years since the introduction of the Long-Term Care Insurance (LTCI) system – there was a 77.9 per cent increase in the number of people receiving support either at home or in a specialist institution (MHLW 2003). For more information on LTCI and some useful references, refer to Vogt and Holdgrün 2012: 73.
19. For a summary of possible negative and positive effects of population decline, see Kono 2011: 43. For a broader perspective on population ageing in Asia, refer to Goodman and Harper 2008b.
20. For a similarly critical analysis of the concept, see Burgess (2004) 2012.
21. See also Chin 1997; Anderson 2000; Rudnyckyj 2004; Williams and Gavanas 2008.
22. According to data published in 2009 by the World Association of Newspapers and News Publishers (WAN-IFRA 2009), out of the three titles, the *Yomiuri Shinbun* had the greatest circulation at 10.020 million copies, followed by the *Asahi Shinbun* with 8.049 million, and the *Nihon Keizai Shinbun* with 3.052 million. The *Yomiuri Shinbun* is considered to be centre-right, or conservative; *Asahi Shinbun* centre-left, or liberal; and *Nihon Keizai Shinbun* economics- and business-oriented.
23. I did not include here those short telegraphic news items that report on the arrival of a new group of candidates, on the schedule of programme

information sessions, or simply provide a short explanation what the term 'EPA' or its Japanese equivalent stands for.

24. This is also the reason why I do not include these texts in calculation of the frequency of references to the EPA Indonesians appearing in the media. I cannot claim that this set represents a comprehensive sample of the material available on the internet. Rather, it is a collection of different voices coming from a range of individuals and sources.

25. See also Gubrium 1995 for the use of life narratives in his eldercare home-based research.

26. It was a thickener added to liquids to prevent choking on too runny a liquid among the elderly who had problems with controlling their swallowing motion.

27. Parts of this Introduction have previously been published in Świtek 2014.

 1

IMAGINING LIFE AND WORK IN JAPAN

Recruitment in Indonesia

In January 2010, a television report by the Japan Broadcasting Corporation showed a group of Indonesian nurse candidates who had come to Japan under the Economic Partnership Agreement (EPA) two years earlier. They were recalling stories they had heard of people signing their EPA contracts on the bus to the airport, just as they were about to leave Indonesia for Japan. With a possible exception of some forty successful caregiver and nurse candidates who at the time of the recruitment process were reaching the end of their education or had recently graduated from one specific school of health sciences in West Java province, the majority of the 208 Indonesians from the first EPA batch were said to have found out about the programme only about a week to ten days before the deadline for submitting the required documentation. Having considered in the Introduction how the acceptance of Indonesian care workers came about, I now turn to the very individuals in question to see what motivated them to use the sudden opportunity to migrate that had been opened by the government-led EPA scheme. Aiming towards one of this book's objectives to show the ways in which the structured nature of the acceptance shaped the Indonesians' encounters with Japan, I examine in this chapter how the particular mode of the programme's implementation affected the Indonesians' outlook at their sojourn – their hopes, expectations and imaginations.

Those who hurriedly applied for the programme did not necessarily desire or plan to work abroad, in particular in Japan, before the information about the opportunity reached them. For those who were considering, if not actively seeking, employment opportunities outside of Indonesia, one of the main and feasible destinations of choice was Australia. There, however, one of the eligibility criteria was proven proficiency in the English language, and the recruitment procedure presented itself as more complicated. Hence, when the Japanese government made a relatively condition-free offer (that is, with no language proficiency requirement), many of the potential candidates for overseas labour seized the opportunity and redirected their consideration towards Japan. My Indonesian informants unanimously recalled that as the information about the programme only reached them just before the application deadline, it left them almost no time to really dwell on what successful selection would entail. They simply grasped the opportunity without much emotional or intellectual investment in the process. Only about a week later, they found themselves qualified for the programme. The decision had to be swift; those who took the chance were sent to a pre-departure training centre in Jakarta, and left for Japan only two weeks later. Such sudden decisions also meant that there was no time for in-depth investigation into the actual content of the work on offer, or into the nuances of the Japanese payment system. This lack of knowledge became a source of disillusionment.

Financial Disappointments

When advertised and published by the media in Indonesia, the information about the salaries the candidates could expect was presented as 'will be paid up to 200,000 yen' (about £1,600 at the time). Such a formulation was said to have misled the candidates into thinking that this was the amount they would receive. Their assumptions were not clarified during the recruitment process (whether purposefully or unintentionally was an object of debate); nor were the candidates told of the various standard deductions from their salary, such as the obligatory national insurance contribution, or so at least they claimed. Some candidates also suggested that they were convinced the amount was calculated after expenses such as rent had been deducted. Moreover, despite the Indonesian government's insistence during the negotiations of the programme, there was no guarantee of a minimum amount that each Indonesian candidate would receive. As a result, not only did the monthly salaries vary substantially between institutions, ranging from about 140,000 to 250,000 yen, but they were also reduced by expenditures the Indonesians did not anticipate. Consequently, instead of the expected 200,000 yen, the majority took home about half of that amount each month.

Because the Indonesian candidates were used to the Indonesian system of remuneration, in which deductions from wages do not happen automatically, it did not even occur to them that the system might be different in Japan. They simply expected what they were used to. It was not until they were faced with the reality diverging from their expectations that they realised the assumptions they had made. This did not alleviate their feelings of disappointment, however, as their expectations were high. Those overseeing the EPA recruitment were suspected of having been aware of the misconceptions the candidates held about both the financial and the practical side of the EPA deployment. They were believed to have purposefully withheld any clarifying information, as it was a strategically kept 'governmental secret', or *rahasia pemerintah* (Ind.), in the words of one of the candidates. Just as in the case of the remuneration system, the candidates also used the familiar images of nursing and Indonesian homes for the elderly to construct an image of *kaigo* (care; Jpn.) they were expected to engage in as EPA candidates. In this respect as well, the image did not exactly match the reality they encountered.

Professional Expectations and Confounded *Kaigo* in Japan

As already mentioned in the Introduction, under the provisions of the EPA between Japan and Indonesia, the caregiver candidates were expected to train towards a Japanese caregiver qualification for four years. The examination that was to guarantee the title of 'caregiver' and the right for the candidates to continue working in Japan consisted of two parts, a written test and a practical demonstration. As also explained earlier, administered entirely in Japanese, the written test in particular was thought to present a 'high hurdle' (*hādoru ga takai*; Jpn.) for the Indonesians to overcome. The Indonesian candidates were made aware of the requirement for them to sit the examination when they were recruited in Indonesia. However, when I talked to them shortly before their arrival at the accepting institutions, they were not concerned about the examination's difficulty. At the time, in January 2009, either it was still too far away to even think about, or it did not feature as anything particularly challenging. The information about the level of difficulty did not seem to have reached the candidates, as those to whom I spoke at the time assumed that they would pass the examination and stay on in Japan for a few more years. Some, of course, clarified from the outset that they were in Japan solely for the money, and hence the examination was not anything they worried about.

Around the same time, I asked the Indonesian candidates what their plans were for the future beyond the four-year training period, and whether they were linked to Japan or not. Apart from those few who decided to openly strip their intentions of any other motives and claimed that they were only interested in the financial side of their sojourn, the responses were usually more thoughtful and often suggested a degree of openness to what the future might bring. Settling in Japan was not written off as an option. A 25-year-old man, who was already fairly fluent in Japanese, said that his plan was to work in Japan for ten years, then return to 'his country' and set up a nursing home applying whatever knowledge he was about to gain in Japan. Another equally fluent and eloquent man, of a similar age, planned to remain in Japan for a 'few more' years after the examination, then return to Indonesia and teach nursing. An experienced 33-year-old female nurse wanted to bring her husband and two children to Japan once she was a qualified caregiver. She was looking to learn something new in Japan, and also wanted her family to have greater prospects than they would in Indonesia. Another woman, in her early twenties, said that she was not sure if she would stay in Japan or go to another country. She planned, however, not to return to Indonesia for 'many years', her goal being to obtain a diploma as a certified nurse, which did not exist in Indonesia at the time.

The caregiver candidates who arrived in Japan in 2008 were all trained nurses. This was a requirement to qualify for the programme in the first year it ran, because at that time the training course for care workers was not yet established in Indonesia, nor did there exist a profession of caregiver. Hence, familiar with nursing in Indonesia, the candidates imagined the tasks of a Japanese caregiver to be similar to those they were performing in hospitals and clinics as nurses. Therefore, despite embarking on care work in Japan, some of them still planned for their future careers to be in nursing, and imagined that the expected experience in Japan would add to their array of nursing skills. Others imagined that their work in Japan would be 'talking to the elderly', a view that was based on experiences they had had in the eldercare homes in Indonesia, where the majority of residents were independent and did not require bodily care.

Development of **Kaigo**

The Japanese *kaigo*, care, as an occupation is in itself a fairly new phenomenon. The qualification of caregiver (*kaigofukushishi*; Jpn.) that the Indonesian candidates were required to obtain by the end of their training was established in Japan in 1987. At the time of my research, *kaigo* as a profession was still perceived as in need of better definition, a suggestion made to me by Professor Itō Ruri from the the Hitotsubashi University in Tokyo during an interview in July 2009. This underspecification of what counted as *kaigo* as a profession manifested itself in the care institutions I visited. There was virtually no difference between the tasks performed by personnel with and without the qualification of caregiver. The differences in pay levels between these members of staff were also very small, and sometimes there was no difference at all. In fact, only around 30 per cent of care workers in Japan were qualified *kaigofukushishi* in 2009.

According to *The Fundamentals of Care*, a 2011 publication tracing the history of the Japanese caregiver profession and its current premises, not only is the profession relatively new, but so is *kaigo* as a word. It appeared for the first time in a Japanese dictionary in 1991 in the 4th edition of *Kōjien*, one of the most popular and highly regarded Japanese dictionaries. However, the very practice of providing 'personal care/help' (*mi no mawari no sewa*; Jpn.) to those members of society who are unable to do it for themselves dates further back in history. The first recorded official use of the term *kaigo* is found in an 1892 directive establishing the practice of assistance to war veterans who became permanently disabled as a result of injuries sustained on duty. In the 1950s the term sporadically appeared in local and national regulations referring to support for the elderly, people with disabilities, and the sick, when *kaigo* and nursing assistance began to be offered at people's homes. During that time, the term referred to the support of a family in their role of looking after a person who was entitled to public benefits based on the degree of their disability. It was officially acknowledged as a 'human' (*jinteki*; Jpn.) or 'personal' (*taijin*; Jpn.) service focused on an individual rather than on a family with the promulgation of the Elderly Welfare Law in 1963. The law, responding to calls for 'taking measures to provide separate accommodation in order to efficiently provide appropriate treatment to the elderly who need daily *kaigo* due to their considerable mental or physical deficiencies' (Satō, Shirai and Terashima 2011: 3), became a basis for the establishment of specialised care homes for the elderly (see also, Wu 2004).

At that time, the elderly in such homes were looked after by 'matrons, housemothers' (*ryōbo*; Jpn.) who had had no professional training, and it was not until 1987 that the need for specialised knowledge and skills to perform elderly care was codified in a law establishing the profession of caregiver, *kaigofukushishi*. Despite the introduction of this officially recognised qualification, the question of to what extent the work or services offered by the caregivers actually required professional knowledge and skills remained. As mentioned earlier, the majority of people employed in care institutions at the time of this research did not possess the formal qualification, but were nevertheless allowed to perform the same range of duties as those who did. At the same time, many people were caring for their elderly at home, either by choice or by force of circumstances, without any previous training. This type of care is also referred to as *kaigo*, the supposed domain of the certified *kaigofukushishi*. The definition of *kaigo* and therefore of the responsibilities to be performed by its practitioners is also confounded by the practical overlapping of tasks between *kaigo* and nursing.

Kaigo – *Care beyond Nursing?*

It is said that the very term *kaigo* was constructed through a combination of the term *kango*, nursing, either with *kaihō*, attending to, taking care of somebody, or with *kaijo*, support, assistance. Central to the work of Japanese caregivers, *kaigo*, although morphologically tracing its roots to nursing, did not emerge from within this profession. The similarity of the tasks performed continues to blur the boundaries between the two, despite efforts in both camps to clearly define their respective domains. Although more readily recognised as possessing professional (medical) skills and knowledge, in Japan nurses often perform the same tasks as caregivers. This is particularly the case in the care homes for the elderly, where the boundaries, even if formally set, are often blurred when it comes to, for example, administering medicines, preparing a care plan for an elderly individual, or attending to the physiological needs of the elderly. With all the necessary information already written down by doctors for everyone to access, the tacit understanding is that anyone, regardless of professional background, is, for example, able to match the information in a notebook with the elderly person's name and the medicines they require. Similarly, the bodily care associated with 'tidying' (Twigg 2000a: 407), which is more readily associated with the responsibilities of caregivers, is commonly required of nurses as well, even in hospitals. A former nurse engaged in lobbying for improvements to the EPA acceptance programme was indeed worried about the impact this conflation would have on the Indonesian nurses. She feared that they would be disappointed once they found out that they would have to change patients' diapers.

Both *kaigo* and *kango* are considered vocations (*shimei*; Jpn.). This means that regardless of professional training one is expected to apply at work not only one's educated knowledge but also one's personal qualities. In other words, vocation requires one to possess not only training, but a particular kind of human capital as well. While compassion for patients has been an integral part of nursing, the interaction between a nurse and a patient is in a sense limited to the cause of a patient requiring nursing care, either in a temporal or practical sense (see Gubrium 1975: 48–49; Wu 2004: 107). A care worker, on the other hand, is expected to provide support (*kaijo*) regardless of the source of the need for the support, and beyond the immediate needs stemming from the particular condition requiring nursing (*kaihō*). *Kaigo* is imbued with the ideas expressed in the concept of quality of life, which began to be directly linked to the provision of care in Japan in the 1960s. This is not to say that *kango*, nursing, is not concerned with the general well-being of patients, or that nurses do not provide wholesome emotional support alongside their more specialised, medical care. The shorter temporal engagement with patients is also particularly hard to argue as a distinguishing factor in eldercare homes, where both nurses and caregivers (and other care workers) provide the same care to the elderly on an everyday basis. In general, however, *kaigo* seems to be imagined as encompassing all areas of an individual's life to a greater degree than *kango*, aiming at providing the highest possible quality of life for the elderly, sick and people with disabilities, regardless of and beyond their physical or mental incapacitation. This requirement of wholesomeness imbued in *kaigo*, and its lack of direct connection to a medical condition of those requiring support, contributes to the ambiguity of the definition of *kaigo* and therefore to the definition of the scope of tasks to be performed by *kaigofukushishi* but not by others. This usually means that the *kaigo* personnel attend to any and all bodily functions in order to support not only the physical but also the mental well-being of the cared-for. Julia Twigg provides an astute description of the ideas behind the distinctions between medicalised and non-medical engagements with the cared-for body. It is worth quoting at length:

> Though medicine deals with the body, it does so in a particular and circumscribed way, constructing it in terms of the object body of science, distant and depersonalised (Lawler 1997). Medical practice is presented in such a way as to limit involvement in the body, and professional status is marked out in terms of distance from the bodily. Doctors perform

relatively little direct bodywork and, where they do, it is largely confined to the high-status activity of diagnosis, or is mediated by high-tech machines. Where it is part of treatment (with the exception of the elite virtuosi activity of surgery), it is often delivered by lesser practitioners like physiotherapists or nurses. Nursing ironically shares many of these ambivalences. Though bodywork is at the heart of nursing, it has an uncertain status. Nursing is organised hierarchically so that, as staff progress, they move away from the basic bodywork of bedpans and sponge baths towards high-tech, skilled interventions; progressing from dirty work on bodies to clean work on machines. Dunlop (1986) argues that the recent emphasis on psychological dimensions of the patient and indeed the whole educational project, with its tendency to academicise nursing, represents a further flight from the bodily in pursuit of higher status forms of knowledge and practice. (Twigg 2000a: 389–90)

Care workers such as the EPA candidates are at the end of this chain of shifting the work on the body, through various distancing techniques (Dyer, McDowell and Batnitzky 2008; see also Douglas 1966; Jervis 2001; Wolkowitz 2006), down the hierarchy of professions. In Indonesia, too, the medicalised side of care is delegated to nurses, and the bodily tasks associated with the given medical condition are attended to by family members, even if the patient is in a hospital. The apparent scarcity of explanation of what would be expected of the EPA Indonesians as *kaigofukushishi* candidates in Japan caused disillusionment in some of the candidates to whom I talked. Iffah, a young woman I introduce more closely later in this chapter, started looking for learning materials on the internet in order to keep up with the latest developments in the nursing field. For several months after her training began, she did not tell her father what she was actually doing, and kept him believing that she was developing her nursing skills, feeling uneasy or even *malu* (Ind.), ashamed, of what she was doing in Japan.[1] In Indonesia when I met two of Iffah's friends who were going to work at the same institution as her, I asked them how they imagined their future work in Japan. They answered that it would be just talking to the elderly. When I prompted them for a more elaborate answer, they added that there might be some help with eating involved, too. Iffah did not seem to have conveyed any information about the more challenging, 'dirty' aspects of bodywork involved in caring for the elderly. When back in Japan I asked Iffah why she did not tell her friends the whole truth about the kind of work they were going to embark on, she replied that she did not want to discourage them. Although once in the care institutions my Indonesian informants wanted, in general, to learn how to provide care to the elderly, the taste of disappointment remained. Two female candidates based in central Japan enjoyed their work and the people they worked with, but felt that they had been 'lied to' (*dibohongi*; Ind.) during the recruitment process about what being a caregiver candidate would entail, and what their conditions of employment would be.

The expectations and disappointments of the Indonesian EPA candidates point to the saliency of the organisation of their move to Japan in the experiences of the sojourn. They embarked on a pre-organised scheme, run by the government, which seemingly guaranteed a certain level of income and a particular kind of employment. Had it not been an officially organised enterprise, their expectations about its outcome might have been more provisory and therefore less susceptible to disappointment, and most likely the individuals who grasped the sudden opportunity would not have decided to travel to Japan (or to any other country) in search of work. The majority of my informants expected to obtain 'respectable' employment in Indonesia anyway, and so the decision to go to Japan was based on the promising and seemingly guaranteed conditions of the EPA employment. Faced with a different reality to what they expected, it was relatively easy for the candidates to resign from participation in the programme, especially as the majority of the costs associated with the deployment were covered by the accepting institutions, not by the Indonesians or their families. Were they to return,

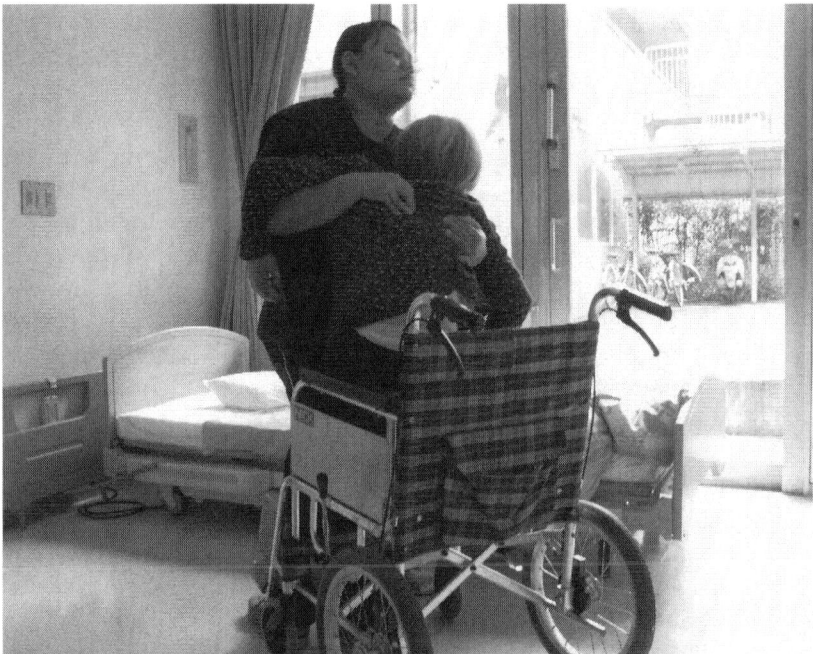

Figure 1.1: Lifting an elderly person. Photo by author.

the loss of incurred costs would not be theirs. Several of the candidates, although none of my informants, chose to return to Indonesia before the end of the training period, something to which I return in Chapter 3 where I deal with the Indonesians' relationships with their employers. However, to say that their arrival in Japan was, for my friends, a chain of disappointments would be foreclosing the importance of other sources of motivation that also contributed to their choice.

Japanese Dreaming

One weekend in November 2008, my husband and I were sitting on a sturdy wooden bench in the middle of a spacious concrete balcony surrounded by an Indonesian family. Although we had just met, we played several rounds of cards without any extensive introductions, and during the game nothing more than comments about how to play were exchanged. Only once our zeal for the game died out did we begin investigating each other's stories. We all had come to this seaside hotel at Pantai Baron (Baron Beach) for a short break, but while for my husband and I it was just a weekend away from Yogyakarta where I was taking an intensive course in the Indonesian language, for the family it was the only holiday they could afford to spend together each year. Inevitably perhaps, our conversation took us to explore where we all came from and where we were heading, two days from that point in time, as well as in our lives. Poland, my country of origin, did not feature prominently in the imagination of the family members; New Zealand, my husband's native land, appeared somewhat more sharply – but Great Britain, where we had both conceded to settle down for the time being, was seen as a prominent representative of the affluent Europe. None of the family members had been to any European country, but they had all heard stories, seen films, or watched the news conveying images of Europe on which they could build their imaginations. A distant relative had actually left for *Belanda*, the Netherlands, in search of work.

I protested against being thought of as leading an affluent life back in London, although we agreed that with the exchange rate between the British pound and the Indonesian rupiah, my husband and I were in a better financial position while in Indonesia than many of the Indonesians working there and earning standard Indonesian salaries (for example, my Indonesian language teacher was earning one million rupiah a month, the equivalent of around 60 pounds sterling; this was, however, a very low salary, albeit one not putting a person below the poverty line at the time). The crux of our conversation about money that is most relevant here was, however, the argument presented by one of the men that the difference between us was not just the amount of disposable income at home, but that a trip like ours from Britain to Indonesia in a reversed direction was simply out of their financial reach. Moving from one coast of Java to the other was the ultimate excursion the family could imagine possible for themselves, as they were acutely aware of the insurmountable financial limitations that living in Indonesia with an average salary imposed on them. The price of travel between Indonesia and Europe would be the same for them as it was for my husband and me, despite the differences in the purchasing power of our respective salaries on the global market. No matter how much they worked, they did not expect to be able to ever venture to Europe. It was not just the cost of the flight but also the extremely low exchange value of the Indonesian rupiah that would have made a holiday in Europe prohibitively expensive, especially if they were to travel as a family.

It felt uneasy to answer the next question about where we were heading after my language course was over. I was coming from an affluent Europe and going to another fairly wealthy country, merely stopping in Indonesia on my way there. From the reaction to my reply, it seemed that Japan, although geographically much closer than Europe, felt even less attainable to them. Although, like Indonesia, an Asian country, Japan was an entirely different world (*dunia yang sama sekali berbeda*; Ind.), the family would say. They knew Japanese cars, which they thought were good and which indeed were plentiful on the Indonesian streets. They imagined Japan as a country of advanced technology and prosperous economy, signs of which they could see around them in the form of various kinds of electronic equipment and through the proliferation of Japanese restaurants in the shopping malls of the bigger Indonesian cities. Perhaps it was the combination of Japan's relatively close geographical proximity and presence in the mundane artefacts, yet with its simultaneous inaccessibility, that made it seem even more elusive than the more geographically distant but not so mundanely present Europe. Merely hinting at its own existence somewhere out there through everyday objects, Japan was like an invisible ghost. Leaving only traces of its presence, it seemed even more of a mythical land to which one was even less likely to go than the unreachable yet somehow more real Europe.

This image of Japan as a kind of mythical promised land was shared by my informants. Two Indonesian care workers from the second batch of the EPA acceptance told me in January 2010 that they had chosen Japan as their destination because it was so inaccessible: 'Usually [outside of a programme such as EPA] it is impossible to go there, only in dreams' (*biasanya mustahil pergi kesana, hanya bisa dalam mimpi*; Ind.). Japan, un-viable as a migration destination due to the travel costs involved and fortified by highly selective immigration regulations, was now opened by the EPA scheme, presenting an opportunity like no other. This did not mean that it was easy to get through the selection process and beat other candidates for acceptance to the programme. As one of the young women put it, she chose to come to Japan because there were so many people who went to the Arab countries for work, and so few to Japan. With the 'thousands' (*ribuan*; Ind.) of people who applied for the EPA programme, she felt it would really be 'something' (*sesuatu*; Ind.) if she were to find herself among the selected candidates. That she and her colleagues succeeded meant that their achievement would be valued even more highly on their return to Indonesia, and should guarantee far better career prospects in comparison to those who went to work in other, more common emigration destinations, such as the Middle East or even Canada or Australia – or at least, so the women believed.[2] The image of Japan as technologically superior to all the other countries and regions the two young women mentioned, and the perception of Japan as leading in *modernisasi*, modernisation, were to aid the value of their work experience and further elevate them above an average *TKI, tenaga kerja Indonesia*, Indonesian (migrant) worker.

Admired from afar, Japan was also, not least of all, the homeland of the locally well-known comic book and anime character *Doraemon*, a cat-like figure with supernatural powers. A wide selection of various series of the comic book translated into Indonesian were commonly available in book stores, and garments with *Doraemon*'s likeness could be found in clothing bazaars when I visited Indonesia in 2008 and later in 2009. One of my teachers at the language school in Yogyakarta asked me to send her a few copies of the comic book in the original from Japan. She already had a collection in Indonesian and harboured a wish to one day learn Japanese, perhaps with the help of the comic book. When a colleague of Iffah, my female informant, presented her with one of the ten *Doraemon* soft toys he had received on the occasion of his marriage, he made Iffah's day. The large size of the toy only added to the joy. The friendly looking blue-and-white figure received a central position in Iffah's small apartment, and the information about her new acquisition spread rapidly among other candidates. When, shortly after this, Iffah found out that her elder sister was in hospital, the large *Doraemon* was an obvious choice for a present to take with her during a planned visit to Indonesia two months later. With *Doraemon*, Iffah had received not just a toy but a physically tangible proof of her presence in Japan. She probably would not have bought the toy for herself, and if she had, it would not have been such a large one (as the size came with an equally ample price tag). A symbol of the world of which she knew but had never expected to be a part had materialised in her hands, and she now *was* in this world: the *Doraemon* had dotted the *i*s and crossed the *t*s for her. 'Iffah was there', the toy seemed to be saying when she delivered it to her sister. Iffah and her EPA friends went to Japan not only to gain professional experience and for financial reasons, but also to enjoy this distant and usually inaccessible but somehow familiar place.

In Okushima Mika's edited volume *Indonesian Community of Japan* (Okushima 2009), Fukihara Yutaka notes that despite a significant increase since 1998 in the Japanese language as the second or third, after English, most popular foreign language taught in Indonesia, there remained very limited options for finding employment using it. This is notwithstanding the close political and economic links between the two countries. Similarly, despite Indonesia hosting the greatest number of Japanese learners in South East Asia (about 85,000 in 2003), the opportunities for them to go to work or to study in Japan were still limited to short-term sojourns under such schemes as those run by the Japan International Training Cooperation Organisation (JITCO) under which Indonesian and other nationals could undergo on-the-job training in various areas of Japanese industry (Fukihara 2009: 69–84). The contrast between the popularity of things Japanese and the widely spread desire, or at least aspiration, to visit Japan, and the comparatively low probability of this ever happening, seemed to have created a phantasmagoric image of the country. The EPA acceptance programme provided a path to enter a country that not only promised financial and professional bounty, but also, due to its inaccessibility, conferred a kind of status on anyone who managed to go there.

Sarah Mahler, in her book *American Dreaming: Immigrant Life on the Margins*, focusing on the experiences of undocumented Salvadoran and South American immigrants living in Manhattan, shows how the vision of migrant life in the United States is constructed by the narratives of those who have already been there, and by media representations. Both of these channels, Mahler argues, produce 'unrealistic dreams', especially given the fact that even 'if the information does arrive in a pure state, people do not accept the bald truth' (Mahler 1995: 84). A similar observation is made by Johan Lindquist (2009: 27) about the information fed back to prospective migrants who contemplated searching for work on the 'fantasy island' of Batam in Indonesia. Indeed, Iffah's refusal to disclose to her friends the details of their job in Japan was an act of such illusory construction. However, when the first batch of

Indonesian EPA candidates were deciding to go to Japan in 2008, they had no obvious predecessors (perhaps with the exception of two candidates who I know had siblings working or studying in Japan; none of them, however, was employed in care provision, and hence they could not reflect on this particular environment). It was therefore the more diffused image of Japan on which the EPA candidates relied. Given the frustrations caused by the disappointments discussed earlier and throughout this book, these other incentives of going to Japan were an important source of consolation for the candidates. Admittedly, the way the EPA programme was structured served to maintain, at least initially, this dream-like vision of Japan.

Introduction to Life in Japan

As mentioned earlier, before arriving at their respective institutions of employment, the Indonesians spent six months in language training. At the time of my first visit to one of the centres towards the end of the introductory training for the first EPA group in early January 2009, the fifty-six caregiver candidates living and studying there were already well accommodated to their environment. They moved around the complex with the familiarity of people who managed to appropriate its spaces through various experiences that had taken place there. The candidates' weekdays were organised around the Japanese classes lasting from 9 a.m. until 4 p.m., with an hour and a half break for lunch. Some of them used these breaks also for prayers. The late afternoons and evenings were meant to be devoted to self-study while utilising the computer laboratory and materials to be found in the adjacent library. When during my visit to the centre I was given fifteen minutes to talk to a group of candidates during their Japanese speaking class, I asked what they were doing during their free time at the centre. The responses I received were univocal. They would either go together to a nearby shopping mall, or would stay at the centre because there were 'enough Indonesians there'.

The training centre provided somewhat sterile surroundings where the Indonesian candidates lived in a community of Japanese language learners and did not really need to use the Japanese language to go about their daily lives; nor did they need to know how to navigate in the outside (Japanese) world. They were enjoying their time in Japan, but in the intimate Indonesian space of the training centre. Situated next to a narrow strip of pebble beach in one of the suburban areas of a large metropolis, the centre was accommodated in a purpose-built hotel-like 18-storey building complete with a library, computer labora-tory and karaoke room. With a roller-blind-shaded glass wall forming cosy lounges and a large refectory overlooking the bay, the students had a comfortable place to live and study. In the centre's refectory the daily menu was displayed in the form of photographs accompanied by cartoon-like images of animals to depict the meat used in a given dish. Alongside the pictures, each meal carried a description in Japanese, translated into Indonesian as well. Every day there was a selection that allowed the Muslim candidates to choose food not containing pork or its derivatives. During my tour of the centre, guided by a member of staff, I was shown two spaces specially selected for the purpose of prayer. They were small, empty tatami rooms, with arrows glued to the ceiling in one of the corners pointing in the direction of Mecca. The Indonesian candidates enjoyed their time spent in very agreeable conditions, without responsibilities other than attending the classes. Pocket money was already entering their bank accounts (set up on their behalf), food was provided by the refectory, and trips and other activi-ties were organised by the centre's staff. All in all, the experience of the young Indonesians in this training centre seemed to be more reminis-cent of a group package holiday rather than of the training of migrant workers-to-be. Thanks to this relaxed prelude to their deployment to the accepting institutions, the Indonesians' tourist-like excitement about being in Japan did not die, although the imminent separation and metamorphosis from semi-tourists into workers with real respon-sibilities did produce anxiety, arising especially from the fear of not being able to communicate in Japanese, and the expected loneliness.

The initial comforts of the training centre allowed my informants to enjoy Japan as they imagined it. For the majority of the candidates, this was their first ever experience of a country other than Indonesia, and the employment which followed was to become their first 'proper' job. The freshness of experience for those for whom these first six months in Japan opened their careers and initiated independent lives added to the bustling excitement among the candidates when I met them in the train-ing centre. Such an initially hospitable environment, where there was no need to pay much attention to the various impediments to everyday life that migrant workers arriving in a foreign country on their own ac-count experience, increased the candidates' expectations towards what was still ahead of them in Japan. This was so even if thinking of the future was linked to the prospect of being separated from the group of friends that had formed during the training. The imagined Japan of *Doraemon* and *modernisasi* presented itself as a hospitable place in these first months of the candidates' Japanese sojourn. When it later turned out to be less perfect than expected, the friendly group, which extended beyond the EPA candidates, became a safety net, especially when their social life in the accepting institutions was not going smoothly. As I discuss later, the relationships forged during training also played an important part in negotiations in which the Indonesians engaged, such as when an apartment did not feel suitable, or when the candidates found themselves living on their own in an isolated village, or indeed when not all of the stated provisions of the EPA programme were granted or were what the candidates expected them to be.

Figure 1.2: Enjoying Japan. Photo by author.

Protagonists

At the beginning of their sojourn in Japan, the youngest of the group of friends who became my informants were Jasir and Lanny, who were both twenty-three; of the others, Daris was twenty-four, Iffah and Lazim were both twenty-five, Amir twenty-six, and Irdina thirty-three.[3] Amir, Jasir, Iffah, Lanny, Lazim and Daris graduated from STIKes (Sekolah Tinggi Ilmu Kesehatan) in Indonesia, a tertiary-level School of Health Sciences and, like everyone who came to Japan under the EPA in 2008, had a diploma in nursing. They had some practical experience of nursing as well, gained through the various placements during studies or while employed in community clinics and hospitals, be it in intensive care units, paediatric wards, or indeed in *panti jompo* (Ind.), live-in institutions for the elderly in Indonesia. However, they all graduated from STIKes in 2008 (in 2007 in Amir's case) and hence did not have a sufficient length of practical work as nurses to come as nurse candidates to Japan in 2008 under the provisions of the EPA. Only Irdina, the oldest in the group, who had graduated from a nursing academy, had the necessary minimum of two years experience working as a nurse to qualify as a nurse candidate under the scheme. In fact, before coming to Japan, she had worked as a nurse for twelve years, some of which was in one of the most prestigious hospitals in Jakarta. She chose the EPA caregiver track, however, because she calculated that she would have a greater chance of being selected for the programme.

Often referred to as elite (*erīto*; Jpn.) in Japan, many of the EPA candidates from the first intake hailed from the more privileged echelons of Indonesian society. The short period of recruitment meant that the information about the programme mostly reached, with sufficient time in which to apply, those who were in some way close to the source of the information. A few of the candidates learnt about the programme from commercials broadcast by Indonesian television, and some had the information conveyed to them by friends who saw the commercials. Many, however, received the information via their 'connected' parents or via teachers. This was because those whose parents occupied administrative positions were more likely to learn about the EPA acceptance. Hence, many of the candidates who arrived in the first EPA group came from families of a better than average economic position, since in Indonesia working in the state administration means better income and more secure employment. In such a way the very organisation of the EPA acceptance preselected the individuals who arrived in Japan, something that affected how the individuals imagined and later experienced their Japanese sojourn.

Among the seven friends, the family backgrounds of Iffah and Amir were prime examples. Amir's father was the head of a village, a position that came not only with material prosperity, but elevated social standing for the family as well. Iffah's mother ran a business of her own while her father was a director of a local hospital. One morning after Iffah and Lazim, who came from a more modest background, spent a night at my apartment, they had a discussion about the relative wealth of their families. When I objected upon seeing Lazim washing up his cereal bowl he responded that people in Indonesia are taught to wash up after themselves. To my comment that some of them have helpers (*pembantu*; Ind.) to do it for them (hinting at what I knew about Iffah's family), he stressed that since both of his parents were retired school teachers, his family was not as rich (*kaya*; Ind.) as Iffah's to have a *pembantu*. Iffah objected by saying that having home help was a matter of necessity (*kebutuhan*; Ind.) for her family: one person was needed to clean the house, one to look after her sister and one to look after Iffah herself. She admitted also that before coming to Japan, she had never travelled alone, even to the city centre, because she was always accompanied by a *pembantu*. On another occasion she talked at length about the house that her parents had bought for her and which she would possibly convert into a dormitory or small guest house with the money she was expecting to save in Japan. Effectively, despite denying the label, Iffah had to admit that she grew up in a rather affluent environment. While Iffah, Lazim, Daris, Jasir (a son of rice shop owners) and Amir still measured their economic standing by the prosperity of their parental families, Irdina had already a family of her own by the time she arrived in Japan, and it was this unit that she used as a reference when assessing her socio-economic standing in Indonesia. Irdina did not come to Japan forced by economic need. Married in 1997, she was a mother of two. Her husband, an IT specialist in Indonesia, took on the full parenting responsibilities when Irdina left for Japan, but their plan was that ultimately the whole family would relocate there. While she was sending back remittances from Japan to support her family, this was not the main aim of her sojourn. She did not feel that in Indonesia her family was living in unsatisfactory conditions. However, she knew that she would not have developed professionally any further in the job she had been in, and was hoping for broader prospects for her children when they grow up as well. She hoped that Japan would open up opportunities, both for herself and for her children. Hence, when she found out about the EPA programme through a friend, she decided to take the chance.

Inside Eldercare Homes

Once the language training was over, the group of friends was sent to work in six different eldercare institutions in various parts of Japan. Jasir and Amir worked and lived together in the countryside of the Chūgoku region. Training in the same special nursing home *tokubetsu yōgo rōjin hōmu* (commonly referred to as *tokuyō*; Jpn.) I call here 'Ajisai', the two men were placed in different wards. Ajisai hosted ninety-six permanent residents, with a more or less equal number living on each of its three wards. There, the elderly were looked after by an average of twenty-five staff, working in shifts. Where Jasir worked, the majority of the elderly were bedridden, and mostly in advanced stages of dementia. Amir attended to elderly who, although limited in their capacity to live independently, were still by and large fairly mobile and lucid. Although, if needed, they would sometimes go over to the other ward to help during meal times, Jasir and Amir would spend most of their working days separately.

Several hours north-east on a night bus, in the Kantō region, a small town Blue Bara special nursing home was where Iffah worked. Iffah's ward in Blue Bara accommodated thirty of the 150 residents living in the institution as a whole, and she worked alongside a team of ten staff members. The elderly people Iffah was working with were mostly in advanced stages of dementia, some of them bedridden and unable to communicate. Every now and then, when her shift included going to a ward on the second floor, she also attended to elderly who were in good mental health and with whom she was able to have short conversations.

Lazim could be found on the outskirts of a larger city about two hours away on public transport from Iffah. He worked in Tsubaki Nursing Home where together with twenty members of staff he was in charge of thirty-five residents on his ward. The condition of the elderly here varied, ranging from residents with advanced dementia to very lucid individuals.

These were the three locations where I was able to follow the Indonesians at work inside the care homes, and where I made most of my observations relayed in this book. On the opposite shore of Japan's main Honshū Island, in the costal Hokuriku part of the Chūbu region, Irdina was based in Tachibana Group Home. The elderly here required some assistance with everyday activities, but overall were able to or-ganise their own lives within the group units set up by the institution. I visited this place only once, but stayed in touch with Irdina throughout the fieldwork and beyond. Lanny and Daris worked in two separate special nursing homes not far away from Lazim, but there too I have only been once, despite the frequent interaction with both Lanny and Daris outside of their working hours.

Under the EPA scheme, only selected publicly funded eldercare institutions whose services fell under the provisions of Long-Term Care Insurance (LTCI), introduced in 2000,[4] and whose residents were entitled to public assistance could accept the Indonesian candidates. These were special nursing homes for the elderly, or *tokubetsu yōgo rōjin hōmu* (*tokuyō*), Long-Term Care Insurance Institution (*kaigo hoken rōjin shisetu*) providing temporary care and rehabilitation for the elderly recovering from illness, day service centres, and group homes for those with dementia. The latter were institutions that accepted residents for permanent stay in units where small groups of residents, supported by staff, led group lives as a community. The elderly living there were comparatively able physically, but could not function independently due to the progression of dementia. Irdina worked in such a group home. Jasir, Amir, Lazim, Daris, Iffah and Lanny worked in *tokuyō*s. Under the provisions of LTCI, the fees for residence and care received in these homes were divided between the individual and the local authority. The *tokuyō* accepted only those over sixty-five years of age, and the majority of the residents there had dementia to a degree that obstructed communication with them. Many were also bedridden. Admission to *tokuyō* institutions was based solely on the health condition of the elderly, and there was no income threshold set as a qualifying requirement. *Keihi rōjin hōmu*, where admission was income-based, and the privately founded *yūryō rōjin hōmu* available only to those in the higher income bracket, were excluded from the EPA scheme.

All three of the care homes I visited regularly were divided into wards where typically the elderly were accommodated according to their health condition. Although the physical space of the wards differed in detail, each of them was structured in a similar way. There was a dining area, which was the largest open space in each ward. Some of the elderly would spend all day sitting there watching television (a common element in all care homes), or just simply sitting. The more lucid residents would cluster together and have short conversations punctuated by easy tasks, such as folding towels, and visits to the toilet. A space where all the members of staff could gather was the nursing station. This was where the staff briefings took place when shifts were changing. It was also where most of the residents' documentation and daily reports were produced and stored. In Iffah's institution, the nursing station served as a place to go for a short break and a snack, although lunch was to be eaten in a staff canteen. At Lazim's institution there was a small *tatami* room adjacent to the nursing station where most of the staff ate their lunch. Lazim, however, preferred to return to his flat for lunch as it was only a few minutes away from the institution. Where Jasir and Amir worked, the nursing station had a small rest area separated by a curtain, but it was only used by the night shift staff. Lunches were eaten in a rather small *tatami* room near the main entrance to the institution, which was used by staff from all wards.

Life and work in an eldercare home are regulated by a tight schedule detailing tasks for the staff and activities for the residents. The following is an example of a morning shift schedule in Lazim's accepting institution. Although details of tasks were different in other care homes and during later shifts, this example offers a glimpse into a typical day at a care home, and the kind of tasks the Indonesian candidates were performing (the translation reflects the telegraphic style of the original morning schedule sheet).

7:15 Collect individual information (from daily reports and personal files).

Check residents for bowel movement, prepare enema.

7:20 Distribute breakfast, assist with eating, distribute medicines (if nurse not present).

Mouth care – help with brushing teeth; take residents back to the rooms.

Collect dishes.

Room visits – administer enemas planned for the day.

Blood and urine sample collection – take samples to the doctors' room on 1st floor.

Respond to nurse calls during morning report.

8:45 On 2nd Monday of each month, hairdresser arrives – take residents to the west wing hallway.

9:10 Change diapers, support in getting up.

Change bedsheets.

Heat up tube feeding for midday meal, take out mouthwash cups.

Turn on the *oshibori*[5] machine.

10:00 Distribute tea.

10:45 Break.

12:00 Midday meal – distribute plates, assist with eating, mouth care.

Take residents back to the rooms.

One member of staff collects the dishes, wipes the tables, washes utensils not returned to the kitchen.

12:45 Day and late shift break.

Room visits.

Bath preparation (fill up the bathing pool); respond to nursing calls; if late shift did not manage, help prepare change of clothes for bathing residents (Wednesday and Saturday).

Take residents to the afternoon activity clubs they participate in.

If time allows, clean those residents who cannot bathe on the day.

13:45 Write reports, staff meeting, respond to nurse calls.

14:00 Change diapers (those residents who do not bathe on the day).

Bathing preparation – assistance before bathing, bringing residents to the bath, assistance with removing clothing.

15:00 Turn on the *oshibori* machine.

Distribute pre-meal snacks (one member of staff), on the day of *kikaiyoku*[6] one member of staff responds to nurse calls.

Heat up tube feeding for evening meal, take out mouthwash cups.

15:30 Planned X-ray checks – deliver X-ray images and booking forms, collect X-ray images from external examination; respond to nurse calls.

16:00 End of shift.

What the above schedule does not show is the intimate knowledge of each and every resident that was required to fulfil the listed tasks. For example, knowing on which side of a tray to place a bowl with *miso* soup; what bodily ailments to look out for when toileting or moving each individual in order not to harm him or her; and being aware of the various tastes and preferences the elderly might have, their dietary requirements, and a plethora of other information not included on the schedule was indispensable to fulfil the assigned tasks. The schedule does not indicate the requirement to note down on a specially prepared chart how much of each meal each elderly person ate, or the type and amount of their excreta, either. Nor are there mentioned here such tasks as cutting nails of the elderly, shaving or providing any additional support, however minute. The staff were expected to pay attention to these additional needs and to meet them between the prescheduled activities. How baffling the initiation into care work can be was described by Neil Henderson (1995), who reflected on a number of mistakes he made within the first seven minutes as a Certified Nursing Assistant at the beginning of his fieldwork in a nursing home. In the care homes I visited, the multitude of small adjustments and pieces of information that needed to be applied to every task was further confounded by the almost constant pressure of time, or what Henderson refers to as a 'cult of time and task' (ibid.: 46). From waking up the residents and bringing them to the dining room for breakfast and feeding, through toilet visits, changing diapers, tidying the rooms, changing bedding, arranging toothbrushes, and emptying trash bins, to bathing and changing the clothes of the elderly, every activity needed to be finished within a specified time frame and in a given order.

***

The package offered by the joint Indonesian and Japanese governmental scheme seemed quite appealing to the young Indonesian workers keen to seize the opportunity not only to develop professionally while making substantially more money, but also to gain independence and experience living in Japan. However, the reality of working in the Japanese eldercare home and the financial conditions that transpired only after the candidates took up employment, were often at odds with what the young Indonesians had imagined. The work performed by care workers in eldercare institutions involved support of the elderly in the aspects of life very often taken for granted and possibly rarely given any thought. Such basic actions as turning in bed to one side or the other, scratching an itching spot, or the more arduous activities such as standing up, sitting on the toilet, wiping one's bottom, brushing one's teeth, cutting nails, washing – all this was (at least implicitly) in the job description of an eldercare worker. This was not how my informants imagined their role when they signed up for the EPA programme, but it was something that ultimately had a prominent influence on the way their sojourn in Japan was interpreted and how they themselves experienced it.

Notes

1. See Lindquist 2009 for a broader discussion of the *malu* concept.
2. In reality, the nursing association in Indonesia was considering banning those Indonesian nurses who had spent their time as EPA caregiver candidates in Japan from working in Indonesia as nurses without additional examination that would confirm that they had not lost their nursing skills and knowledge while working in Japan as caregivers. Moreover, at the time the first batches of Indonesian workers were making their decision whether to apply for the programme or not, there was no mutual recognition of qualifications between Indonesia and Japan that would ease transition to a new job for those who ultimately returned to Indonesia.
3. This age range corresponded roughly to that of the entire batch of 104 caregiver candidates, while the nurse candidates were in general slightly older. According to my own questionnaire survey, the average age of caregiver candidates was twenty-four and a half.
4. See Vogt and Holdgrün 2012: 73 for more information on LTCI.
5. Small dampened and heated towels used before and during meals to wipe one's hands.
6. A bathing method used for bedridden residents who are washed with dampened towels while lying on a horizontal board which, once the soap is rinsed off their bodies, submerges into a bathtub of warm water.

 2

WORKING INTIMACIES

Despite a noticeable presence of foreign workers in several other sectors of the Japanese labour market at the time of the first Economic Partnership Agreement (EPA), the vast majority of staff employed in the eldercare sector were Japanese. In many of the accepting institutions, the Indonesian candidates were the first and only non-Japanese among the staff as well as among the elderly. Sometimes, in smaller towns, they acquired a presence akin to local celebrities whose faces, known from television screens or from newspaper pages, were recognisable in the streets and who were greeted by the local residents as 'our Indonesians'. Inside as well as outside of the accepting institutions, the Indonesian workers were a novel presence attracting attention for better or for worse.

This chapter offers a glimpse into the day-to-day social interactions of the Indonesian care workers with their Japanese colleagues and the elderly for whom, and about whom, they cared together (Tronto 2001). Bearing in mind the expectations the candidates harboured about their employment in Japan, as well as remembering under what conditions they arrived at the institutions, as discussed in Chapter 1, I show here how, thanks to the particularities of the working environment, the tasks in which the Indonesians were involved, and the way the EPA acceptance programme scattered them among the eldercare homes, the candidates and their colleagues, as well as the elderly, were able to form meaningful and intimate interpersonal relationships. I start off situating the accepting sites against the background of other working environments where foreign workers in Japan have had a prominent presence; then I have a closer look at the discursive construction of an eldercare home. Finally, I devote the largest part of this chapter to considerations of how intimate interpersonal relationships in the care homes where the Indonesians worked were denied or precluded, on one hand, and what allowed for their emergence, on the other.

Non-Japanese Workers in Care Sector and Beyond

Since the 1950s, comparatively large numbers of foreigners (about 80,000 in 2004), coming primarily from Asian countries such as China, Thailand, the Philippines, Malaysia and Indonesia, have been undergoing training in various branches of Japanese industry. Since the 1990s, *Nikkeijin*, or people of Japanese origin, have similarly been entering manufacturing and automotive industries, sometimes concentrating in such cities as Hamamatsu to the extent that they have become widely associated with a given region or industry. Indonesian workers were only a small fraction in both of these groups. There were only over 35,000 Indonesians residing in Japan in 2007, a year before the arrival of the first EPA group (Okushima 2009: 15).

The number of foreign-born carers employed in Japanese eldercare institutions was difficult to establish since there was not a visa category for this kind of work at the time of this research. However, while no official estimates existed, circumstantial information suggested that the proportion of foreign care workers was indeed very low. According to a survey conducted by Nissōnet, a temporary employment agency specialising in placing people in the care sector, among care institutions in the Tokyo Metropolitan Area and the three adjacent prefectures, Kanagawa, Saitama and Chiba, nearly a quarter of the institutions that returned responses to the survey (427 out of the 2,898 contacted) claimed that at that time, or in the past, they employed non-Japanese (Nissōnet 2008). Although the exact number of these employees was not evident in the survey results, anecdotal evidence suggested that typically there had been one or two such employees in an institution. It was also likely that, as shown by a survey of eldercare institutions in the UK (Cangiano et al. 2009: 69), the capital city area was characterised by a higher number of foreign workers than other areas of the country. Moreover, the low response rate (just below 15 per cent) to the survey conducted by the Nissōnet possibly stemmed from many institutions never having employed foreigners. If they had not, the majority of the survey questions were irrelevant to them and might have led to them disregarding the exercise altogether.

Overall, the situation presented itself as nothing like the contemporaneous state of affairs in institutional eldercare provision in the UK, for example, where, according to a 2009 report issued by the Oxford-based Centre on Migration, Policy and Society (COMPAS), migrant workers, understood as those who were born abroad, accounted for around 18 per cent of all social care workers, with the proportion rising to more than half in London (Cangiano et al. 2009: 58 and 70–72). In the United States the percentage of foreign-born nursing assistants rose from 6 per cent in 1980 to 16 per cent in 2003 (Fisher and Kang 2013: 167).

In Japan, one foreign group has been known to somewhat naturally stream into care jobs – a limited but growing number of Filipina women, who originally arrived in Japan as 'entertainers' (Nissōnet 2008), that is, equipped with a visa that allowed them to work in the entertainment industry (now significantly curtailed).[1] These women met their Japanese husbands-to-be in bars where they worked but eventually decided to move away from the original occupation, either as a result of a request from their husbands or because they felt that they had reached an age when they should turn to a more 'respectable' occupation. They have been able to do so because holding the residency status of 'Japanese national's dependent' gives them freedom of employment in Japan. Having received the entry-level qualification of 'domestic helper level two', the lowest and relatively easy to obtain care-related qualification in Japan, they have been taking up employment in care facilities for the elderly.[2]

In a kindred sector of medical care, as of April 2008 there were only 120 non-Japanese doctors and nurses working in Japan (Japan Economic Research Institute 2008: 147). This datum was collected by Nimonjiya Osamu from the Asia Human Power Networks (commonly known as AHP),[3] which had been implementing a training programme for Vietnamese nurses in Japan. Since 1992, the network had been running the scheme for Vietnamese nurses-to-be willing to undergo professional education and complete their work experience in Japan before undertaking employment in Vietnam. Under the AHP scheme, high school graduates who successfully passed through a screening process of the Vietnamese Ministry of Health underwent a 17-month training programme in Japanese and other subjects, such as maths, chemistry, English, and composition writing. Having completed the training, the trainees went to Japan to sit the entry examination to Japanese nursing schools or universities on par with the Japanese candidates. Those who passed the examinations remained in Japan as foreign students for three or four years, depending on the type of educational institution they entered in Japan. Upon graduation, the Vietnamese trainees sat a regular Japanese national nurse examination, and if successful they were placed as nurses under the same working conditions as their

Japanese counterparts in one of the cooperating Japanese hospitals for four years. In 2006 this period was extended to seven years. After that time, the Vietnamese nurses had to return to Vietnam and, having their nursing qualifications recognised, were able to take up employment as nurses.[4] Between 1992 and 2010, the organisation successfully trained fifty-six Vietnamese nurses out of a total of 174 candidates who passed the screening by the Ministry of Health, and entered the first stage of the preparatory education in Vietnam. Unlike the implicit opportunity presented by the EPA to allow the Indonesian workers a chance at permanent residency in Japan, the fifty-six Vietnamese nurses who have been trained by the AHP Networks have never been considered a potential part of the future Japanese labour force.

Type of Work and Physical Proximity

Thus, the novelty of the Indonesian care workers was not only a function of the relatively small number of Indonesians already in Japan. It was also the type of work in which they came to be involved there. In contrast with such groups as the technical trainees placed in various branches of Japanese industry since the 1950s and the *Nikkeijin* discussed in the Introduction, the EPA Indonesians were placed in a sector where their roles as care workers made it very difficult if not impossible to segregate them from the Japanese members of staff and/ or elderly. They found themselves in far greater physical proximity to the Japanese than any of the other foreign worker groups. Until then, Indonesians working either as technical trainees in factories, in the countryside, or as seamen on Japanese fishing or merchant vessels, had limited opportunities for socialising (*kōryū*; Jpn.) with Japanese at work. This was partially due to the insufficient level of Japanese language among the Indonesians, who would reside in Japan only for short periods and were not obliged or stimulated to learn it (Okushima 2009: 19). Moreover, as one of the technical trainees I met through an Indonesian church in Tokyo told me, he barely met any Japanese at work anyway, since all of his work team was made up of other trainees of various nationalities, and a Japanese team leader would only come to their assembly line to convey official information. A similar case regarding the spatial and relational divide in the workplace can also be made for the many *Nikkeijin* who were primarily employed in Japanese industry. For example, Tsuda Takeyuki (2003a: 161–63) describes the separation between the Japanese and the Brazilian *Nikkeijin* workers in the factory where he conducted his fieldwork. Daniela de Carvalho (2003: 204–5) made similar observations of *Nikkeijin* and their relations with the local Japanese community. The EPA Indonesians (and later Filipinos and Vietnamese) entered a predominantly Japanese environment where no separate space or role was designed for them. Because they were in Japan to provide the 'interpersonal service' (*taijin sābisu*; Jpn.) of care (Satō, Shirai and Terashima 2011: 3), there was no niche where the Indonesian candidates could be tucked away out of sight. On the other hand, the technical trainees and *Nikkeijin*, operating assembly lines in automotive factories or fishing away from the Japanese shores, would often find themselves working in an entirely non-Japanese team, engaged in performing jobs shunned by Japanese workers, and interacting with a machine rather than a human being.

The other group of workers who, in a comparable way, worked in close proximity to Japanese co-workers and in direct contact with customers as well were the Filipina women who entered Japan on entertainer visas. As Lieba Faier (2009) illustrates in her ethnography I mention earlier, these women, who were originally employed as performers, dancers and hostesses, and sometimes trafficked into prostitution, have been marrying Japanese men whom they met as customers. In recent years, these Filipina–Japanese unions have come to account for the majority of the so-called international marriages (i.e. marriages between a Japanese and a non-Japanese citizen) in Japan (Yamamoto 2010). Faier does not delve into the nitty-gritty details of how exactly these relationships emerged in the rural Kiso where she based her research, or how the kind of work performed by the Filipina informed their relationships with Japanese co-workers. However, the processes she documents are suggestive of a particular type of negotiation (accompanied by more rationalising calculations) in establishing one another as a potential life partner or a friend. In a different setting, less sexualised and perhaps less readily open to abuse, the EPA candidates entered jobs that similarly situated them in direct proximity to their co-workers and the cared-for elderly, preparing therefore a stage for similar interpersonal encounters, which were reportedly less common on factory shop floors.

Hence, although there might have been significant numbers of foreign workers in other workplaces, and although a certain number of Indonesian workers were concentrated in some of them, they seemed to offer limited possibilities for forging intimate relations with one's colleagues. On the other hand, workplaces with a greater potential for interpersonal interactions, such as hospitals or care institutions, had not seen a significant presence of non-Japanese at the time of this research. Where these interactions had been possible, such as in hostess bars, they were of an explicitly eroticised (or romanticised) nature, and were less open to public scrutiny within Japan than eldercare. It is against this background that the sense of novelty surrounded the EPA care workers. The accepting eldercare institutions became new sites of encounters, where both cultural and interpersonal intimacies needed to be negotiated and fitted into the wider imaginations of the Japanese and Indonesian selves. It was here that the generalising cultural representations were gradually filled by the nuances of personalities, individual stories and engagements.

Cultural Intimacy in Eldercare

Unlike the by-then popularly spread ideas about the Filipina women working in bars as entertainers, common to the extent that one could choose to go to an exclusively Filipina bar (Faier 2009), and about the factory lines of the automotive industry operated by the Brazilian *Nikkeijin*, the occupation of care worker was not associated with foreigners/foreignness. If anything, I would be more inclined to describe the care homes I visited as falling under the rubric provided by Yongmei Wu in her ethnographic study, in which she concedes that 'the main characteristic of Japanese institutional care for the elderly is its emphasis on Japanese traditions and cultural values' (Wu 2004: 185). Wu's observations that 'food and annual events are provided in traditional ways; club and recreational activities focus on forms of traditional arts; there are traditional religious rituals for death; values such as endurance and cooperation are promoted to maintain harmonious human relationships; the norm of collectivism is promoted to form a familial atmosphere, and "dependence on indulgence" (*amae*) of the sick elderly is acceptable when providing care' (ibid.; emphasis in the original) would have to be mine as well.

The 'Japanese traditions and cultural values' observed in the care homes, through mimicry recreated a simplified and essentialised image of the past and present, but mostly inaccessible to the elderly, Japan. 'It is in this cultural environment that the residents can lead comfortable lives in the institution', claims Wu (2004: 185), and indeed the elderly residents I talked to seemed to derive pleasure from such details of their lives in the care homes, as if the small events of brewing green tea, or watching the *omikoshi* (a palanquin used to move a deity from the main shrine to a temporary one during a festival) procession performed by children from the local school in the care home's car park, were confirming their Japaneseness – the elderly's lasting belonging to Japanese society, despite the isolation of their lives in the care home.

Tasting Culture

Some of the residents took delight in repeatedly introducing the Indonesian workers and me, both equally foreign figures, to the Japanese 'traditions and values', showing us how to properly roll an *oshibori*, a small dampened and heated towel, or how to tie the bow of an apron the 'proper Japanese way', or encouraging us to definitely try *kakigōri* (flavoured shaved ice eaten primarily in summer) during a summer festival, or *natsu matsuri*, organised by a care home, as something that we could have a chance to taste only in Japan. Another time, during *ocha kurabu* (tea club; Jpn.), an occasion when some of the residents would prepare green tea for others to enjoy together with Japanese sweets, a set akin to that used during traditional tea ceremonies, Amir was helping to distribute the treats to the residents. After everyone had been served, a member of staff suggested to the elderly woman preparing the tea that she should make one for Amir as well, so he could 'taste the Japanese culture' (*nihon no bunka o ajiwaeru*; Jpn.). On a different occasion, on Jasir's ward, a female resident astonished all members of staff with a morning greeting performed in English. When the ensuing conversation turned to the topic of *enka*, traditional Japanese ballad songs, often sung by the resident, she was instructed to 'teach the foreigner about things Japanese' (*gaikoku no kata ni nihon no koto o oshiete agete*; Jpn.). Manifestly, therefore, even the most mundane everyday activities and items in the eldercare homes were constructed as markedly Japanese, while the EPA Indonesians needed to accustom themselves to and 'get used to Japan' (*nihon ni narete morau*; Jpn.) and its traditions and customs (*nihon no shūkan ni narete morau*; Jpn.). The bathing method, represented as uniquely Japanese, using a miniature hot spring or *onsen*-like pool of hot water installed for the elderly to immerse in after having their bodies cleaned; the insistence of the elderly to use chopsticks instead of the cutlery set associated with more Western arrangements, and the stressing of the importance of time-keeping among the staff were all particularly emphasised as traditionally Japanese, and contrasted with what the Indonesian or, more generally, foreign ways were thought to be.

The quality of care resided in the ability to maintain these minute Japanese ways of life, although, ostensibly, it was also measured by its responsiveness and mouldability to the individual elderly's preferences. The care homes I visited advertised their services as personalised and crafted to provide 'comfort and peace of mind' to each resident individually. '*I ni semari, i ni soeru*' was a motto displayed by one of the homes I visited briefly, with an appended explanation that '[if you] recognise and anticipate another person's desires, [you can] meet their hopes/expectations'. The pledge continued, 'in an environment where both the mind and the body can be at ease, we would like to provide every day life support, functional training, and health supervision in order that the [service] users can lead a life they wish for themselves and in accordance with their own ways'. Another care home set as their objective a provision of service that would allow 'each and every [service] user to spend their time to their liking, safely and enjoyably'.[5] While such declarations stressed the need for personalised care, both in its physical and mental aspects, the arrival of the Indonesian workers gave rise to concerns that the care they provided might not be fully 'Japanese', or might jeopardize the efforts to offer the elderly dignified conditions to live in.

Dignity of the Elderly

Dignity of the elderly was one of the ideas that persistently reap-peared in the discussions surrounding the Indonesians' engagement in Japanese eldercare. One particular occasion on which I heard a defi-nition of what specifically Japanese eldercare was meant to be about was during a board meeting of one of the support organisations. At the end of the meeting a Japanese language teacher, in concluding an already fairly relaxed discussion about how the Indonesian can-didates were doing at their institutions of appointment, said that in Japanese eldercare the most important thing was *songen* (Jpn.), dig-nity, or regard for the elderly. I do not think that she meant to im-ply that dignity was solely a Japanese ideal of eldercare, or that the Indonesian candidates would in some way lack the respect or the intention to sustain (or provide) dignified living conditions for the Japanese elderly for whom they were caring, particularly in light of her oft expressed admiration for the Indonesian (cultural) aptness for care work. Instead, she seemed to be pointing to the possibility that the cultural differences could lead to the environments in those care homes employing the Indonesian candidates losing some of their Japaneseness. In consequence, the elderly's comfort of living in accor-dance with their preferences as Japanese might be compromised. This in turn could preclude the sustenance of regard for these preferences, and therefore deny the elderly the familiarity of an environment in which they could navigate in a dignified way, without bumping into unknown elements with which they may not know how to deal. The personal preferences of the elderly were therefore once again con-nected to the cultural comforts of predictability (Mahler 2013: 31).

The commonly uttered triad of *kotoba, shūkan to bunka no chigai* (Jpn.), that is, the differences in the language, custom, and culture, accompanied concerns over the differences in the professional knowledge and skills of the foreign staff.[6] This connection of personalised care with the need to preserve a Japanese cultural environment suggested that certain individual preferences were seen as shaped by, or embodying, the cultural milieu of Japanese lives. Conversely, the connection and the related concerns relied on the categorisation of the Indonesians as fairly uniform in their difference from the Japanese. Such categorisation did not allow for personal idiosyncrasies or intellectual involvement or intervention.

Indonesian Novelty and Discomfort of the Japanese Elderly

One morning, nearly a year after her assignment began, Iffah was leading a morning exercise session for the residents on her ward. Surrounded by the elderly sitting and standing in a semi-circle around her, she stood in the middle of an empty space in front of a large television set. Other members of staff dispersed themselves among the gathered elderly to assist those more fragile or confused. Shortly into the session one of the men, who had been looking curiously at Iffah, asked the worker assisting him who that person in the middle was. The worker replied, 'It's Iffah, she came from Indonesia'. 'Indonesia, *hee*?!' responded the elderly man, seemingly surprised and astonished at the information.[7] The elderly man, suffering from dementia, apparently did not remember his previous interactions with Iffah, who had fed him many times during meals, and he was now reliving his initial surprise at seeing a face so ostensibly atypical to a Japanese person. I never encountered or was made aware of a similar situation involving a Japanese carer. On the contrary, I was myself once shouted at by an elderly woman residing in one of my main research sites. It happened on the fourth day of my first visit, when I was passing her in a corridor. I noticed that she had been anxiously eyeing me from her seat in the day room, where she spent most of her time, while I was following Amir and talking to those elderly with whom he chatted the most. Seeing the woman coming from the opposite direction, I decided to smile and greet her to try to break the ice. In response she quite aggressively shouted, 'What are you looking at?!', and carried on, saying things that I was unable to understand. News of the incident spread quickly, and during the lunch break a physiotherapist asked me whether I had been scared today, referring, as it turned out, to my earlier encounter. When I replied that it was rather disconcerting, he suggested that I should not worry because this particular resident always became anxious on seeing a new person, and her reaction was to be expected since I was a 'particularly unusual occurrence' (*toku ni mezurashii sonzai*; Jpn.). It took about a year's worth of visits for me to be accepted by this resident. One day she simply invited me to join her in folding the *oshibori* towels before dinner. Such reactions of the elderly as those towards Iffah and me just described should not be dismissed as coming from individuals who might have lost their decisional capacities and thus are unable to express their stance on a given situation. As Lynn Mason admonishes, 'even chronic confusion is not necessarily a bar: the trick is not to accept the local assessment … Often persons who do not know where they are, are perfectly clear about how they feel' (1995: 82 after Schmidt 1990: 546). The elderly who could not otherwise express their opinions, preferences or befuddlement in relation to the presence of, and/or being cared for by, the Indonesian workers, or perhaps forgot that they should not be wondering anymore, let their surprise and sometimes anxiety be known in the ways and at the times suitable to their own feelings.

I heard several stories of elderly residents who had felt discomfort or anxiety during their early encounters with the Indonesian candidates. However, all of these accounts were conveyed to me as matters of the past by the Japanese members of staff and by the Indonesians. Such was the case involving one of the elderly female residents suffering from dementia who lived on Iffah's ward. The elderly woman used to react aggressively towards Iffah, some days worse than others. However, by the time I started my visits they already had a friendly relationship which, according to Iffah, began when the resident learnt her name after Iffah defended her from what she saw as abusive treatment from a Japanese member of staff. Defending the elderly resident gained Iffah the resident's trust, which seemingly overshadowed the former feelings of unfamiliarity and fear, and singled her out from both categories: a member of staff and an unfamiliar foreigner (although it is hard to assess to what extent the resident was actually making a distinction between Japanese and non-Japanese, rather than simply between familiar and unfamiliar).

Iffah's experience did not seem unusual. At Ajisai, one of my other main research sites and the one where Jasir and Amir were based, the floor manager told me that there were several elderly who had initially refused to be looked after by the Indonesians. In response she organised the roster in such a way as to avoid assigning the Indonesian candidates to tasks around those particular residents. However, with time, these residents changed their attitudes and were cared for by the Indonesians as well. In another institution, which I visited only for one day, I was told that there were indeed some residents who, seeing the Indonesian candidates for the first time, would call them *kuronbō* (a derogatory term for a dark-skinned person; Jpn.); but they, too, all became used to them and there were no such problems any more (see also Foner 1994: 38).

The requirement for the Indonesian workers to attend to the Japanese elderly's physical and mental well-being was unlike the technical, impersonal jobs heretofore imagined accessible to non-Japanese. The extraordinariness of the EPA assignment consisted therefore in the directness of the workers' engagement with the Japanese bodies – the immediate medium of social interactions and the 'primary site of both privacy and display' (Herzfeld 1997: 20). However, despite their professionalised proximity, the Indonesians were neither related nor familiar to the elderly in cultural terms, and yet they were put in a relationship where it was desired, if not indispensable, that the 'carer and cared-for can connect and identify' (Milligan 2003: 462) on a very intimate level, usually accessible only to the most heartfelt individuals, if to anyone at all. Rather, the Indonesians represented that which was unfamiliar and non-familial. Alien to the Japanese culture, the Indonesians were not expected to be able to tap into the culturally specific knowledge to attend to the Japanese needs and therefore to support the elderly in achieving the highest possible quality of life. They were hence unfamiliar strangers who could not share with the elderly in the intimate knowledge of their experiences as Japanese.

Thus, the Indonesians were not imagined as intimate – at least not in cultural or national terms. Despite this, the Indonesians were expected to provide intimate bodily care. Implicated in an intimate relationship, and yet unfamiliar, unpredictable, and not sharing in the same likeness, the Japanese and Indonesians were potential witnesses to each other's ruefully (or not) recognised qualities. The original proponent of the concept, Michael Herzfeld, writes: 'Embarrassment, rueful self-recognition: these are the key makers of what cultural intimacy is about' (Herzfeld 1997: 6). Although he acknowledges that 'nationalism and cultural intimacy are caught up in a mutual dependency' (ibid.: 8), he explicitly does not limit his definition to intimacy among co-nationals (ibid.: 174n2). The potential for embarrassment should the knowledge gained through intimacy be shared with a third party is what distinguishes intimate from other relationships, national communal imaginings being just one of these. In bodily care, the directness of physical contact can be a source of embarrassment, as the cared-for needs to grant access to the most private aspects of his or her being (Twigg 1999, 2000a); in intimate emotional relationships, the knowledge gained through shared memories or through access to knowledge that otherwise would have remained confined to an individual is also a potential cause of embarrassment if disclosed (or could 'damage the other', in Viviana Zelizer's words [2005: 15]). In all of these cases, embarrassment is a function of disclosure beyond the relations of a group considered intimate.

In this sense, care work can be considered as (at least) doubly intimate. As a profession, or a professionalised vocation, care work has emerged from the domestic domain, where it was primarily the role of women to attend to other members of the family, the children, the unwell and the elderly. As a function of familial life, care work continues to carry strong associations with emotional attachment between the individuals involved in the relation of care. Such links underlie the distinction identified by Joan Tronto (2001: 62–63) between 'caring about' and 'caring for', where the former points to emotional and intellectual practices and the latter to the practical or physical actions taken for or on the other person (see also Tronto 1993; Williams 2001). This distinction suggests the possibility of one practice occurring independently of the other. With more women taking up paid employment in the market economy, the relations formerly imagined as domestic and based on an emotional bond had to be transferred and transformed into relationships not solely between familiar family members but also between strangers. In such a context, the possibility of 'authentic' care – that is, combining caring about and caring for someone – has been denied since it has been argued that care, if formalised, may become merely 'substitute services' (Graham 1983: 29), especially if its provision is exchanged for money. Therefore, care work has been understood in 'either/or' terms as labour and as love (Finch and Groves 1983; Graham 1991; Folbre and Nelson 2000), denying the claims to intimacy of care work done in exchange for money. In this context, intimacy has been understood as being built on the basis of emotional attachment. This emotion-based intimacy of care has been particularly stressed in relation to care for elderly family members since, as Simonetta Simoni and Rossana Trifiletti (2004) argue within an Italian context, attending to the elderly is an 'intergenerational pact' in which the character of exchange takes the form of 'delayed reciprocity' in a 'chain of obligations' (Fine and Glendinning 2005: 612, in Huang, Yeoh and Toyota 2012). As a duty among family members intimacy of care cannot be easily conferred upon a hired stranger, even less so upon a foreigner. However, Viviana Zelizer (2000: 821), focusing on 'sexually tinged relations' as based on intimacy, dismisses the 'hostile worlds' approach to the (in) commesurability of intimacy and money transfers. She proposes to look at the two as coexisting in a variety of social contexts and relationships (see also Zelizer 2005). Similarly, reflecting on the contemporary shift towards commercialisation of the personal and intimate relationships, particularly those linked to the domestic sphere as a (traditional) locus of reproductive labour, Nicole Constable defines intimate relations in the following way:

> The term intimate relations refers … to social relationships that are – or give the impression of being – physically and/or emotionally close, personal, sexually intimate, private, caring or loving. Such relationships are not necessarily associated with or limited to the domestic sphere, but discourses about intimacy are often intertwined with ideas about gender and domesticity, gifts as opposed to markets. In many cases, intimate relations are related to reproductive labor or care work in the broadest sense including, most notably, child care, nursing, and hospice care (Hochschild 1983; Russ 2005) and also to entertainment such as stripping, erotic dancing, hostessing, and other types of sex work. (Constable 2009: 50)

For Zelizer and for Constable it is, therefore, possible to think about intimate relations not in opposition to the economic exchange outside of the family realm, but in relation to it. Such commensurability makes it possible to talk about 'intimate labours' (Parreñas and Boris 2010)[8] that '[entail] touch, whether of children or customers; bodily or emotional closeness or personal familiarity, such as sexual intercourse and bathing another; or close observation of another and knowledge of personal information, such as watching elderly people or advising trainees' (ibid.: 2). Julia Twigg's (2000b: 151) interlocutors stressed the importance of skin-to-skin contact and touch in the 'bodywork' of care and the construction of 'bounded intimacy' (ibid.: 47) between the carer and the cared-for. Similarly, Japanese studies highlight the achieving of 'intimacy through touch', or 'skinship' (Tahhan 2010; see also Clark 1994; Lebra 2004). The intimate labour of care, also referred to as 'emotional work' (Lee-Treweek 1996) or 'affective labour' (Lopez 2012), is therefore predicated on touch, but also incorporates emotional attachment (or its appearance), and eldercare in particular connotes intergenerational obligations. This is particularly true in Japan where, despite ongoing changes, the ideals of filial piety remain powerful (Wu 2004: 7).[9] The emergence of eldercare institutionalisation in Japan has been perceived as a 'disjuncture between a cultural norm of filial piety and a changing social reality' (Bethel 1992a: 109; see also Wu 2004), and is still experienced by some elderly who have to spend the autumn of their lives in a care home, as equivalent to having failed in achieving this cultural ideal (Wu 2004: 80). This disjuncture is sometimes invoked in figurative representations of eldercare institutions as *obasuteyama* (Jpn.), meaning literally 'a mountain, or mountainous place to abandon old women', where according to an old Japanese folk tale, the elderly (often women) who became a burden on their families would be taken to perish (see Bethel 1992a). Some of the residents in the care homes I visited would also describe themselves as living in *obasuteyama*, although their comments seemed to be humorous, at least on the surface. The Indonesian care workers who arrived to care for (and care about) the Japanese elderly were therefore invited, or expected, to partake in bodily and emotional intimacies still very much laden with familial and culturally framed values closely associated with Japanese national belonging.

The reactions of the elderly when they first saw their new Indonesian carers in the institutions I visited attested to the unusualness of the latter. It seemed that the presence of individuals with whom the elderly were unable to identify could easily become a source of anxiety. This was true at least in their reactions to the early encounters, which probably most forcefully brought to light the apparent unfamiliarity and therefore unpredictability and suspended trust otherwise granted to more familiar – that is, Japanese – strangers (see Simmel 1950; Ringmar 1998). The elderly's reactions, ranging from joyful anticipation of a chance to interact with somebody different to fearfulness at the sight of the unfamiliar appearance of the Indonesian candidates (the latter prevalent particularly among those elderly with progressed dementia), had their roots in the perceived extraordinariness of that foreign element which disturbed the usual order of things. A non-Japanese care worker was a categorical confusion, matter out of place. In the eldercare homes constructed as and considered inherently Japanese, the Indonesian EPA care workers represented that which was not Japanese. Odd, surprising and interesting, or unknown, unwelcome and threatening to the elderly (and, as I will also show below, 'illiterate' in Japanese culture and the everyday routines in the eyes of their co-workers), the candidates disrupted the fabric of social relations and imaginations within the institutions. The presence of Indonesians in positions usually occupied solely by Japanese was a kind of anomaly. Despite the still rare exceptions of the Philippine or *Zainichi* Korean home helpers employed in the care homes, or the Vietnamese working as nurses, the prevalent image of care workers in Japan was fused with their Japaneseness. A typical care worker, or any other employee of the institution for that matter, was Japanese. The Indonesians were care workers, yet they were not Japanese. Their proximity to the bodies of the Japanese elderly, and their status as colleagues in relation to the Japanese staff, went against the usual state of things. The Indonesian candidates disrupted the routine associations, the naturalised relationship between the spaces of eldercare homes and Japanese bodies (Puwar 2004: 143). As in Nirmal Puwar's book, *Space Invaders*, the EPA workers became 'space invaders' in the care homes where the relatively closed, small-scale societies of the elderly and the staff reproduced the dominant ideologies of Japaneseness, performing (more or less consciously) its uniqueness and homogeneity. The 'invasion', however, allowed for new constellations of relationships to be negotiated. The camaraderie that developed between Iffah and the elderly woman mentioned above penetrated the cultural categorisations and brought out the individuals, rather than stereotypical representations, as anchors for mutual engagement. I will return to this topic later in this and the following chapter.

Given their new and often sole presence as foreigners in the eldercare institutions, the Indonesians were acutely aware of their extraordinariness and thus scrutinised their own actions and positioning in relations with their co-workers. In certain contexts, such assumptions of difference precluded the formation of close relationships. This was the case when essentialising notions of the other (and the self), a quite common medium of making sense of the surrounding world, dominated mutual representations and modes of engagement.

Divisive Differences

Unappreciated

At the end of November 2009, during an event officially launching a regional branch of one of the support organisations directed at the EPA Indonesians and the accepting institutions, a group of care worker candidates were asked to reflect on their situation at work. Apart from voices of disenchantment with the very system of acceptance and the perceived low probability of anyone passing the national examination, many of the candidates voiced their disquiet with the attitudes towards them that they had observed among the Japanese members of staff. Several of the remarks referred to the unjust judgements that the Indonesians felt had been made about them by some of their co-workers, supervisors and employers. The fact that many institutions would not allow the Indonesians to perform all the tasks specified for the *kaigo staffu* (care staff; Jpn.) was often interpreted as being thought of as *bodoh* (stupid; Ind.) or as if they were *dari hutan* (from a forest; Ind.), that is backward and unsophisticated when it came to, for example, handling various pieces of equipment or using desktop computers. They felt that the image that the Japanese held (or at least seemingly acted upon) about Indonesia as a country lagging behind Japan in such areas as common access to technological gadgets, was unfairly equated with a lack of savvy, or even with an inability to acquire relevant knowledge and skill. As Amir and Jasir, whose reflections open this book, have been frustrated over the limits imposed on their ability to acquire an independent standing at work, so were those who took part in the November meeting sensing that they were not recognised as fully comprehending human beings. In one of the institutions I visited at the beginning of 2010, it was only after nearly a year into their employment that the Indonesians started to be introduced to tasks involving any direct contact with the elderly, and in a very sporadic manner at that. Otherwise, they were confined to housekeeping jobs before and after meals or in the bedrooms, but nothing involving handling of the elderly.

When faced with their superiors questioning their ability to provide adequate care, the Indonesians saw the limitations imposed on the range of activities they could perform as emblematic of a lack of trust in their abilities. This was something also alluded to by Amir as presented

Figure 2.1: Toothbrushes ready for use after lunch. Photo by author.

in the vignette opening the book. Under such conditions, Amir felt that he was not performing at the top of his abilities because of the continuing lack of freedom to act and the pervasive feeling of unreliability. The restrictions and the practically constant supervision, Amir claimed, made him wary of doing anything according to his own judgement, lest it was to be deemed improper. Such concerns ultimately led him to avoid showing any initiative. This, in turn, contributed to his image as being someone unable to perform various tasks autonomously. He felt caught up in a vicious cycle of dehumanising representations and his own attempts at navigating within (or against) them.

Less Human

The relationships were further affected by the limited opportunities to communicate in a way that would convey information about who each of the individuals involved was on a personal level, what their idiosyncrasies were, according to what values they operated, what they liked and disliked, and so on. The linguistic barrier contributed a great deal to this situation with one of the young Indonesian women admitting: 'I rarely communicate with colleagues because my Japanese language skills are still limited'. Another one understood the impact that the lack of linguistic fluency had on her relationships with the Japanese staff. She observed: 'Because I just started working, there is nothing special about our relationship, not very intimate, but good. Perhaps it is because the language obstacle becomes a hassle [rebut; Ind.] when I try to express something'. Indeed, initially, the still imperfect Japanese language of the Indonesians made it a daunting exercise for both the Indonesians and the Japanese alike to achieve understanding on anything more profound than basic information that required little more than several set phrases to accomplish communication. A lack of commitment to engage with their Indonesian co-workers beyond the superficial and occasional probing into random areas of their lives was a common, albeit not surprising, attitude among the Japanese employees. At work, usually occupied with their duties, the co-workers had little time for extensive conversations. Sometimes this lack of verbal communication affected the degree to which the Indonesian and Japanese workers were able or willing to perceive each other as comprehending individuals. Consider the following situation. Mr Yamada, a team leader, had been told to instruct Jasir how to transfer a bedridden elderly from his bed to a wheelchair and back. They practised on one of the residents. Mr Yamada was mostly showing Jasir the whole process with the help of another member of staff. When Jasir's turn came, he picked up the legs of the elderly man, Mr Yamada picked up the upper body, and they transferred the man into the wheelchair. It went rather smoothly. Jasir started pulling down the jacket of the resident's pyjamas, and placed his hands in a safe position, as previously instructed by Mr Yamada. At this moment Mr Yamada made the following statement, as if he were talking to himself: 'Clothes have to be put in order. Then, a cushion should be placed. There is a meaning to the cushion. But you, Jasir, have not grasped the cushion's meaning and so you don't know [what to do with it]' (*Fuku o totonoeru. Sore kara kusshon o ateru. Kusshon ni imi ga aru. Jasir wa kusshon no imi ga ha'aku shite nai kara wakaranai*; Jpn.). Hearing this statement, Jasir, surprised and confused, looked up as Mr Yamada was placing the cushions around the resident's upper body. As I later found out, Jasir did not fully understand Mr Yamada's words, partly because he misheard the word *kusshon* (cushion; Jpn.) for a word which he had learnt earlier that day, *fushu* (swelling, oedema; Jpn.), and partly because he did not expect Mr Yamada to suddenly make a comment like this because he knew perfectly well what the cushions were for and simply could not imagine anyone suggesting it was difficult or impossible to comprehend the cushions' practical application. He was planning to put the cushions around the resident once he made sure that his arms were in a safe and comfortable position.

The imperfect sentences, unusual pronunciation, and need to repeat the same information several times or to rephrase one's words distorted the usual communication practice, and there was still no guarantee that the intended message would come across. In the case of the Indonesian workers not fully competent in the Japanese language, the need to simplify the sentences used for communication seemed to have brought about, even if unintentionally, the assumption that they were incapable of understanding the meanings behind what was being said (rather than just the words), or that the simplicity of the language reflected the simplicity of the thoughts or minds behind it. A complaint to the same effect was made by non-native English-speaking domestic workers in Toronto, Canada, researched by Kim England and Bernadette Stiell (1997). Transposing one inability, in this case the linguistic incompetency, onto the perception of the totality of a person, served to represent the entirety of the Indonesians as dissimilar, and therefore unknowable to the Japanese. Such representations were not structured on the basis of a cultural stereotype of what the other *is*, but rather what they *are not*. In other words, the stereotype was that of a non-Japanese who could not speak the language or comprehend the complexities of Japanese customs and ways of thinking. As Michael Herzfeld (1997: 157) argued, such reductive representations imply a lack of certain valued characteristics in the person described, and serve as a 'discursive weapon of power'. The less complex the image of the other, the less human and therefore possessing less of an active agency they are made to be. The lack of appreciation for the Indonesians' skills or indeed for their maturity to think for themselves, and the presumed distrust of the Indonesian care workers, kept them at a distance from the areas where their non-Japaneseness could be expressed and could potentially (re)shape the established practices and relationships. The more depersonalised, the less powerful were the Indonesians made out to be, and thus they were the less able to disrupt the natural order of things. The Indonesians could be ignored as viable working partners needing to be engaged with as equals and whose personal wishes or preferences should be taken into account. Of course, safety considerations were behind the delays in introducing the Indonesian workers to tasks involving handling of the elderly as well. The difficulty of conveying crucial information about the health condition of the elderly was an important issue. (However, the need for linguistic explanation was often questioned by both the Indonesian workers and other supporters of their quick involvement in the handling of the elderly. Their arguments rested on the perception that it was possible to learn such tasks through demonstration. In some of the accepting institutions, the Indonesian workers, Iffah among them, were allowed to perform all the tasks from the very beginning of their employment. For Iffah it happened within the first two weeks of her arrival at the institution. She was soon performing her tasks confidently, and was even occasionally asked to instruct new Japanese members of staff.[10]) What was most problematic in the eyes of the Indonesians, however, was not their removal from some of the tasks per se, but the systematisation of this overarching denial of agency. What Herzfeld called 'nationalistic feelings of distrust' (1997: 43) based on the perceived unfamiliarity of the Indonesians, perpetuated, justified, fossilised and put into action the simplifying and hence dehumanising image of the Indonesians through the way work was organised in the accepting institutions. Such acute division of representations made the Indonesian difference all the more unsettling for both the candidates and the Japanese negotiating their coexistence inside the institutions.

Embarrassments

Aware of their unusualness, the Indonesian workers felt uneasy about openly engaging in practices common to them in Indonesia. None of my friends ate with their hands when at work. They would all prepare an Indonesian meal in the form of *bentō* (a set meal in a lunch box; Jpn.) to have during lunch break, which they usually spent at the institution. They always used chopsticks or cutlery, because it would have been *malu*, embarrassing (Ind.), to eat with their hands. At home, where, in their words, they finally felt *bebas* (free, unfettered; Ind.), each meal, as long as it was not a soup, would have been consumed without utensils. Although not ruefully so (Herzfeld 1997: 6), but self-recognised as particular to an Indonesian person, eating with the hands also had connotations of being 'uncultured', as was once suggested by Iffah's employer during a meal at a restaurant. Watching her eating, Iffah's director commented that it seemed to him that Indonesians could not really use a knife and fork, suggesting that this differentiated them from the Japanese, who, apart from using chopsticks, were well accustomed to using 'Western' cutlery as well. As if confirming the Indonesians' expectations about how awkward and unappreciated the practice of eating with hands would be for the Japanese, one day during lunch on Jasir's ward there was a kerfuffle between two residents over the very issue. One of the female residents, whose mental impairment that came with age left her more or less oblivious to the outside world, started eating rice using her fingers. She was seated at a table together with another elderly woman who, although already senile as well, was sometimes still able to communicate with other people, depending on the day. The latter noticed what the other woman was doing and first commented, as if to herself, that it was disgusting. Then she tapped her on the arm, telling her to stop and use her spoon (the woman was unable to hold chopsticks anymore). When she received no reaction, she raised her voice, repeating her demand, and tried to grasp the hand with which the other woman was eating in order to stop her. At this point Jasir, who was until now observing the situation together with other workers, came up to the table and suggested to the agitated woman that she change tables. She took her lunch tray and sat at a table in a far corner of the room together with three other elderly. She calmed down and began eating again, but every now and then she would turn around to look at the woman still eating with her hand, and murmur to herself.

Eating with hands as distinctly non-Japanese was also a subject of a conversation Iffah, two of her colleagues and I had during one lunch break. Iffah had brought some rice and boiled chicken with her. Amidst the comments on who had prepared what for today's lunch, she mentioned that if she were at home she would be eating hers with a hand, not like she was doing at the time, with a spoon. Kenta, Iffah's male colleague, responded with the interjection 'interesting' (*omoshiroi*; Jpn.), and asked if everyone in Indonesia did the same. Iffah explained that yes, but only the right hand should be used, because the left hand is used 'in a toilet'. She then told everyone that I would use my hand, too, when I ate at her house. After an exchange explaining that it is not a custom in Poland, where I was from, but that I did use my hand when eating Indonesian food, our joint story was met with interested acknowledgement expressed by the *hee* token already explained above. At this moment, however, Kenta looked down at his own hands and, surprised at the realisation, said that actually he had just eaten an *onigiri* (a rice ball; Jpn.) with his hands too. Before it was time to get back to work, we finished our conversation enumerating other examples of Japanese foods like sushi, and in particular *temaki zushi* (a cone-shaped sushi wrapped in a flat sheet of dried pressed seaweed; Jpn.), which are eaten with one's fingers or hands. On this particular occasion the apparent difference was the subject of a pleasant discussion that aroused interest rather than consternation or agitation. What this episode also highlighted was how stereotyping representations can lack in reflexivity over one's own actions and habits. Such oversights serve the maintenance of the differentiation between the category in which one declares membership and those considered as different in some salient respects. This episode hints also at how more intimate relationships could serve mutual learning and the formation of nuanced understandings, in this case through discovering similarities where the more stereotypical view produced difference. Nevertheless, the fact that the Indonesians continued to refrain from eating with their hands in the institutions suggests that the uneasy feeling of going against the grain of the dominant practices and expectations persisted on a more general level.

On another occasion, Amir admitted to praying in a narrow diaper storage room because the common room, where he would usually perform his afternoon prayer, was occupied by a group of staff having a meeting. Despite the carers' station (a designated area where some of the smaller equipment, the residents' files and some of their belongings were stored; it was also a small rest area for the staff, with a table and a few chairs) being far more spacious and seemingly more suitable for the purpose, he decided to pray in the storage room because it would have been *malu* (embarrassing; Ind.) to do it where everyone could see him. It was the feeling of an acute difference breaking with the practices commonly accepted in the care home to the extent that they became normalising. Were Amir, Jasir or Iffah to pray in the carers' station or eat with their hands in the presence of their Japanese colleagues or the elderly, they would have been emphasising the distinctive category to which they felt they had already been ascribed. They would be presenting an additional token by which to be classified as different, and hence difficult to trust or be relied on for their judgement. They also knew that such acts could be unsettling, or attracting particular attention at least. This anticipation made them feel uneasy. To avoid putting themselves in such a position, they reacted with self-censorship on where to perform what actions. Sometimes this shielding failed only to disclose how ill at ease the Japanese co-workers might be with the unfamiliar practices engaged in by the Indonesians.

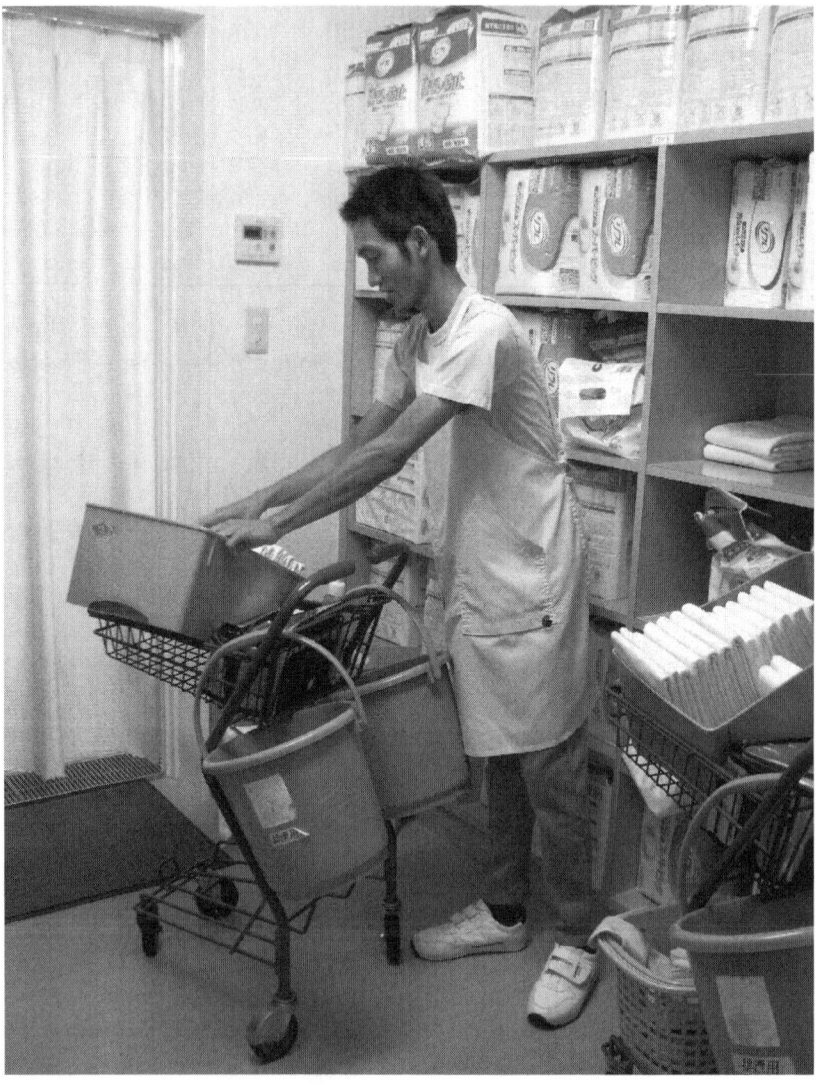

Figure 2.2: In a diaper storage room. Photo by author.

Such was the case when one afternoon towards the end of a study break to which Amir and Jasir were entitled every day after lunch, their floor manager walked in on the two of them while they were praying. The floor manager was planning a meeting with her deputies in the room, which served multiple functions as a lunch room, common room and meeting room. When she opened the sliding door leading on to the elevated tatami floor of the room, she saw the two Indonesians prostrating in their prayers. She quickly apologised and closed the door. From behind the closed door she informed the two men that she needed the room for a meeting when they were finished. Amir and Jasir exchanged glances, somewhat amazed by the reaction of the floor manager, and vacated the room. When passing the floor manager and her deputies waiting outside, they were caught up in almost viscerally tangible shared awkwardness of the moment. In this situation, the floor manager found herself at a loss as to how to deal with the situation of the break room having been temporarily transformed into an unfamiliar space by the Indonesians' prayers. Although the manager knew about the practice, she has not seen either of the two men pray before. Not wanting to disturb, but also not knowing what the appropriate behaviour should be, she found the overall situation uneasy, baffling, and even embarrassing. The uneasiness and discomfort caused by the immediate encounter fleshed out the sense of expected predictability of the eldercare home spaces, and stressed the categorical difference of the Indonesian workers.

Stereotypical Imaginations

Both the construction of the eldercare homes as culturally Japanese spaces and the resultant emphasis of the Indonesians' unfamiliarity with and within the environment so construed operated on common-sense conceptions of what 'Japaneseness' and 'Indonesianness' were. These notions found their instantiations in such everyday practices as eating or praying that at the same time confirmed and accentuated the mutual perceptions of distinctiveness. The frustration expressed by Jasir and Amir, in the opening paragraphs of this book, the feelings of distrust, the excitement and agitation of some of the elderly as well as the surprises and discomforts felt by the Indonesians and the Japanese alike emerged in response to such real-world instantiations of essentialising imaginations that assigned the Indonesian workers and the Japanese they encountered to two separate categories. This categorisation was based on the national, ethnic or even racial imaginations informed by stereotypical, that is simplifying, representations that stood for the whole range of attributes while overshadowing the idiosyncrasies of the individuals. Such common and shared understandings of what a given culture, nationality or ethnicity represents form intuitive theories (Gil-White 2001; Gelman and Legare 2011), otherwise known as intuitive ontology (Boyer 1996) or folk theories (Gelman and Legare 2011). These theories allow people to predict with some degree of certainty what they can expect from encountered individuals on the basis of clues that help to associate them with a given culture. They 'are not scientific theories – they are not formal, explicit, precise, or experimentally tested. Intuitive theories are implicit and imprecise, but as with scientific theories, intuitive theories have broad implications: they organize experience, generate inferences, guide learning, and influence behaviour and social interactions. Most centrally, intuitive theories are causal and explanatory' (Gelman and Legare 2011: 380). Michael Herzfeld goes as far as to say that 'social life consists of processes of reification and essentialism as well as challenges to these processes' (1997: 26). The categories of the 'Japanese' and 'Indonesian' (or more broadly, 'non-Japanese') became a cognitive tool, much in the way theorised by Rogers Brubaker (2002: 174–75), with which to navigate social relations and organisation of tasks inside the accepting institutions.

'Culture' has proven to be 'one of the two or three most complicated words in the English language' (Williams 1976: 76). The breadth and multiplicity of its meanings, as well as culture's relationship to the actions people undertake, have consistently rendered elusive any definite statement about its nature. Talking about the 'nature of culture' may be in itself deemed oxymoronic. However, rather than being concerned with culture as a 'problematic object of description and critique' (Clifford 1986: 3), as it presents itself to its theorists, I want to take it to stand for that which is common sense (Bourdieu 1977: 80) or habitual in the 'performances of everyday life' (Edensor 2002: 88), that which is imagined as a 'way of life' (Eagleton 2000: 112) by people who live or observe it. Without entering the debate about the relationship between social structures or cultural determinacy and the agency of individuals within these structures (see Parsons 1951; Sahlins 2005), I concentrate in this book on the familiarity (and lack thereof) with a given culture-coded sociality, the knowledge this familiarity (or perception thereof) conveys, the imaginations it gives origins to, and the role it plays in shaping encounters between peoples perceiving each other to be of different culture.

Such differentiating perceptions are made possible through the formation of the intuitive theories that rely on stereotyping, essentialising imagery. Social psychologists have studied extensively this human propensity to make distinctions between 'us' and 'them'. For example, prompted by some of the most tragic consequences of such differentiation, namely the Holocaust, Henri Tajfel conducted a series of experiments with British adolescents that showed that any arbitrary attribute can become a source of in-group–out-group differentiation, and what is more, that this differentiation constituted a sufficient factor in deciding who would be treated favourably and who could be gladly seen worse off (Tajfel 1970). Such processes are at work not only in the profoundly disagreeable displays of discrimination on the basis of, for example, someone's skin colour, nationality, religious affiliation, biological sex or sexual orientation, but also in the more benign perceptions of someone's clothing style, the sports they engage in, the shops they get their groceries from, the kind of food they eat, or indeed the way they respond to a pedestrian in their way or to a laundry trolley-basket delivered before the schedule – instances I explore later on in this chapter. Extrapolating information, or prejudging on the basis of some particular characteristic is something we do every day. The very process of stereotyping – that is of essentialising on a basis of often selective and rudimentary information that we are able to categorise in a way meaningful to us – assists our navigation through the everyday, and provides guidelines for distinguishing between those who appear as potentially possible to engage with – that is, viable – and those who do not. Culture and cultural representations, such as those implied by the differentiation between the Japanese and the Indonesians, served as one cognitive tool informing mutual relations and guiding actions. There are objections, however, to using such stereotypical, essentialising categorisations as having an explanatory value in themselves.

The premises of racism, sexism, ageism and classism have long been refuted for the very reason that they discriminate against individuals and groups on the basis of their particular characteristics made to represent some kind of predetermined 'truth', primordial essence-shaping abilities, values, customs, behaviours, and so on, of the individuals and the putative groups in question. For example, and most pertinently to the subject of this book, the reservations to use essentialised notions as tools to understanding interactions between groups defining themselves as ethnically different are well represented by Rogers Brubaker in his paper 'Ethnicity without Groups'. He writes: '[E]thnic common sense – the tendency to partition the social world into putatively deeply constituted, quasi-natural intrinsic kinds – is a key part of what we want to explain, not what we want to explain things *with*; it belongs to our [anthropologists'] empirical data, not to our analytical toolkit' (Brubaker 2002: 165, emphasis in original). In a footnote, Brubaker adds, however, that 'to the extent that such intrinsic-kind categories are indeed constitutive of common-sense understandings of the social world, to the extent that such categories are used as a resource for participants, and are demonstrably deployed or oriented to by participants in interaction, they can also serve as a resource for analysts' (ibid.: 165n4). Both the Japanese and the Indonesians, as I show throughout these chapters, used culture as such a trope to analyse and intuitively theorise the realities of mutual interactions. Thus, I also align myself in this book with Brubaker's latter contention and I look at stereotypical or essentialised notions as representations of how people imagine themselves and the world around them, and which affect the way they act within it.

In doing so, I equate essentialised representations with stereotypes drawing on Michael Herzfeld's understanding of iconicity – that is, 'the way in which meaning is derived from resemblance' (Herzfeld 1997: 56).[11] Stereotypes are the expressions of such iconic connection between the representation and that which is represented. The possibility of such analogy is predicated upon essentialisation of the represented and on masking any internal difference. As Herzfeld argues, 'the rhetorical force of such iconic correspondences resides in their being perceived as somehow natural' (1997: 68), where the stereotypical or essentialised representations gain efficacy through their strategic use (Spivak 1987b: 270–304) in support of the ideologies of likeness, notably among members of national groups.[12] In this book, I aim to argue that instead of merely deconstructing the essentialist notions on which the Indonesians and Japanese operated to prove their manufactured character and simplifying, flattening function, paying attention to these notions' lives can help us to understand how they informed particular actions and reactions, how they shaped perspectives and beliefs, influenced decisions and affected interactions in the most mundane situations as well as on the policy-making level. Essentialising imaginations play an important role in the everyday, and not only when they take the extreme form of violent, hostile, demeaning prejudice and discrimination (see also Tajfel 1970; Turner 1999).

Although the common representations locked the Indonesians into the less potent category of those who needed guidance or had to be excluded from full participation, and although they urged the candidates to weigh their self-presentation in order to underemphasise their own difference, there was a potential resting in the everyday practices to cut through these representations. The remaining part of this chapter focuses on this potential. I show how certain practices and statuses functioned as social adhesive, but also how certain constellations of them could fail to fulfil this function.

Alliances with the Elderly

A part of the carer's job that, in the institutions I visited, was the most tricky to carry out was to verbally engage with the elderly, as, unlike for the manual tasks, there was no scheduled time for it. The conversations needed to take place in between or during other, body-focused caring activities. When the work tempo was fast, the Indonesian candidates did not have the time to pause in order to concentrate on conversation, something that was necessary for them to do, especially in the early period of their employment. Very often they could not count on a Japanese colleague to step in and 'do the talking' for them, either. A carer was expected to be on the lookout for the elderly's wishes and requests, and to attend to them within reason and the care home regulations. Some such requests, no matter how deeply felt or however much a carer might wish to fulfil them, could not be met. It was often the case that the elderly who were suffering from dementia would want to return 'home', maybe one they remembered from their past but that might not exist any more. Sometimes believing that a husband, a wife, or their children were waiting for them to come back home, the elderly would anxiously try to open any door leading to the outside world. Being unable to leave the ward, they would become even more distressed, and it was the role of the carers to ease the elderly's emotions. Without a certain level of language proficiency, soothing their anxiety was nearly impossible. The Japanese carers, provided there was time for such an engagement, would usually strike up a conversation with the anxious person about their family and, to an extent, would enter the fantasy world of the past, playing along while still trying to find a reason acceptable to the elderly for why they would not be able to go back home just yet. Such conversations would either finally drift away in a completely different direction, with the elderly seemingly forgetting about their desire to return home, or end with the elderly having been persuaded to wait until after supper, for example, by which time they were most likely to have forgotten about the whole issue. To be able to engage in a conversation and to calm down the elderly in this way, the Indonesian candidates had to display more than just a basic grasp of the Japanese language. Initially Iffah, who worked on a ward where there were the greatest number of elderly with dementia of all the wards I visited, either avoided engaging with an elderly person wishing to return home, or utilised rudimentary phrases, such as a simple *dekimasen* (you cannot, it is not allowed; Jpn.), or *ato de* (later; Jpn.), and so on, which did not attend to the feelings of the elderly. She felt frustrated at not being able to perform what she knew was her duty, but also because she felt for the elderly separated from their families whom they missed, and she could do nothing to comfort them.

On the other hand, the lack of fluency in the Japanese language meant that the Indonesian candidates would listen carefully to any word uttered by the elderly and ask them to repeat or to rephrase until they were able to understand what was being said to them. When speaking, the Indonesians would not only speak much slower than their Japanese colleagues, but they would also use the polite forms which they had been taught during the introductory language course, and which they were admonished to use when talking to the elderly. In the Japanese language the same information can be conveyed in various styles depending on the relative positions of the people involved in the exchange. Depending on whether one's interlocutor is of a lower, equal, or higher standing, or whether he or she belongs or does not belong to the same group or category as the speaker, or whether the person being spoken about belongs to the group of the speaker or to that of the addressee, the styles used in a conversation alternate. The Indonesian candidates were taught only the forms that could be used to converse politely with people who do not belong to one's group – who, for example, would be their seniors at work even if of the same age, or of a higher standing, such as teachers or indeed the elderly to whom linguistic respect was due, not least because of their age. In the institutions I visited, however, most of the Japanese members of staff when addressing the elderly, especially those with whom communication was difficult due to hearing problems or psychological conditions, would use expressions and forms usually deployed in conversations with individuals of lower or equal standing. The Indonesian candidates, using only honorific expressions and displaying more attention to the words of the residents, were often praised for their politeness and attentiveness. Their inability to speak Japanese fluently was turned to their advantage and secured them the sympathy of the elderly residents. Although not the case for all the Indonesian caregiver candidates, those of them who were confined to a limited range of duties could also afford to spend more time chatting with the elderly, further enhancing their relationships. In this way, the relative marginalisation of the Indonesians in terms of their involvement in performing the full range of tasks expected of the staff turned out to be supportive of their getting to know individual elderly. Moreover, these conversations provided the Indonesians with

opportunities to practise their Japanese language skills in a more relaxed manner than when they were involved in caring duties.

Lazim and Amir had particularly cordial relationships with some of
the elderly on their wards. This may have been due to the fact that, in
comparison with other wards I visited, there were a large number of still
lucid elderly. On Lazim's ward it became his daily routine to dispense
an after-meal cigarette and light it for Ms Arai, a long-standing resident
with a strong personality, known for speaking her mind. The elderly
woman would not engage in a conversation with any other member of
staff but Lazim, and she would often communicate with him through
gestures across the dining room where she spent a large part of the
day. Ms Arai would tell me that there was nothing she wanted to talk
about or to hear from the others, and often commented on their rigid,
martinet-like demeanour. Ms Arai also seemed more approachable to
another young staff member who had just joined the ward team and
was still receiving instruction from others. On Amir's ward, Mr Sawada
was the one who became a friend of the young foreign carer. Although
Mr Sawada was a well-regarded man known in the entire institution for
his readiness to engage with others (despite the fact that he was hard
of hearing and had difficulty speaking after a stroke), it was with Amir
that he would jokingly plot how to get a sip of whisky; he would invite
him to his room, showing different objects he had stashed there over
the years (a small collection of DVDs with Japanese film and television
series classics, old coins and bills, books, and so on), and they would
often communicate through an exchange of looks only. It was also Mr
Sawada who was the most knowledgeable about Amir's private life.
On the day when an interview with Amir, accompanied by a photograph of him, was published in the local newspaper, Mr Sawada rolled
in his wheelchair to every nurse station on each ward, and when the
staff or other residents leaned over the newspaper to see the article, he
would point to the photograph, say Amir's name, and smile proudly,
showing his thumbs up. It was 'his Amir' in the newspaper. Sadly, both
Ms Arai and Mr Sawada have passed away since then. Ms Arai passed
away during my last visit to the care home, after a few weeks of illness.
Although I did not take many notes on that day, I recall reminiscing
with Lazim about Ms Arai during our lunch break, her engaging personality and the feeling of attachment Lazim gained thanks to interactions with her. The news of Mr Sawada's death reached me through no
one else but Amir after I had already left Japan.

Noticeably, the relative position of dependence on the Japanese
members of staff and the occasional inability to communicate their
thoughts effectively created a sense of a bond between the Indonesian

carers and those elderly who were aware of their own situation. For different reasons, both the elderly and the Indonesian candidates needed to be looked after. To an extent, the limited linguistic abilities of the Indonesians were not unlike the impairments of some of the elderly. Being unable to understand the spoken language was not much different from not actually hearing what was being said; being unable to read Japanese was very much like not seeing the text; and lacking words and grammatical structures was not a far cry from being unable to articulate words due to paralysis after a stroke. Hence, in a sense, the Indonesians and the elderly occupied a similar position within the care institutions, where they were dependent on the Japanese members of staff for instructions and explanations, and where they were not always acknowledged as fully comprehending adults. As if in recognition that workers might have the tendency to dehumanise those elderly with whom they could no longer communicate (that is, to deny them viability as people), the management of Tsubaki Nursing Home made a point of displaying photographs of the elderly living there, showing them in their earlier, active years. During my first visit, Lazim's manager, Mr Kawamura, pointed to the photographs hanging next to the ward entrance and explained that the pictures were kept there to remind the staff that the elderly they cared for were people (*hito*; Jpn.) as well – that they also had had lives. The similarity of the position occupied within the institutions by the elderly and the Indonesians led some of the elderly to give the candidates understanding looks and smiles when the latter were in trouble with Japanese members of staff. Just as the Indonesians were there to provide care for the elderly, so also the elderly looked after the young candidates, supporting them through showing that they were on the same side, and making sure to cheerfully accost them whenever they were passing by. Such special relationships were possible precisely because the Indonesian candidates were unusual figures in the institutions. If on occasion leading to negative and fearful reactions from some of the elderly, being extraordinary also meant being recognisable and interesting. These alliances were perhaps even more significant given the typical association of the older generations with a conservative approach to change and novelty.[13] Here, rather than being met with disapproval at being attended to by Indonesian workers and despite the initial negative reactions to the very idea of a 'non-Japanese' carer by some, the EPA candidates acquired personal, if not yet professional, viability in the eyes of the elderly. They came to be recognised for their individual personalities, shedding, sometimes only temporarily and possibly never completely, the indiscriminate category of 'Indonesian' or 'non-Japanese', and as such they became possible to engage with.

One more important factor seemed to facilitate such transition. Because under the provisions of the EPA programme only up to five candidates could be placed in any institution during one intake, the candidates often found themselves the sole Indonesians, and usually the sole non-Japanese, working on a given ward. Such singularity guaranteed that the attention would be focused on the one person who had a kind of monopoly on interesting unusualness. Only 'seeded' (Burgess [2004] 2012) in the institutions in small numbers, the candidates' presence was also less overwhelming and less likely to threaten any sudden or drastic change to the social landscape of the care homes. Such a situation was unlike what Wilbur Watson and Robert Maxwell (1977) observed in an American Jewish nursing home for the elderly, where the predominantly Afro-American members of staff appeared to be kept at a (social) distance by the white Jewish elderly residents, who were sometimes overtly racist. Although the different social awareness of the late 1970s in the United States might be behind such differences of attitudes, similar observations were made more recently by researchers from the already mentioned Oxford-based research centre COMPAS. In their report, the authors note that in the care homes for the elderly in the United Kingdom and in other care-providing institutions they reference, where many care workers were foreign or members of ethnic minorities there was a noticeable incidence of verbal, often racist, abuse by white elderly residents, and a persistent preference for white care providers (Cangiano et al. 2009: 143). In contrast, in the case of the EPA Indonesians, their novelty and limited numbers turned the otherwise disadvantageous position into a factor conducive to more welcoming acceptance. Such seeding also supported the development of intimate interpersonal relationships with their Japanese colleagues, a subject to which I now turn.

Relations with Japanese Colleagues

Intimacy of Bodywork

As mentioned above, in the first year of their employment in Japan, most of the Indonesian EPA candidates had limited Japanese language skills. This often precluded them from being able to represent themselves as anything beyond or more complex than what the stereotypical image of a 'non-Japanese' or 'Indonesian' would invoke. This was, at least, the case with my informants. While struggling to build relationships through conversations, the candidates' involvement in other activities (ones not directly aimed at communication), proved more conducive to overcoming the anonymity of stereotypical categorisations. Cleaning genitalia was one such practice.

When Amir was instructed in the ways of cleaning male genitalia as practised on his ward, it was by his female supervisor, who was, like Amir, in her mid-twenties. The two of them disappeared behind a curtain closed around the bed of a male resident being washed, and after a few minutes of silence I heard Amir comment that the resident's penis was just like his (i.e. circumcised; Amir did not use the word, but, as he later told me, pointed to the removed foreskin instead). Amir's supervisor laughed in a manner that sounded somewhat embarrassed and surprised, but picked up the subject and asked Amir what the word for 'penis' was in Indonesian and why he would be circumcised. I could not hear the details of the rest of the conversation that ensued, but a friendly chat continued until Amir and his supervisor opened the curtain and left the room. On the way back home that day, Amir brought up the subject of his exchange with the female superior and said that although she was shy, *malu*, at the beginning, she then started asking questions, although she kept using the Indonesian term for penis rather than the Japanese. As abrupt as Amir's initial comment might seem, in the situation it served to naturalise, or make appear as common, what was an unusual setting for an interaction between two young people of the opposite sex. It made the situation and the body parts, which were usually embarrassing if displayed and witnessed, into a possible topic of friendly conversation. Amir underwent further similar instructional sessions with the same supervisor, who oversaw him in his first attempts at changing diapers and toilet help, and sup-ported him in transporting the elderly between their wheelchairs and beds. The two developed a system of gestures and a quasi-language composed of mostly Japanese words, but with some Indonesian, which they used to communicate during work. Julia Twigg (2000a: 401) de-scribes various coping techniques deployed by care workers in order to '[get] over the more difficult or embarrassing aspects of silence' when attending to the more intimate needs of the elderly. Witnessing and working within embarrassing situations, or indeed embarrassing body parts and bodily substances, can be in itself a source of embarrassment if done together. 'Direct physical contact, access to nakedness and the sharing of bodily processes are all powerful mediators of intimacy, con-taining a capacity to create closeness and dissolve boundaries between people', writes Twigg about the relationship between the carer and the cared-for, noting that such intimacy in the context of care work is not necessarily welcome and may in fact 'disrupt friendship' (ibid.: 402–3). In the case of the young Indonesian workers in Japan, the shared participation in such boundary-dissolving practices affected the boundaries between the carers as well. There was a clear difference between being there and knowing of it, the former becoming the basis for development of close relationships. When physically put in direct proximity to each other and the naked intimate body parts of the cared-for elderly, disengagement became difficult to maintain. The awkwardness of the moment emphasised and pulled out a viable person in the other that now needed to be engaged with. The moments of embarrassment uncovered the equivalence between the self and the other through making it obvious by the very possibility of awkwardness. When the elderly on whose body the workers were focusing was able to actively partake, they engaged in the exchanges as well. When Amir was helping for the first time to change the diaper of a new female resident (it was also the first time for him to work on a female body), in his nerves he kept forgetting the typical items used in such situations: the protective mat to put on a bed, a change of underwear, and so on. The elderly woman, who had been turned on her side by Amir's supervisor who was instructing him on this occasion as well, opened a friendly chit-chat about

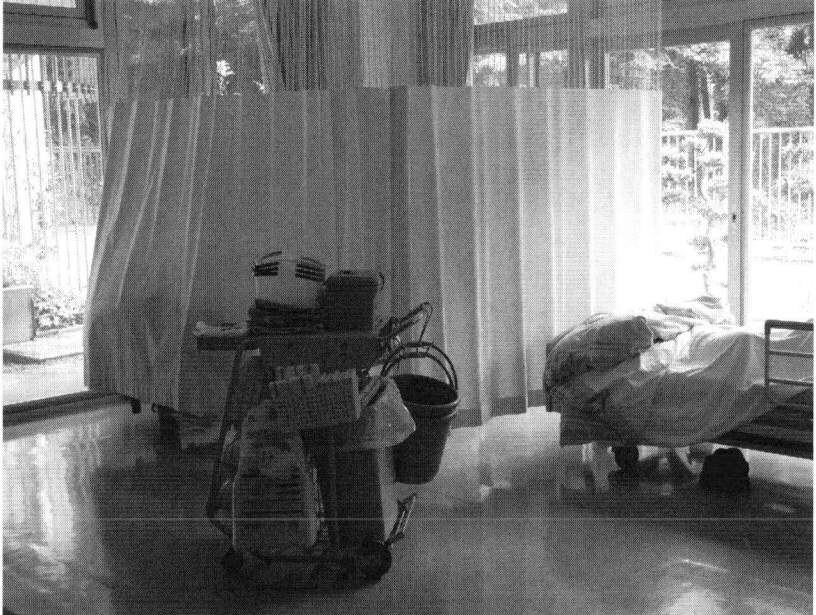

Figure 2.3: Changing diapers. Photo by author.

how the woman's exposed buttocks were getting chilly as she was waiting for Amir to get ready what he had forgotten. The three-way interaction that followed revealed Amir's and the resident's histories of arrival at this particular institution. In the process, the supervisor was skilfully linking Amir's obvious tension and the coldness of the woman's buttocks to Amir's personal trajectory that had brought him to Japan. With the physical boundaries between Amir and the resident already reduced, the conversation was then easily interwoven with the resident directing Amir in his actions. The engagement with each other became more individualised and thus less instrumental. The initially awkward setting for a young man and an older woman to interact was transformed into a more ordinary, and hence more comfortable, one through direct engagement and normalisation of the nakedness and contact with it. Amir's supervisor's understanding support for both the Indonesian candidate and the elderly resident added one more constructive instance of mutual comprehension to the repertoire of their relationship. Later, it was also her who invited Amir and Jasir to join the institution's volleyball team and attend their practice sessions.

In her work in the United Kingdom, Julia Twigg (2000a) noted that young care workers concentrated on the sexual areas in reflecting on their experiences of contact with the nakedness of elderly bodies. For Iffah this was one of the more problematic areas as well. One day when I was following her from room to room during her diaper-changing shift, she sighed that she had not even seen her boyfriend's penis yet, but had seen so many of old men. She then added that the same was true for the two new young female employees. As she told me, closing a curtain around the bed of the next elderly, they had talked about it a few days previously during a short break in a staff room. Somehow the topic had arisen when they were exchanging their impressions of work in eldercare, which was for Iffah's new colleagues a fairly recent and new experience. They found this upsetting commonality, which not only 'broke the ice' between them but also made it possible to discuss the otherwise difficult to express details of the tasks required of them as care workers, and the feelings related to these tasks. Geraldine Lee-Treweek has also noted the female nursing auxiliaries' difficulty in conveying information about the actual content of their work in an eldercare home in the UK (1997: 52–53). One of Lee-Treweek's informants did not clarify to her husband what she was doing at work, and let him believe that she sat there and talked to the patients, whereas she did find it possible to talk about the actual duties with her co-workers. Sharing in such intimately charged experiences meant that it was possible to talk about the otherwise silenced aspects of care work. It was only after I had assisted Iffah with changing the diaper of one of the bedridden male residents who started having a bowel movement just as Iffah was cleaning him that she started discussing with me her experiences of dealing with faeces.

The embarrassments of intimate and 'dirty' work and the tactics used to overcome the awkwardness served as bonding experiences for the care workers despite the distance created by the difficulties of verbal communication and the shield of 'non-Japaneseness'. Other commonly shared experiences included back pain due to the strenuousness of lifting the elderly bodies, exhaustion from attending to the elderly in a hot bathroom, and chapped skin on hands from using detergents. Such non-linguistic activities or states contributed to the development of closer relationships between the Indonesians and their Japanese colleagues. These somatic experiences served as markers of solidarity in the same plight of working with one's body to care for others, and obfuscated the generalised differentiating discourses.

Buddies in Sport, Buddies at Work

When Amir and Jasir joined their institution's volleyball team, their relations with those co-workers who were also on the team became more personal. The camaraderie of the volleyball pitch spilled over into the workplace as well. When Amir in particular turned out to be an asset to the futsal (football played on a small indoor pitch) team and a committed goalkeeper, he sealed his position as a valued companion as well. This is not to say that he was only welcome on the pitch. Rather, his performance on the futsal field reflected on him as a person with particular skills and interests, enmeshed him in relationships with the other players, and hence provided ground for further mutual explorations, even if linguistic communication remained as challenging as before. In contrast, during a *sōbetsukai* (farewell party; Jpn.) for a member of staff leaving the care home to give birth to her first child, organised in a local *izakaya* restaurant, Amir and Jasir sat at one end of a long table, where, even if remaining attentive and trying to understand the ongoing conversation, they mostly stayed quiet, only sporadically exchanging a few words between themselves, or answering questions about whether they liked the food. They remained outside of the main conversations.[14] On a futsal pitch or volleyball field, on the other hand, they were able to fully join in, and communication and bonding happened despite the scarcity of words. Such physical activities in which the Indonesians engaged outside of work conveyed information about them despite the non-verbal content. James Roberson too, in his study of work relationships in a small Japanese factory, emphasises the need to distinguish between 'work-related associations' and 'work-established friendships' (Roberson 1998: 157). He suggests that in order to fully account for the relations salient in a workplace it is necessary to look not only at the formal divisions of individuals according to their role allocation within the workplace, but also at the formation of relationships, sometimes cutting across the formal affiliations, which form

Figure 2.4: Evening futsal game. Photo by author.

more intimate groups of *nakama*, based on a 'common interest or some other relationship' (Atsumi 1979, cited in Roberson 1998: 157). Nancy Foner (1994: 125), for example, notes that purchasing Avon products from a member of staff cemented social relationships within the care home where she conducted her research. In a similar fashion, Amir and Jasir managed to forge close interpersonal relationships through their involvement in futsal and volleyball teams.

Social Status Connection

On a different level, Kenta, a young male colleague of Iffah, suggested an affinity between him and Iffah on the basis of them both being care workers in a broader socio-economic context. That evening he took Iffah and me for a ride to a nearby creek to watch fireflies. The conversation arrived at our respective decisions of what to do in life. Kenta considered himself a bit of a rebel against the prevailing conception of what was a desirable job in Japan. He came to be a care worker after several years as a manager in a successful company. He grew tired of the cold corporate environment and, thinking of his ageing father, turned to care work and remained proud of his new profession despite his former corporate friends' ridicule and his ultimate alienation from them. He definitely looked like he was enjoying his job when I saw him in the institution, and when during the ride he described Iffah and himself as both having a 'tough, socially low status but honourable job' (*kitsukute, shakaiteki chii hikui shigoto da ga, rippana shigoto da*; Jpn.), Iffah was quick to pick up on it, too. She agreed wholeheartedly and explained that she thought of what she was doing now in similar terms, although she found the job very hard to adjust to, both physically and mentally. The conversation continued along the same lines (as much as Iffah's language skills allowed), with Kenta and Iffah exchanging thoughts on different ways of dealing with the unpleasantries of their work and why they should carry on doing it.

Kaigo's, or care work's, provenance, in what was traditionally assumed to be an unpaid responsibility of women who in their reproductive role within a family possessed a 'natural' ability to attend to other humans' needs, fed into the representation of care as not requiring professional (i.e. obtained through systematised training or schooling) skills. That possession of a formal qualification was not a requirement for working in care provision in Japan added to this image of *kaigo* as unskilled, and excluded *kaigo* workers from a category of 'knowledge workers' (Nishikawa and Tanaka 2007). Also, in the case of eldercare, as Lise Widding Isaksen (2005) has argued, it is its association with disgust, disease, and decay of the body that continues to classify care work as devalued and undesirable (see also Lawton 1998). Combined with the stigma attached to eldercare as 'dirty work' (Hughes 1962; see also Anderson 2000) through its dealing with the unbounded, disintegrating bodies of the elderly, and with death, the perceptions of care work as 'unskilled' place it on the socio-economic margins of Japanese society. As illustrated by Kenta's story, it is particularly alienating for men who are valued against the still relevant ideal (or folk model) of a Japanese man as a white-collar company employee, a salaryman, which, as James Roberson (1998: 6) suggests, 'may perhaps be seen to constitute a hegemonic cultural symbol of masculinity [in Japan]' (see also Dahle 2005: 130). Working in an eldercare home, not only was Kenta performing a 'female-coded' (ibid.: 136) role and dirty work, which was stigmatised in itself, but as a non-white-collar employee and therefore non-representative of the ideal of a uniformly middle-class Japanese society (Lie 2001: 28–35) he was also aware of his undesirable and somehow stigmatised lower-class status which he experienced in his alienation from his previous colleagues. Iffah, too, experienced what Tsuda Takeyuki (2003a: 172) has described of the Brazilian *Nikkeijin* factory workers performing blue-collar jobs in Japan: 'shame and damaged pride' after being middle-class white-collar workers in Brazil. University educated and used to high-middle-class life, complete with live-in domestic workers, ashamed and afraid of the reaction of her father (himself a hospital director), Iffah did not tell him what exactly she was doing in Japan for several months. Similarly, unused to the tasks involved in eldercare provision, sometimes she found it difficult to justify to herself the kind of work in which she was engaged. She told me how she cried at work, asking herself what she was doing there (in Japan), when, one day, already tired towards the end of her shift, she still needed to change the diapers of every elderly on the ward – and right on that day, nearly all of them were soiled with faeces.

The mutual assurances of worthiness and ethicality (or seeking to 'valorize their activities'; Fox 1999: 95) of care work expressed by Iffah and Kenta during our drive to the firefly creek were what Blake Ashforth and Glen Kreiner (1999: 428) call 'ennobling ideologies' through which the 'dirty workers … are more likely to embrace the work role'. They served as a means to rationalise and add positive value to what the two realised was perceived as low-status and undignified work. In particular, for Iffah, it was also a way to deal with the psychological burden that the nature of eldercare carried with it, and with which she still needed to come to terms.[15] Her effort to do so was further suggested during a morning shift following our trip to the firefly creek, when she asked me to remind her the Japanese word for *mulia* (noble; Ind.), which Kenta had used the night before to describe eldercare work. Importantly, what this shared realisation and strife to explain away the negative connotations of the work they were performing achieved was recognition of a correspondence between Iffah's and Kenta's positions and experiences, something that allowed them to imagine each other as somehow similar.[16]

Discovering one another through intimate practices or through a particular positioning within the hierarchy of institutions and dominant ideologies, and the distancing through the unfamiliar, was happening within the confines of the same space and within the same social relations. Therefore, the feelings of relatedness and solidarity, curiosity and compassion, existed alongside the discomforts, embarrassments, and distrust of the unknown. Although discussed here as separate issues, it is important to remember that in everyday life all the alliances and divides described above mixed into one multifaceted sociality. Essentialising disabling views and practices, and negative mutual valuations at a general level, coexisted with the development of closer interpersonal bonds and individual-specific knowledge. The Indonesian candidates perpetually moved between those realms, where at one moment they were able to cast aside the broad interpretations based on their nationality (ethnicity, non-Japaneseness, Indonesianness) to become viable working or conversation partners, and where they would be subsumed under these interpretations in the next. They could be immersed in negotiations of awkward situations, being a part of a sports game, or exchanging comments on the different afflictions caused by working in the care home, but then not be invited for a drink after a futsal game on the assumption that they would not drink anyway. They could be excluded from a conversation once they had moved to a different task or room, be rebuked for allegedly not understanding a simple task, or be the cause of embarrassment or agitation through their religious practices or purely by the way they look.

Sociality of Alcohol

Issho ni osake ga nomeru to ii naa (it's good to be able to have a drink together, isn't it?; Jpn.), commented one of the former Japanese language teachers, Ms Ito, as she was making herself comfortable in a corner between a bed and a small *kotatsu*[17] in Irdina's rented flat. The idea of not being able to share a drink with the Indonesian candidates in an informal setting seemed to be unnatural or at least uncomfortable to some of the Japanese with whom they worked, either as colleagues in the care homes or as teachers turned friends. As Stephen Smith remarked in his earlier work on alcohol drinking in Japan, 'a man who does not drink does not partake equally in the rituals of drinking. Equally important, he does not share in the emotional warmth and camaraderie that goes with drinking and therefore inhibits others who do drink' (Smith 1988: 150 quoted in Roberson 1998: 163). The comment made by Ms Ito referred to the visits that she regularly paid to other Indonesian candidates, either at their homes or when she would invite them out for a meal. In the majority of cases, no alcohol would be consumed, or even suggested, with the meals or as a drink over which to exchange mutual stories about what had been happening in the lives of the candidates and Ms Ito between the visits. During Iffah's birthday dinner – organised and sponsored by her employer, and attended by the employer, his deputy, Ms Ito, Iffah, and me – everyone but Iffah ordered beer with his or her meal. Although otherwise an undisputed practice, this time the ordering of beer was preceded by a discussion of whether or not we should do it because Iffah was with us and she was not intending to drink anything alcoholic. Ms Ito's and my ordering of beer was particularly noted by Iffah, who asked if we would not get dizzy (*pusing*; Ind.). Although an informal gathering, it felt as if a degree of formality or seriousness remained because not everyone at the table was joining in what was for the employer, his deputy, Ms Ito and me a token of a separation between the formal, professional relationship we had and the more personal, informal conversations on which we were about to embark. That becoming more relaxed was associated with drinking alcohol was hinted at by an exclamation that had been made by another person involved in the language training of the Indonesians a few months earlier. On our way back from a visit to a care home when the candidates were getting on a bus to take us back to the language centre, one of the teachers commented with appreciation on the cheerful behaviour of one of the EPA candidates with these words: *sake nashi de hai ni naru*, or '[he] gets high without alcohol' (Jpn.). The comment implied that being cheerful without alcohol was somewhat unnatural, and that such unrestrained chirpiness belonged to a drinking situation rather than to what was essentially a work setting.

Therefore, since drinking alcohol was associated with relaxation and unrestrained socialisation, abstaining from it (or the expectation that they would abstain), seemed to be an important drawback for the Indonesians in their ability to form closer relations with their Japanese colleagues, and indeed it often figured in conversations about socialising. At the institution where Amir and Jasir were employed, the majority of their Japanese colleagues were of a similar age to the two candidates. There was also a good mixture of men and women on each ward, although the formal affiliations did not seem to play an important role in the way the interpersonal relationships formed; as I already mentioned, the volleyball and futsal teams cut across the institutional divisions. When taking turns eating lunch, everyone would gather in a small room of about sixteen square metres (the same one where Amir and Jasir were praying when their manager wanted to use it for a meeting), sit around a low table, and talk about anything that seemed interesting on the day. These conversations would often revolve around how everyone spent their days off work. Some of the Japanese employees were socialising outside of work, and these events, usually involving going out for drinks and/or to karaoke bars, were discussed as well. With certain regularity, when talking about such outings in the presence of either of the Indonesian men, someone would ask them, as if to confirm once again, whether it was true that they did not drink alcohol. These questions were rather rhetorical in nature and seemed to serve as a justification for not involving the Indonesian colleagues in the more private activities associated with drinking alcohol of some of the Japanese workers. For the length of my research, neither of the two men, despite participating in various other activities, such as the sports games, joined a private social outing with his Japanese colleagues. James Roberson (1998: 164) also provides an example of a young female Japanese factory worker who was excluded from joining in *nakama* events because she chose not to drink alcohol, based on her Christian faith. Such exclusion of Amir and Jasir from events involving alcohol consumption affected the extent to which, on a personal level, the Indonesian and Japanese co-workers were able to engage in what Befu Harumi (1971: 164–65) refers to as the 'emotional interpenetration' that accompanies the drinking of alcohol together.

Irdina was one of those of my Muslim informants who decided to drink alcohol openly in Japan. She considered her arrival in Japan to be the beginning of a much longer phase in the life of herself and her family, whom she planned to bring to Japan once she had obtained the required certification. Therefore, it was important for her to attend to her social life in ways that would secure future inclusion. Irdina decided to adapt to the behaviour that was par for the course in Japan. She argued that when in Japan she should behave as the Japanese in order to create better relationships, and that her God would understand it. She also found it enjoyable to be able to socialise freely with her Japanese colleagues without being perceived as the odd one out in the group, and seemed to have successfully achieved her goal. Irdina made it clear to her colleagues that she would join in, and soon she openly shared drinks with her Japanese colleagues during outings and karaoke evenings, and began to form closer relationships with several individuals who would join her in other, less group-oriented activities, such as shopping on their days off.

When we were talking about Japanese members of staff in their institution, Amir and Jasir would comment on who was and who was not *orang baik* (a good person; Ind.), often referring to those stories they heard and could understand during lunchtime when the Japanese workers sometimes exchanged impressions of their nights out. In the course of this research, my friends often mentioned with disapproval how being *mabuk* (drunk; Ind.) took away one's ability to reason. These statements were, I was told, based on observations of other people either in Indonesia or in Japan. When mentioned in relation to the observations from Indonesia, alcohol consumption was directly linked to the individual's poor economic performance. His (as the narratives referred solely to men) economic failure was explained by a lack of virtues needed to achieve success, and drinking alcohol was proof of such a character flaw. The negative perceptions associated with drinking, or getting drunk (as one seemed to imply the other), did not present the drinking Japanese in a positive light, either. To an extent, drinking alcohol (or refraining from it) was sometimes used as an essentialising indicator of what kind of a person one was, or could be, and suggested the potential direction of interactions. Alcohol consumption was therefore not only a means of excluding the Indonesians from the socialising circles of the Japanese staff, but the exclusion had the potential to work the other way round as well. Indeed, the knowledge of the assumption on the Japanese side that, as Indonesians, the candidates would not be drinking alcohol was sometimes used by the latter to decline social invitations from individuals with whom they did not feel like socialising.

Despite the disapproving narratives about individuals drinking alcohol produced by the candidates, even those of my friends who were most vocal in their criticisms would try alcohol at least once while in Japan. In several instances, the first encounters and explorations took place while in the language training centre. Still, even those who decided to have a beer with other EPA Indonesians after language training would not always admit to it in front of their Japanese colleagues or employers. They were not sure if the Japanese would form a negative opinion about them if they found out about their 'untypical' for Muslim Indonesians practice. They also did not always want the Japanese co-workers to know about their drinking in order to be able to decline any unwelcome invitations. In this way the Indonesians were able to manipulate the perceptions, and therefore the potential ease or possibility of engagement.

Joy Hendry (1994: 184) notes that 'consumption of alcoholic beverages in Japan is for the most part quite an acceptable pastime'. Indeed, apart from those already mentioned above, several anthropologists also have noted the close link between alcohol consumption and sociality in Japan (for example, Embree [1939] 1946; Befu 1974; Bestor 1989, 2004: 301; Edwards 1989; Allison 1994; Roberts 1994: 106–7; Moeran 1998, 2005; Borovoy 2005; Christensen 2014; see also Ando and Hasegawa 1970; Douglas 1987; Oliver 2008: 91). When I spent my first year as a foreign student in Japan in the early 2000s, I came across many a poster hanging on the university corridor walls campaigning against *aruhara*, a popular name given to 'alcohol harassment' (*arukōru harasumento*; Jpn.) and publicised alongside *sekuhara*, or sexual harassment. *Aruhara* was particularly affecting first-year students who, having joined one of the popular interest circles or sport clubs (part and parcel of Japanese university life, akin to the perhaps more widely known fraternities and sororities of North American universities), were often forced to drink large amounts of alcohol, sometimes in a quick succession of *ikki nomi* (drinking in one breath, in one go; Jpn.), to establish themselves socially within the new *nakama* group of a circle or club.[18] The more prowess one had in drinking, the more easily one could be accepted as a socially desired member. Unfortunately, some such attempts had tragic consequences, with students dying of alcohol poisoning.

Where drinking alcohol was so closely related to socialising, it had to feature in one way or another in the Indonesians' experiences in Japan and in their relationships with their Japanese co-workers. By choosing not to drink, or not to share drinks with their Japanese co-workers, the Indonesian candidates attended to a certain image of how an Indonesian Muslim should, or would, behave. Those candidates who felt that not drinking was not a matter of choice for them could find themselves on the social margins of the accepting institutions. On the other hand, they were able to manipulate the extent to which they partook in the 'emotional interpenetration' allowed for by drinking alcohol, and were therefore better positioned to decide which relationships they wanted to foster and which to forego (see also Onishi 2008: 228–30 on what she calls a 'separation strategy'). Apart from whether or not drinking alcohol was a matter of choice, there were also other factors that affected the degree to which this particular form of interpersonal engagement would result in building more intimate relationships. This had to do with the more objective characteristics of the staff.

Impeding Demographics

James Roberson (1998) argues that, in the factory where he located his research, the *nakama* groups that were based on involvement in a shared activity, while shaped by individuals' age, life stage, and marital status, formed on the basis of individual personalities (see also Roberts 1994). In the case of the EPA Indonesians, a degree of their social engagement with the Japanese members of staff was linked to age and life stage, too, but it was also affected by gender and the educational levels of the co-workers. For example, Lazim, a 25-year-old candidate, was working as the sole male among fifteen females aged forty and older. He was at the time a bachelor, and did not have children. During lunch breaks he would go back home because he did not want to eat in the break room as his co-workers often used it as a changing room, which made him feel uncomfortable. Before *mōshiokuri* (reporting on the situation to the next shift; Jpn.), when all members of staff on duty gathered around a table in the nursing station, there usually ensued a free discussion on a range of topics. Issues discussed were the children of the women, their school stories, preparing *bentō* (lunch boxes; Jpn.), sometimes husbands, shopping, and so on. These were subjects difficult for Lazim to engage in (even disregarding his lack of the linguistic ability necessary to follow and contribute to a changing and fairly fast-moving flow of conversation), so he usually just sat there, trying to smile when appropriate. There was a male Japanese part-time worker who worked on Lazim's ward twice a week. When their shifts overlapped, these were the good days at work for Lazim. They talked a lot; they joked around. Lazim would say to me, on passing me in a corridor, that *otoko ga iru to tanoshii desu* (when there is a man around it is fun; it is nice to have a guy around; Jpn). In contrast, in the institutions where Iffah and Idrina were employed, the gender and age of staff were more varied, which made it easier for the two women to identify with those colleagues who were of similar age and/ or professional status. As shown earlier in Iffah's case, such identification, combined with the bodily aspects of their work, supported the formation of meaningful interpersonal relationships. By far the most outgoing of my informants, she was quick to suggest joint shopping excursions to her young female colleagues, and when one of them was scheduled to work an early morning shift, Iffah offered to let her stay at her apartment overnight since she lived only several metres away from the care home. The colleague accepted the invitation, and for the next couple of months this became their routine, until the roster was changed.

Another factor was the difference in educational levels. The EPA Indonesians who arrived as the first batch in 2008 held higher education degrees, while the majority of the Japanese care workers with whom they worked were educated to high-school level, but with a supplement of a care-specific vocational education (usually one or two years). Given the extent to which my Indonesian friends could communicate in Japanese, it was more an assumption than an actually felt incongruity that the educational difference precluded some of the Indonesians from forming closer relations with their Japanese colleagues. However, it was Amir who once pointed it out to me. He still had difficulties trying to follow the conversations of his colleagues, but from what he could gather, he told me once on our way back home, he did not find many of these conversations interesting. He then added that he had recently found out that people working as care staff in Japan were not really educated, and maybe that was the reason for his lack of interest.

Privileged Alienation

Finally, one other aspect that influenced the Indonesian workers' relations with their Japanese colleagues was the former's relationship with the employers. I explore this issue in more detail in the next chapter, here focusing solely on how it shaped interactions between the Japanese and Indonesian co-workers. For example, Lanny did not enjoy living in the flat arranged for her by the accepting institution. Although size-wise it offered a comfortable living space, it was only a 1DK *apāto* (one-room apartment with a combined dining and kitchen area; Jpn.) in an old building, deprived of sunlight. As with most housing of this type one could hear one's neighbours through the thin walls, and during the winter months the cold and dampness were hard to ignore. Wanting to move to a warmer and brighter place, Lanny had been collecting information about rental prices and the procedures for renting a place in the area adjacent to her workplace. One day after work, three of us – Lanny, her female colleague who had joined the institution only a few weeks earlier, and I – went to have a look at the colleague's flat. The walk took us about twenty minutes, most of which was filled by a conversation on the cost of living in the area and the need for keeping a balance between the price of rent and the commuting time. Lanny's current flat was situated directly opposite the institution where she worked, which meant that it took her literally a minute to walk to work. The colleague asked Lanny how much rent she was paying at the moment and the amount of her monthly bills. Instead of giving a direct answer, Lanny began to muddy the waters and avoid answering. She was paying half of her rent and none of her bills, as these were covered by the institution. Although she knew the total amount due from her each month and could have given it as the answer, she did not know how much the bills were and she knew that the low number she would have to cite as her payment would lead to further questions as to why she was paying below the usual amount expected for the area and the type of accommodation. Making up a total number would have meant lying to a person whom she had started considering a friend. Instead, she preferred to say that she was not sure since the amount differed each month and the rent went out of her account automatically. This was a lie as well, but one which was partially based on Lanny's real lack of knowledge about what her bills added up to, and one which did not disclose the favouritism offered to her by the common employer. The colleague expressed surprise at Lanny's lack of knowledge about her own living costs, especially given Lanny's usual scrupulosity about money, but she gave up further questioning, apparently sensing Lanny's apprehensiveness.

The financial provisions offered to (some of) the Indonesian carers were a welcome gesture, easing their efforts to save and remit as much as possible. However, receiving special treatment from their common employers remained something that created a distance between them, and was something they could not share. As Lanny grew closer with her Japanese colleagues, they began to share sometimes very intimate information about each other. Consequently, Lanny, and other candidates in a similar situation, had to manage the double allegiance: to their employers with whom they shared secrets, and to their Japanese colleagues whom they began treating as friends. The inability to combine the two stemmed both from the clear admonition by the employers not to give details of their financial dealings to anyone from the staff, as well as from the uneasy sense of the unfairness of the differentiation between themselves and their Japanese colleagues. Although privileged in some respects, some of my informants who were receiving the additional favours from their employers were set apart from the rest of the staff by the very privileges they were offered.

At the same time, the limited capability of the Indonesian candidates to engage in the full range of the care worker tasks (at times due to the imposed restrictions as discussed earlier) and to perform them with at least a similar result to that achieved by the Japanese workers was a bone of contention. The lack of full command of the Japanese language limited the Indonesian candidates in various administrative tasks that were a part of their duties as well. The system varied slightly in each care home, but in general each member of staff was responsible for reporting on the condition of the elderly assigned to him or her. In order to assure that the information reached every member of staff on any shift, the information had to be reported in writing by the end of a shift. The staff of the incoming shift would read out loud what was reported about each elderly during a meeting before dispersing to their respective tasks. The ability of the Indonesian candidates to fully participate in the process was thrice limited. Firstly, they were still unable to write by hand in Japanese. Even Lazim, who was by far the most literate in *kanji* (Sino-Japanese characters; Jpn.) among my main informants, was unable to hand write the reports quickly and accurately enough to allow for an unobstructed work flow. Neither were the Indonesians able to read what had been written by the previous shift's staff. Finally, they all had problems understanding what was read out loud as well.

Their co-workers, as well as individual observers who had been following the EPA acceptance in the media, found it questionable that the Indonesians, whose ability to work in a similar manner to Japanese workers was limited, should receive the same amount of pay as the Japanese workers. This was one of the conditions specified in the EPA programme, which stated that the EPA candidates would receive pay equal to that provided to the Japanese employees. Aware of the statutory level of remuneration offered to the Indonesians, some of their colleagues were dismayed at the idea that despite being able to perform only a part of the usual care worker duties, the Indonesians were receiving the same amount of money, a situation that in their eyes amounted to preferential, if not unfair, treatment. This was particularly visible in the care home where the two male candidates were not only confined to general housekeeping activities rather than personal care of the elderly, but, in addition to the two-hour-long language classes with a teacher each Thursday, were also granted a two-hour-long break every afternoon designated for self-study. All this was included within their working time and paid accordingly. On the several occasions when I managed to have conversations with the more favourably disposed Japanese colleagues of my Indonesian friends, I was told about two general approaches towards such an organisation of the Indonesian training in the institution. Some co-workers saw the situation of the candidates as very demanding, and expressed admiration for their efforts and bravery to take up the challenge of working and studying in a foreign country. These individuals perceived the studying time as work. But the same situation was interpreted in a less accommodating manner by others. Because the stated goal of the language training was to prepare the Indonesian candidates for the national examination, the time during working hours that the Indonesians spent studying was seen as privileging the candidates. The argument went that if Japanese workers wished to prepare themselves towards the same examination, they had to do it outside of working hours, were not paid for it, and sometimes had to take a temporary leave off work if they could not manage their responsibilities otherwise. Combined with the perception that the two candidates did not contribute much to the work of the team, the dispensation from being on the floor did not go down well with this part of the staff. I know about these attitudes from my conversations with the more positively inclined staff who were willing to talk to me, but I was unable to investigate the origins of such attitudes any further. Those who resented the treatment the Indonesians received were less likely to engage with the candidates on a personal basis, and they also seemed to avoid closer encounters with me, perhaps due to my association with the Indonesians.

The extent to which the Indonesian candidates were able (or willing) to relate to their co-workers was influenced by such characteristics as age, gender and educational level. Similarly, the alienation experienced by some of the candidates was also a function of perceived financial unfairness. They coexisted with cultural representations and perceived incompatibilities as well as with the bodily engagement in certain practices, the sociality of alcohol, the recognition of shared socio-economic status of care work, and the recognition of shared positioning within the institutional hierarchy. The accepting institutions were therefore not solely sites of cultural negotiations. Instead, the different areas of human engagements and orientations intermingled, providing or removing common ground for recognising commonalities through which to 'open up' an individual for interpretations beyond reductive stereotyping.

Familiar Safety Net of Fellow Indonesian Candidates

This opening up could be successful on one day and a failure on another. The EPA Indonesians found somewhat disorienting the way socialisation in public spaces was organised in Japan. The streets were boring (*bosan*; Ind.), with no *warungs* (food stalls, often mobile; Ind.) inviting people to stop for a quick meal and to socialise in a direct manner. A group of five women employed by the same institution located in a rural area of the Kansai Region cited a lack of relationships with their neighbours beyond formal exchanges of salutations in the street. They perceived the location in which they were accommodated as *desa* (village, countryside; Ind.), which was rather desolate (*sepih*; Ind.), and expected that the few inhabitants would form closer relationships, as would have been the case in Indonesia. Instead, they rarely saw anyone interact in the streets. They, too, to their disappointment, did not manage to go beyond a morning greeting with their neighbours. A similar observation about the lack of neighbourly bonds was made by Lazim, a male Indonesian candidate, who, eight months after moving into his flat in the suburbs, contrasted his lack of local acquaintances with what he had imagined would be the natural course of things in Indonesia, were he to live in a *kecamatan* (a sub-district administrative unit in Indonesia; Ind.) for that long. Used to socialising in streets enlivened with *warungs*, the Indonesians also found it intimidating to enter such enclosed spaces as *izakayas* (popular places for Japanese people to socialise while drinking alcohol and eating a variety of small dishes) without knowing what awaited on the other side of the door and/or *noren*, a short curtain usually bearing the shop's name and hanging at the entrance, obstructing the view of the inside even if the door itself is transparent. Daniel Linger made similar observations during his work among Brazilian *Nikkeijin* factory workers in Toyota city. He wrote, 'Japanese men often gather in closed settings, in small bars and clubs, behind opaque sliding doors. To a Brazilian such places seem uninviting, even forbidding' (Linger 2001: 87). Similarly, Joy Hendry, in her considerations of the intercultural varieties in 'the wrapping of space', notes that, 'in the use of space, ... a community may be relatively open or closed to the exploration of outsiders' (Hendry 1995: 116). The EPA Indonesians, and presumably the *Nikkeijin*, used to more open public and communal spaces, found it difficult to navigate the unfamiliar Japanese surroundings.

When the Indonesian workers arrived in Japan they, on par with the Japanese, took recourse in juxtaposing sets of images to make sense of the day-to-day experiences that were quite commonly marred with misunderstandings and surprises. In order to introduce some predictability into the encounters, the Indonesians, for example, described the differences in the ways they and the Japanese interacted with other people through a set of two exclusive metaphors: heart and head. The *hati* (heart; a seat of emotions; but also: liver; Ind.), or in Japanese *kokoro* (heart; spirit), was to guide the behaviour of an Indonesian person, while the *kepala* (head; Ind.), or *atama* (head; mind; brain; intellect; Jpn.), would guide the behaviour of a Japanese. Sitting around a table in a family restaurant in Tokyo, four of the EPA Indonesians – Lanny, Daris, Iffah and Lazim – feverishly discussed questions that they found problematic during the Japanese Language Proficiency test they had just taken a few hours earlier. Soon the conversation moved on to job-related matters. That day it seemed like everyone felt a need to divulge what was weighing on their hearts. Although Iffah was dominating the conversation, everyone else was admitting to having had the same kind of experiences and observations. Iffah presented a series of situations at work in which she was taken aback by the Japanese staff's attitudes towards the elderly residents and towards herself. She claimed that whenever she noticed any abnormal symptoms, like discolouration of skin, a rash or a sore on an elderly resident's body, or an unusual weakness, she investigated the issues as far as she could and promptly reported any worrying signs to a nurse on duty or to a team leader. The Japanese members of staff, on the other hand, in her opinion, would ignore any changes in a resident's condition. They would also easily forget any related care instructions. This could lead to, for example, making a resident who should not be walking by herself walk to a bathroom, an action that, in Iffah's narrative, resulted once in a resident complaining about pain in her legs. For Iffah it was an example of how the Japanese members of staff do not 'really care' for the elderly. In addition, they were *tidak senang* (unhappy; Ind.) seeing Iffah being more proactive in her duties. Daris added that *ada yang senang* (there are those who are happy; Ind.), but admitted that he had been experiencing similar attitudes at work as well. Lanny nodded in agreement while listening to Iffah and Daris, and finally asked whether the Japanese did not use their *perasaan* (feeling, compassion; Ind.) in interactions with people. The question was directed to me (as someone thought of as being more familiar with 'things Japanese'), but as I shrugged my shoulders, Iffah went on to explain what she thought about Lanny's question. She presented yet another story.

One day at work, she took a laundry trolley-basket to the laundry room in the basement. She had managed to finish her duties quickly, so this time she went to the laundry room about twenty minutes earlier than usual before going to accompany the other carers in *mimamori* (overseeing patients' activities in the day room; Jpn.). The next day, her team leader called upon her and explained that the laundry trolley-basket should not be taken to the laundry room earlier than specified in the roster. Iffah took notice of the remark. However, what she found unnerving was the fact that the woman from the laundry had not said anything to her directly at the time when she brought the trolley-basket. She concluded that the difference between Indonesians and Japanese is that 'Indonesians think with their hearts, *hati*, and Japanese think with their heads, *kepala*'. The rest of the friends around the table agreed and expanded on Iffah's statement, saying that indeed Indonesians, if they had something to say to somebody, would do it there and then, face to face, while Japanese would avoid such direct engagement and instead resort to official structures to communicate any issues.

The two sets of stories seemingly referred to different aspects of Japanese behaviour as observed by my friends at work. One of them alluded to the Japanese lack of compassionate engagement (*perasaan*; Ind.) in the care of the elderly, and the other to the formalised attitude towards interpersonal interaction at work. Both of them, however, signified an absence of *hati* (heart; Ind.), whether manifested in the lack of compassion for the elderly, or in the unwillingness to engage in conflict resolution in a person-to-person manner. For the young EPA candidates, letting one's *hati / kokoro* be the principal guide for one's actions was the prerequisite of forming close and 'real' relationships with others. It enabled the weaving of a close-knit web of friendships where human emotions were given priority over rules (*aturan*; Ind.), making the world friendlier and easier to navigate. If there were only *aturan* and no *hati*, there would be no flexibility for individuals to negotiate the best options within the system (as in Japan). If it was the *hati* that prevailed, it would be possible to get to the core of people's problems without being diverted away from them by the complexities of a rigidly applied system. This unwillingness, or inability, to directly engage with other people by Japanese was brought up on many occasions outside of the work environment as well. The lack of flexibility of a saleswoman in a mobile phone shop where Lazim and Iffah wanted to buy a phone was framed in reference to the *atama*-driven, *aturan*-abiding, unsociable attitude of the Japanese. Incidents as small as people not using their bicycle bells when trying to overtake a pedestrian on a pavement and waiting for the pedestrian to notice them coming from behind were also given as an example of Japanese people lacking the ability or willingness to communicate directly with others. It was also visible in the perceived lack of intimacy between people, pointed out by Irdina, who was amazed at the story of her Indonesian friend married to a Japanese man, according to whom many Japanese married couples have separate bedrooms. In such a different social environment, difficult (*sulit*; Ind.) and tiring (*capek*; Ind.) were the omnipresent rules (*aturan*; Ind.). The perception was that the *aturan*-restricted life was obliging the Japanese to use only the *atama*, the non-emotional, non-compassionate judgement, to direct them through various social situations, thereby distancing them from other people.

Thus, from interpersonal relations to the organisation of workflow, the Indonesians glossed the differences between Japan and Indonesia according to the *hati–kepala* opposition as a 'cultural difference' (*bunka no chigai*), an expression widely adopted by the candidates from the

Japanese language. Operating on such generalising classifications, the Indonesian workers were making sense of the everyday experiences in relation to that which they perceived as already familiar. By promoting whatever unexpected experience they had to cultural difference, the Indonesians formulated new stereotypes through which to differentiate between Japanese and Indonesian nationals. Such production of stereotyping representations played an important part in making sense of the surrounding world. When the candidates arrived in Japan, and even more so once they had left the training centre, they lacked the 'knowledgeability' (Giddens [1984] 2011: 21–22) needed to decipher and successfully reproduce social interactions and to predict the workings of the surrounding world. The minute habits of thinking, interacting and socialising heretofore taken as a given proved to provide a misleading guide to life in Japan. The discomforts and frustrations that arose from this incompatibility of 'interactional styles' (Linger 2001: 292–93) were dubbed by the Indonesians in terms of a couplet of oppositional and exclusive metaphors of *head* and *heart*.

When the day experiences at work seemed to be hindered by the culturally understood differences, the Indonesian candidates relied on a safety net of friends from the language training centre discussed in Chapter 1. Photographs from the time spent in training decorated the rooms of the candidates long after they had been dispatched to their respective institutions, and the stories of the good times spent with friends from the centre and memories of rooms, karaoke sessions, and teachers often resurfaced in conversations, all suggesting a lasting attachment among the candidates. Not surprisingly, the news of a three-day follow-up training course organised by their home language centre a little over a year after the candidates' first day at work spread quickly among my informants as being a 'reunion'.

The friend group formed during the language training supported those candidates who had failed in establishing satisfying personal relationships with their colleagues, or anyone who had simply had a bad day at work. Even after a tiring shift, all of my informants would without fail sit on the floor in front of their laptops, resting on low tables or put directly on the floor, and would log in to an instant messaging application. Almost always they would simultaneously talk on their mobile phones to some other friend who perhaps did not have an internet connection yet, or simply preferred to use the phone at this particular moment. If the candidates shared a flat, it was unusual for them to have only one-to-one conversations, or electronic chats, unless with a partner or family members. Everyone present would at some stage be talking to the person or persons on the other end of the connection, or would at least shout something over the shoulder of the person currently holding the handset if the conversation was being held over the phone.

Those evening conversations revolved around individual experiences at work, and featured accounts of the candidates' encounters with their Japanese colleagues and the elderly residents they looked after. Whenever somebody had a story to tell, either about some frictions with their colleagues at work or, quite the opposite, about a pleasant surprise, it would be conveyed almost instantly to a large number of candidates. But even the most distressing stories, such as when one of the candidates was found to have been responsible for an elderly patient falling out of her bed without anyone from the staff noticing, were quickly transformed into humorous exchanges filled with light-hearted sarcasm making the candidates themselves the butt of the ridicule. The basis for the ridicule was the extraordinary situation in which they found themselves. They operated in an environment where they had to live and work among people whose language and culture they barely understood. This often left little room for the candidates to ascertain their own personalities or unmask their actual selves, that is, persons with very specific reasons for actions. Instead, they were perceived through blanket representations or met with outright disengagement.

Apart from the everyday experiences, the candidates exchanged more practical information about the amount of money they were receiving, the number of days off to which each of them was entitled, the extent of financial support granted by their respective institutions, and so on. Sometimes the conversations did not go beyond the exchange of information about each other's dinner menu, or simple friendly banter. Whatever the content, sitting in a room where sometimes three laptops and three mobile phones where simultaneously in use, it was hard not to imagine a web of invisible threads running across the sky over the Japanese archipelago (and beyond), forming multiple intersections and headed for the points marked by the presence of the Indonesian care worker candidates. When the need for intimate social interactions was not satisfied in their dealings with the Japanese, this web provided a virtual space where the candidates could retreat and offset the deficiency. Admittedly, these interactions were particularly intense during the first few months of employment, after which my informants began to visit each other and establish new friendships with other (non-EPA) Indonesians living in their area, and with the Japanese. Nevertheless, the core of the friendship networks seemed to remain unchanged, and the regular exchanges continued throughout the time I spent with my informants.

This enduring connectedness between the candidates suggests that they needed these contacts as a respite from the still volatile social relationships within the institutions. Being able to converse in their native language about shared experiences, memories, and often simply food or television programmes that the Indonesians knew their friends would appreciate, offered a familiar environment enjoyed for the comfort of speaking in Indonesian (or in one of the local languages) as much as for the predictable 'interactional style' (Linger 2001: 292–93) and the opportunity to express oneself and to be listened to. Just as the candidates would feel *bebas*, free (Ind.), at home to eat with their hands, so did they revert to the comfort of interactions with known Indonesians to offset any troubling experiences at work.

***

The Indonesian workers were bodies out of place (Puwar 2004) in Japanese eldercare institutions. They were an anomaly both in terms of their novelty as foreign care workers and in terms of being non-Japanese figures in the care homes imagined and constructed as Japanese spaces. Encounters with and displays of difference, an index of unfamiliarity, such as the Muslim prayers or simply a recognisably non-Japanese physiognomy, served as reminders of different cultural intimacies in which the Japanese and the Indonesians partook. The differences, sometimes a source of embarrassment and therefore to be hidden, at other times provoked conversations. The fact that the EPA Indonesians entered the accepting institutions in small groups, and sometimes alone, meant that their entrance into the Japanese care spaces did not appear to threaten the latter's Japaneseness to the extent that most likely would have been the case with large numbers of foreigners simultaneously entering the eldercare homes. It also meant that the candidates were unable to retreat to the comfort of their own, Indonesian circles at work and were therefore more inclined to seek relationships among their Japanese co-workers. Such a situation was directly linked to the way the acceptance was organised. This is, of course, not to say that the relationships formed solely because of a lack of other alternatives, or that they were predestined by political and administrative regulations governing the Indonesian acceptance. Rather, the seeding of the Indonesians in the eldercare institutions across Japan provided an environment more conducive to the development of intimate interpersonal relationships between the Japanese and the Indonesians. This was a situation unlike the ones observed by Linger (2001), Roth (2002), Tsuda (2003a), or Carvalho (2003). Tsuda (2003a) notes, in fact, that in smaller factories with fewer *Nikkeijin* workers, the relationships between the

Japanese and the *Nikkeijin* were more intimate, too. The essentialising ideas of differences between the Japanese and the Indonesians did not cease to affect their mutual interactions. However, cultural representations and reifications coexisted with more intimate knowledge of individuals, and the two were not exclusive. The cultural was paralleled, if not overridden, by other, intimately informed and shaped identifications and ascriptions. The cultural was also a resource into which to tap when convenient or necessary. The perceived cultural differences could be negotiated through a prism of intimacies built on other, non-culture specific engagements. In the process, an individual person would emerge from within the images painted with a broad brush. Some of these themes reappear in the following chapter, which turns to the relationships between the Indonesian candidates and their employers. The difference is in the focus on the function that an (asexual) intimate relationship may serve in the context of employee–employer relations.

Notes

1. For a more detailed account of these women's experiences, see Parreñas 2011.
2. Domestic helper level two requires 132 hours of theoretical and practical training, no examination, and no minimum educational level.
3. Formerly known as Asia Human Power Network, the cooperative gained the status of a non-profit organisation (NPO) in early 2010 and changed its name to AHP Networks. The change in legal status was made in order to enable engagement of the NPO in the expected intake of Vietnamese candidates under the Vietnam–Japan EPA.
4. This is according to an AHP outline of the preparatory education offered to the Vietnamese candidates, *jizen kyōiku*. The document can be accessed at http://www.ahp-net.org/jizenkyouiku001.pdf.
5. I provide only English translations here to prevent identification of the actual research locations.
6. See also Friebe 2011 for similar considerations in a German context.
7. *Hee* is a 'news-receipt token' in the Japanese language which is frequently used in response to deliveries of news (see Mori 2006).
8. Although the terms used in this section in particular, and throughout the book, encompass a range of work types, from sexual services through eldercare to manicure, I consider them interchangeable as referring to the kind of work that requires the ability to combine the 'care-about' and 'care-for' aspects of care work (Tronto 2001). I also do not, in general, differentiate between 'work' and 'labour', although in my usage of the terms I maintain the nuance of labour as being a subject of economic exchange, a fictitious commodity (Polanyi 2001); work, on the other hand, is the very action performed, which may not necessarily be labour.

9. See also Croll 2008 for a broader discussion of filial piety in Asia.
10. She was, however, excluded from writing reports and reading them out loud during staff meetings, as her Japanese language ability was still considered insufficient to perform such tasks.
11. See Eco 1976 for a critique of the concept.
12. Herzfeld 1997 provides an elaborate explanation of the process of naturalisation of stereotypical representations.
13. My thanks to Professor Roger Goodman for drawing my attention to this point.
14. I could not participate in this outing, as I was scheduled to be at a different institution at the time, but I saw a ten-minute-long video recording, and later talked about it with Amir and Jasir.
15. See also Bolton 2005; Stacey 2005; Kreiner, Ashforth and Sluss 2006; see Jervis 2001 for an account of workers who were unable to rationalise away the stigma of care work.
16. See Foner 1994: 123 for an account of the bonding force of class belonging between nursing aids in a New York eldercare institution.
17. A table with a heater attached underneath its top.
18. The difference between a circle and a club at the Shizuoka University I attended lay in the source of funding for the activities. While the circles relied solely on contributions from members, clubs received subsidies from the university and would represent a given university in tournaments if their activities involved an element of competition. The greater formality of the clubs meant also that there was a stronger emphasis on the *jōge kankei* (lit.: relations between the above and the below; Jpn.) – that is, relations between members of different seniority in terms of belonging to the club.

 3

Intimate Management

'*"Nihon ni kite yokatta!", "Nihon de ukeirete yokatta!" to kokoro kara omoeru yō sapōto shite ikitai'* (We want to provide support in order that [the EPA Indonesians] could think: "I am glad to have come to Japan!", "I am glad to have been accepted [to work] in Japan"; Jpn.). Such was the objective outlined in the second paragraph of the charter issued by one of the grass-roots support organisations that formed on the occasion of the Economic Partnership Agreement (EPA) acceptance. 'So that [they] had good memories [of Japan]' (*ii omoide o tsukutte moraeru yōni*; Jpn.) was another common phrase uttered by people associated with the same organisation, and often used by the mass media as well. These hopeful declarations were followed by propositions of changes to the acceptance programme in order to make it more feasible for the Indonesians to obtain the Japanese qualifications and to avoid disappointment with the organisation of the programme in Japan. The activities of the grass-roots support group I cooperated with and the plethora of other similar groups were not limited to lobbying for the systemic changes. They were also very much concentrated around the idea of making sure that the Indonesian candidates would feel comfortable in Japan and appreciate their experiences there. Previous chapters provided several examples of the difficulties the Indonesian candidates had in adjusting to everyday life in Japan, where not only socialising spaces and interpersonal relations but also eating habits were unfamiliar and taxing to negotiate. All these observations feature in this chapter as well, and are presented as having jointly contributed to the development of extra-professional relationships between the Indonesian candidates and their employers that aided the influence they had on each other. What becomes visible through this relationship is how intimate interpersonal relationships can serve to stabilise professional relationships in a situation where the usual means of knowledge and professional control are not accessible.

Alongside the hardship of care work, it was the physical and psychological strain of working and living in a foreign country compounded by the isolation from one's friends in Japan and family in Indonesia that were also widely discussed aspects of the Indonesian candidates' lives in Japan. Examples of how some of them found it difficult to adjust to life and work in Japan abound. Irdina, for example, developed a skin condition that resulted in a near-constant appearance of boils on her face. A doctor told her that this was stress related. When I went to visit her for a few days in the early part of 2010, she told me that she would cry almost every evening, feeling lonely at her flat, which she did not like too much, and because she was missing her children who at the time were still in Indonesia. Such images circulated among the grassroots support organisations. The following description reflects actions taken by one such group.

This particular organisation worked towards helping both the accepted Indonesian candidates and the accepting institutions in dealing with any problems they might face. Once the activity of the group had brought its members into closer contact with at least some of the EPA candidates, they began to have a clearer picture of what kinds of issues the Indonesians were facing in their day-to-day lives, as well as what the problems were in terms of their training aimed at passing the national professional examinations. It soon became apparent to the members of the group that the main means of communication among the Indonesian candidates and between them and their relatives in Indonesia were mobile phones and internet-based communication channels, such as VoIP (Voice over Internet Protocol) programmes and chatting tools. The support organisation saw a need to secure access to these methods of maintaining contact to support the candidates' mental well-being, particularly for those who had been dispatched to remote areas or those who ended up working as the sole Indonesian in their accepting institution. Thus, the group launched an initiative to provide the EPA Indonesians with laptops and mobile phones free of charge.

The initiative to distribute mobile phones was primarily aimed at the second batch of the EPA Indonesians since the vast majority of those who had arrived in Japan in 2008 were already in possession of phones by the time the idea was born and the preparation for its implementation was under way. The plans were officially announced during a meeting organised at the beginning of January 2010. In the announcement, the mobile phones were presented as an important means to maintain the mental health (*mentaru herusu*; Jpn.) of the candidates who, as Indonesians, were believed to be very sociable and so did not take well to being isolated from their friends. By the end of my fieldwork the mobile phone initiative was not fully under way yet, but the very proposal to provide the Indonesians with free mobile phones suggested that creating an environment as convenient as possible for the Indonesian candidates to live and train in Japan was high on the agenda of this particular organisation.[1]

The project to provide the Indonesian workers with free-of-charge laptops was ultimately not carried out, only because the founder of the group had received information that the Nursing Division of the Ministry of Health, Labour and Welfare (MHLW) and the Kenkō – Ikigai Development Foundation were pursuing similar plans.[2] The latter was an organisation selected by the MHLW's Division for the Promotion of Social Welfare (Shakai Fukushi Suishin Jigyō) to implement a programme aiming to support the EPA Indonesian caregiver candidates in passing the national professional examination. Both units, as a part of the ministry or through the funding received, used public resources to finance the provision of laptops. The devices were not presented to the Indonesians as planned by the support group; rather, they were lent to them for the purpose of access to the internet-based Japanese language and *kaigo* (care; Jpn.) course organised by JICWELS (Japan International Corporation of Welfare Services), the organisation responsible for overseeing the implementation of the foreign workers' acceptance on behalf of MHLW. The cost of the lease was covered by JICWELS, and the language tuition was provided to the candidates free of charge.

The actions undertaken by this particular grass-roots organisation and other similar groups showed that the concern about the quality of the EPA candidates' experiences in Japan was not only related to their passing the national examination, although this too featured prominently in the discussions over the acceptance. Efforts were therefore made by these organisations to attend to the various needs the candidates might have. They also, for example, organised home-stay visits, invitations for home meals, and other social gatherings for the Indonesians. Although relying in part on the particular image of the Indonesians as exceptionally sociable and ill disposed to lone existence, such efforts as those presented above were of course welcomed by the people at whom they were aimed. The consideration given to the well-being of this particular migrant group in Japan could, in fact, be regarded as an ideal (if perhaps utopian) approach to be taken by host societies the world over to facilitate newly arrived migrant workers achieve a smooth(er) adaptation to the organisation of life in the new environment. However well intended, the ideas of support were still closely related to the image of Japan as occupying a prominent position in a hierarchy of countries most worth living in. *Nippon no subarashisa o shitte kudasai ne*, or 'please do learn about (lit. know) the marvel of Japan' (Jpn.), were the words directed to a class of Filipino candidates who, just like the Indonesians before them, were undergoing six months of Japanese language training prior to their dispatch to the accepting institutions. The worth-knowing admirable qualities of Japan and its people were something to educate about, and to be enjoyed by those perceived as new to, or visiting, the Japanese world. The expected outcome of experiencing the Japanese 'wonderfulness' by foreigners was for them to appreciate the value of Japan and to take its good image back to their own country. The supportive actions were thus based on the premise that if unsatisfied with the conditions of life, the candidates might come to the conclusion that it was not after all a good choice to come to Japan, despite all the marvel it had to offer. In such a situation the acceptance would fail, exposing Japan's lack of readiness to accept foreign workers. This is something to which I return in the next chapter.

Acceptance Manual

In preparation for the arrival of the Indonesian candidates, JICWELS (2008) prepared a manual, which was distributed to the prospective accepting institutions. This 68-page-long A4-size booklet, alongside factual information on Indonesian geography, economy, labour market organisation, and so on, contained descriptions of the 'Indonesian character' and specific Indonesian traits, together with instructions on how to interpret and respond to them. A similar management manual was issued on the occasion of the later acceptance of workers from the Philippines, and from Vietnam as well.

In the preface to the Indonesian Nurse and Caregiver Human Resources Management Manual (henceforth 'Acceptance Manual' or simply 'the manual'), after a short introduction reiterating the basic facts about the EPA programme and a reminder that the Indonesian workers would be practising in the accepting institutions under the same financial conditions as their Japanese counterparts, the authors laid out the intended aim of the manual:

> On the occasion of employing people who grew up within an Indonesian culture and who have lived taking for granted an outlook different to that of the Japan[ese], it is conceivable that one will feel various differences

such as in the manner of working between the Japanese members of staff and the Indonesian nurse and caregiver candidates. In this situation relying solely on the usual employment supervision and guidance management methods used with the Japanese will not allow for a successful preservation of the motivation of the Indonesians who came to Japan with ambitions. Moreover, [such usual methods] will unavoidably bring about a situation in which [the Indonesian candidates] will not be able to showcase their full potential, despite having excellent dispositions.

Therefore, believing it necessary for the hospitals and the care facilities to familiarise themselves with the state of affairs [*kokujō*; Jpn.] in Indonesia, with the living circumstances there, the Indonesian worker mentality [*hataraku indoneshiajin no kishitsu*; Jpn.] and values [*kachikan*; Jpn.] in order to manage Indonesian nurse and caregiver candidates and later nurses and caregivers appropriately, here at JICWELS we arrived at a decision to issue the present manual. (JICWELS 2008)

The second chapter of the Acceptance Manual, 'Characteristics of Indonesian Workers Working in Indonesia', was based on a questionnaire survey and interviews with Japanese who were deployed to Japanese companies based in Indonesia, and who assumed supervisory positions over Indonesian employees. The information presented there ranged from the Indonesian working time regulations, the system of financial bonuses, and the social insurance system to the provisions required from employers guaranteeing workers the possibility of maintaining the conduct prescribed by their professed religion and the customary practices commonly encountered at work. In the latter section, the authors of the manual pointed out that Indonesian workers, 'just like Japanese', tended to abide by the rules at work, but unlike Japanese did not keep to the time. They were also more likely than Japanese to, for example, make private use of company computers. Importantly, throughout the Acceptance Manual, the highlighted differences were followed by advice to the Japanese employers and co-workers to understand and embrace the different needs and conduct of the Indonesian workers, either by providing them with a designated space for prayers, or by not treating their lateness as a sign of personal negligence but rather as a culturally informed action (and therefore somehow out of the Indonesians' control). Only in a section on forbidden food items, after a reiteration that, depending on the person, some may not consider it a sin if they consume, for example, pork without their knowledge, the suggestion was that sometimes it may be 'advisable, wise' (*kanmei*; Jpn.) not to disclose the ingredients of a dish offered to an Indonesian (JICWELS 2008: 49). In such ways, the attention to cultural differences was inscribed in the formal directives regarding the approach to the Indonesian workers within the accepting institutions.

In the spirit of the Acceptance Manual, the institutions made various facilitating adaptations to the working environment of the EPA candidates. One of the measures taken to assure that the candidates arrived into as friendly an environment as possible was to address and mitigate some of the foreseeable challenges. For example, some of the managers sent out a letter to the families of the elderly residents informing them of the institution's participation in the EPA programme. Although the elderly themselves seemed to have less room for expressing their opinions on the prospect of being looked after by Indonesian workers, which was in many cases due to their already limited cognitive abilities, the employers felt it was only fair that the families be consulted on, or at least informed about, the planned acceptance of foreign workers. This in itself suggests that an unexpected arrival of Indonesian candidates could have become an object of contention, and needed to be dealt with through some special measures. The deputy floor manager and a training section supervisor of one care home that had informed the families in advance told me that she was glad that the reaction was positive, that the families were supportive of the institution's decision and that some had even replied with encouraging messages. As an institution, they would have found themselves in an awkward position should the reaction have been negative, she added. Here and in other care homes, the staff were also informed about the forthcoming scheme, and some of the institutions organised induction meetings about what to expect from working alongside Indonesians. When I took part in one such meeting organised by a hospital about to accept two Indonesian nurses from the second batch in 2010, the information offered to the gathered employees very much reflected that contained in the Acceptance Manual. In addition, the meeting organisers suggested their audience imagine trying to write or read upside down, and to remember the uncomfortable, unnatural feeling. This, they suggested, would be how the Indonesian nurse candidates would feel working in a Japanese hospital. It was therefore important to make sure that this discomfort was mitigated as much as possible while the Indonesians accustomed themselves to the new working culture. Moreover, the organisers stressed that the Japanese should be on the lookout for any misunderstandings that might arise, not only from the linguistic side of the communication but also from different customary ways of thinking about things in Indonesia. The audience was, therefore, advised to also try and find out the motives behind any behaviour that they might find dubious, before judging the Indonesians as acting in an inappropriate manner. Such informative and pre-emptive steps indicated the extent to which the Indonesian candidates were constructed as 'unfamiliar beings' who

required particular attention, and whose arrival called for special measures to sooth the impression it might have on the elderly or their families. They were unlike any new workers employed by the institutions,
and therefore their imminent arrival needed to be announced, prepared
for and accommodated by those involved. At the same time, such measures aimed to alleviate the initial disorientation that the Indonesians
were expected to experience in the new working environment shaped
by different mentalities (*kishitsu*; Jpn.) and values (*kachikan*; Jpn.).

When the EPA candidates finally arrived at the care homes, they received an official welcome, sometimes with the staff and the elderly
residents gathered outside the institutions with bouquets of flowers.
Amidst applause, the Indonesians were given formal welcome notes,
sometimes contracts, and neatly folded working uniforms, handed to
them by the managers of the institutions. In Blue Bara special nursing
home where Iffah came to work, in the hallway of the main entrance a
Japanese flag and an Indonesian flag hung side by side. They remained
there throughout my fieldwork. In Ajisai, a manager of Amir and Jasir
told me once about her strategy when, after a few months into the
Indonesians' on-the-job training, she noticed that most of her Japanese
staff were not communicating sufficiently with the Indonesian candidates. She sent out emails to all the Japanese staff to remind them to use
easier language and speak more slowly when talking to the Indonesians.
This communication was to remain secret from the Indonesians themselves so as not to make them feel uneasy and patronised. Through
such actions the accepting institutions aimed to prepare the social environment for the arrival of the Indonesian workers, one which would
make them feel comfortable and welcome. Alongside such social engi-
neering, more practical adjustments were made as well.

The supportive adaptations were visible in such details as additional
labels with transcriptions of the Japanese names of facility rooms put
on almost every door. It also seemed to be a common practice among
the accepting institutions to make sure that their staff canteen, if there
was one, served at least one pork-free meal each day. I have heard stories both from the Indonesian candidates and from their Japanese supervisors about institutional canteens completely withdrawing pork
from their menu options, but I have never managed to confirm such
statements. In a sense, whether it was a fact or not did not much matter.
What mattered was the imagination of the length to which the accepting
institutions could go to provide hospitable living and working conditions for their Indonesian workers. Through such means, the accepting
institutions, imagined as representing an environment alien to the arriving candidates, attempted to become more familiar and welcoming.

Accommodating Islam

One of the greater concerns about accepting the Indonesian workers was caused by their religious (read: Muslim) observances and how the Japanese working environment could and should accommodate them. These concerns were pertinent to most of the accepting institutions since most of the EPA candidates were indeed Muslim. For the majority of Japanese, conceiving of themselves as without a religion 'in particular' (usually expressed as *toku ni nai*, none in particular, rather then *mushinkyō*, without religion), foreigners devoted to a single religion were already different in this very respect, but foreigners professing Islam were an even greater rarity, and an unknown. In its first chapter, the Acceptance Manual provided basic factual information on Indonesia. Attracting attention was the ordering of the presented information. Interestingly, the reader learnt first geographical, then historical information, directly followed by an introduction of the religions practised in Indonesia. Areas such as the political and administrative organisation of the Indonesian state, the Indonesian languages, and the educational system come only after the section devoted to religion. While it may be reading too much into the design of the manual, with the descriptions of religions tacked between geography and history, on the one side, and economy, politics and administration, on the other, the place of religion within the Indonesian reality appeared to take on a more objectified existence, one which can be verified and measured in the same ways as the physical area of the state or its main export destinations.

In the section on the religions, where one could find a table comparing the three major world religions practised in Indonesia, namely Buddhism, Christianity and Islam (Bali Hinduism is mentioned later in the chapter), arranged in this very order (JICWELS 2008: 3), the manual concentrates most, in terms of length, on Islam. Organised in bullet points, the table introduces the Qur'an, the Six Pillars of Islam, the Five Islamic Practices, the main Islamic celebrations, and the taboo items – that is, 'pork, dogs and alcoholic beverages' (ibid.: 5). Bali Hinduism is briefly outlined following the more detailed description of Islamic precepts and practices. While justifiable that the religion whose officially registered professors amounted to just over 86 per cent of the Indonesian population should be allocated the most space, or that the specificities of Bali Hinduism, despite its numerical minority within the Indonesian population, should be briefly compared against the, perhaps better known, Indian version, the decision not to include in the manual any mention of the doctrinal or practical details of Christianity or Buddhism as practised in Indonesia can also be read as dictated by an assumption (well grounded) that these two religions were less alien to the Japanese working in the accepting institutions and therefore did not call for an explanation. The overwhelming stress on Islam as one of the Indonesians' most prominent unfamiliarities was later resented by those of my informants who identified themselves as Christians (three Batak women and one man referring to himself as Indonesian–Chinese). Often being assumed to be Muslim was somewhat annoying (*ira ira*; Jpn.), not because they found the misconception offensive in any way, but because they felt deprived of a piece of their self-representation and did not feel comfortable being assigned characteristics with which they did not identify. To an extent, they were surprised by the naivety of the Japanese who were readily making the ill-informed generalisations.

Made aware of the precepts of Islam, the accepting institutions tried to accommodate the candidates' needs. As mentioned above, canteen menus were revised, special breaks were assigned for prayers, and all of my main Muslim informants who did not live close enough to use lunch breaks to pray at home had a designated prayer space within the institution. Ramadan, the Muslim month of fasting, was one of the Indonesian Muslim traditions that worried their employers. The concern was that because the fasting period coincided with a very hot season in Japan (in 2009 it began on 21 August), the Indonesians would become physically too feeble to perform their assigned tasks without sufficient intake of nutrients, and water in particular, and might collapse. Of particular concern was the Indonesians' participation in bathing the elderly – a duty that required spending a prolonged time in a hot, steamy bathroom, and was often considered the most physically demanding area of the care work in the institutions. Some of the supervisors of the Indonesian candidates decided to exempt them from partaking in bathing duties altogether, in order to ease the expected hardship which the Indonesians would be going through during Ramadan. In other institutions the rota during the fasting period was organised in such a way that the Indonesians were assigned only early morning or night shifts. Such working hours minimised the time the Indonesians had to spend at work between sunrise and sunset. There were Indonesian candidates who were required to work as usual as well, but it needs to be remembered that during this first Ramadan in Japan, many of the Indonesians were still assigned only assistant duties, limited to helping during meals, changing sheets, and keeping the common areas tidy – duties that were not as demanding physically as bathing.

What perhaps evoked the most emotion among the Indonesians was the issue of acquiring permission to return to Indonesia to celebrate Lebaran (festivities marking the end of Ramadan) or Christmas together with their families in Indonesia. This was an area where the expectations of the Indonesians and the usual working practice in the accepting eldercare institutions conflicted. It was a commonly accepted practice among the Japanese staff and the management to refrain from requesting holiday leave for longer than a few days. It was presumed and seen as appropriate and fair towards the employer and one's co-workers to abide by this unwritten rule, since any long absence from work would increase the burden on the rest of the staff. Often struggling with a shortage of staff, the institutions were usually opposed to their employees taking prolonged holidays, even if they were formally entitled to do so. Simultaneously, the employees aware of the situation would not consider it feasible, if appropriate at all, to receive or demand a week or so off work. The Indonesians on their part were expecting to be able to visit Indonesia at least once every year or two, and did not share the Japanese perspective on absence from work. To make the trip to Indonesia worthwhile, my informants calculated, they would need more or less ten days off work – a length exceeding the usual leave duration in the institutions. The first significant confrontational moment came with the end of Ramadan 2009 when many of the EPA candidates wanted to return to Indonesia to celebrate the week-long festivities of Lebaran. Although in 2009 Lebaran began on 20 September, and thus overlapped with a national 'long weekend' in Japan (19–23 September) when already many of their Japanese co-workers had requested the weekend off, my informants still managed to secure a full eight days of holiday (meaning six days off work). Moreover, the timing was set by the four concerned institutions to enable all the candidates to travel together. Why such arrangements were possible will also be made evident in the following sections where I discuss the nature of relationships between the Indonesian workers and their employers.

Adapting to the Islamic practices within the institutions was, therefore, one way to ensure that the Indonesian candidates could maintain this part of their lifestyle while working in Japan. Of course, such spatial and temporal arrangements accommodating different-to-Japanese conduct did not always go together with personal readiness for encounters with the unfamiliar practices. The institutional preparations coexisted with the more complex interpersonal relationships and attitudes discussed in the previous chapter.

Before moving on, one qualification is needed here, which is that not all accepting institutions were as engaged in the private affairs of the Indonesian candidates, or indeed in their training required by the EPA scheme, as I describe here. Perhaps the institutions whose candidates decided to return to Indonesia before the end of the training were such places. Some of the candidates I encountered in various locations in Japan, but with whom I only had sporadic contact, also mentioned that no provisions whatsoever had been made for them in order to, for example, be able to work and study at the same time. One such candidate, whom I met in Osaka, complained that he was simply expected to work, and any attempts he made to arrange language tuition had failed because any arrangement he suggested would mean that he would need to sacrifice a few hours of his working time. Living in a rural area, he did not have many options to choose from in terms of Japanese courses. Hence, after his institution declined his consecutive suggestions, he focused on self-study, but remained disgruntled by the approach of his employer, who, in the candidate's eyes, did not fulfil his part of the deal. He was also covering all his living expenses on his own, and did not relate to me any situations in which his employer offered any kind of financial or practical support in the ways I describe below. My account here is, therefore, an example of how the relationships between the Indonesians and the employers developed in the institutions where this support existed. Perhaps, it was the same approach to the support of the Indonesians that has made it possible for me to conduct research in the institutions, and thus what I observed had already been preselected by the very possibility to access the sites.

Employers' Personal Engagement

How to Spend Money

Although it should not obscure the variety of other motivations, such as enjoying Japan as a country otherwise hard to go to, as discussed in Chapter 1, to be sure, the prospect of earning substantially more in Japan than in Indonesia was a very important factor in my informants' decisions to choose this particular country as their migration destination. *Cari uang* (Ind.), or looking for money, is what Iffah admitted to be her reason for wanting to come to Japan.

The decision to relocate to Japan to work was often a family endeavour rather than one of the individual. Soon after the first remittances were sent to Indonesia, the news of new acquisitions travelled in the opposite direction. Lanny had a look at her sister's new television set during a family conversation over Skype, and Jasir began discussing with his mother where to buy more space for their future, larger family shop. When with my husband I visited Iffah's family house in Indonesia in September 2009, she took us for a drive in a new 4x4 car to which she had contributed with her remittances. Twenty-one out of thirty caregiver candidates who responded to my questionnaire survey, answered that they found being able to support their family by sending some of the money earned in Japan back to Indonesia one of the most rewarding aspects of their sojourn.

The possibility of earning substantial amounts of money had an additional meaning for those for whom employment in Japan was their first job after graduation. Not only did they gain independence from their families by physically moving outside of their parental or familial control, but also, now that they were financially self-sufficient, it was they who were able to bring money into their families, and not just spend it. A young male candidate sent to the north of Japan started supporting his two younger cousins as they moved on to university; Iffah started planning a present for her parents which was to send them together on *hajji* (pilgrimage) to Mecca; and Amir, preoccupied with planning the house he was hoping to build for himself and his newly wedded wife, would spend many evenings flipping through glossy catalogues.

The ability to generate wealth made the second year of the candidates' employment in Japan a year of weddings. I was closely following the marriage negotiations of two of my informants who happened to be a couple, so their resultant wedding plans were not a surprise. But when I learnt that two other of my male informants had set dates for their weddings as well, and that there were more such people in the larger group of the first batch of candidates, I questioned the proliferation. I was told that now they, and the young men in particular, were *berani* (brave or daring, also manly; Ind.) and *mampu* (able; Ind.) to get married. These qualities were ascribed to them because they had shown that they were capable of accumulating enough wealth to form a new family, and, not least, to pay for the wedding.

Remitting money back to Indonesia meant, however, that the candidates had to limit their private expenditures while in Japan. In the first months, from the moment they started working, saving seemed relatively easy and was done without much ado. In fact, my informants seemed to genuinely enjoy putting away the money, seeing the amount grow and calculating how much in Indonesian rupiah the savings in yen would be once converted. The amount of money they were earning was known to their families in Indonesia, who could plan ways of spending it, and not only for the weddings. My informants would also inform their families in advance of any expected bonuses and their timing so that the families could plan any potential expenditures. Some of the investments, like the new car bought by Iffah's family and the new shop space envisaged by Jasir's family, were planned joint ventures.

During the first few months of their employment my friends would often mention that they were bored, not knowing how to spend their time off work. A lack of familiarity with places to go and things to do was one of the reasons, but the perceived lack of things to do was also linked to the limited financial resources they had due to the remittances, and the constant awareness that they should put aside whatever they did not have to spend on necessities. When gradually the Indonesians discovered ways of finding entertainment in Japan, the amount of money they needed for themselves increased. For example, Jasir had been interested in photography. Initially, the camera he bought compromised the optimal quality of the photographs for the lower price of the camera. A few months later, however, he acquired equipment of a very high standard, which came at an equally high price. He and several other Indonesian EPA candidates who lived in the same area formed an informal photography group, and they would go out, sometimes together, for a shooting session, and later post their works on Facebook together with the information explaining under what conditions and at what settings a given picture had been taken. Besides using the time in Japan to develop hobbies, apparently used to a more glamorous lifestyle in Indonesia, the young men and women enjoyed fashionable clothes and accessories. A new pair of shoes, a handbag, or a pair of trousers were the more visible items testifying to the extra cash the Indonesians would spend on themselves.

The Indonesian friend of mine who was supporting his cousins through university would keep the amount of money sent even and reliable. Similarly, Irdina, a mother of two, maintained an unchanged flow of remittances for her family. However, after a few months of diligent saving and close cooperation in financial matters with their families, those of my friends who were funding luxury items for their families and who did not yet have families of their own to support began to conceal a part of their earnings.[3] Iffah, Lanny and Jasir decided on different occasions not to tell their families about bonuses they had received, or else only to declare an amount lower than what had actually entered their accounts. As Iffah told me, she wanted to enjoy her time in Japan, and sending all her financial surplus to Indonesia would significantly limit her options.

It was, therefore, an important part of the Indonesians' Japanese experience to not only be able to remit money back to Indonesia for their families to use, but also to be able to enjoy their stay in Japan. In time, these two goals came to be at odds with each other, as the young candidates learnt where and how to spend time (and money) in Japan. Unsurprisingly, then, financial dealings were a prominent aspect of the relationships between the Indonesian candidates and the employers.

Cooperative Remittances

As already explained in Chapter 1, due to the hastened nature of the EPA recruitment in Indonesia, many of my informants had a relatively wealthy background and came to be referred to in Japan as Indonesian 'elite'. Nevertheless, in their relations with employers they positioned themselves as in need of money. Particularly dear to Iffah and two young men, Lazim and Jasir, all in their early to mid-twenties, the phrase *kanemochi dakara* (because [you are] rich; Jpn.) served as a discursive means to this end. It was uttered whenever their employers offered them a gift of substantial monetary value, or money itself.

The image of the Indonesians as arriving from a 'poorer' country played a role in such positioning. My informants, who had chosen Japan, attracted by (among other considerations) wages that dwarfed the pay they had been receiving or could expect to receive in Indonesia, knew about such ideas and indeed shared them. Therefore, despite their own situation in Indonesia, which was anything but living in poverty, and having sufficient means to live in Japan, they readily accepted any additional financial relief, particularly when they needed to decrease the amount of money sent home due to the increase in their own expenses in Japan. Not without significance here was also the awareness that this Japanese sojourn was likely to be temporary, whether the Indonesians had planned it this way or not. It added to the idea that the gains needed to be maximised now, while the opportunity lasted, because after their return to Indonesia they would have to rely on only a fraction of what they were earning in Japan. Therefore, although it sometimes seemed that the remittances remained an unspoken topic between the employers and the Indonesian workers, it was often a matter discussed in the open and accounted for as one of the expenses that the Indonesians needed to shoulder. In knowledge of this obligation the employers took a sympathetic stance, and through various allowances participated in the Indonesians' efforts to accumulate enough capital to subsidise their families' lives in Indonesia.

As mentioned in the previous chapter, some of the institutions covered parts, and sometimes all, of the candidates' living expenses, such as utility bills or rent. This was a part of making the Indonesians' lives in Japan more agreeable. I also pointed out how, upon their arrival at the accepting institutions, many of the candidates were disappointed not only with the content of their work in Japan but with the financial conditions offered as well. Indeed, aware of such disillusioned expectations and the perceived and observed difficulties the Indonesian candidates had with adjusting to living in Japan, the commentators of the acceptance programme often referred to the need for *mochibēshon no iji* (preservation of motivation; Jpn.) of the candidates, or to *mochibēshon no teika* when referring to the feared 'decline in motivation' (Jpn.). One of the ways to sustain this motivation was to meet, or at least make up for, the Indonesians' unfulfilled financial expectations.

Figure 3.1: Study break. Photo by author.

The employers would, therefore, try to minimise the financial burden carried by the Indonesians. This could take a variety of forms, such as unofficial monetary gifts to cover the costs of leisure travel, the provision of furniture, financial assistance towards rent and facilities, or a contribution towards expenses incurred in relation to language or professional training. As a result, the amount of money at the disposal of the Indonesians was sometimes greater than that of the Japanese staff working in the same position but who did not receive such favours from their employers. During a meeting organised by a group supporting Filipinos in Japan who gathered to discuss their future activities in relation to the acceptance of the Filipino candidates under the EPA programme, a freelance journalist specialising in health- and care-sector subjects noted that, from her own investigation into the Indonesian EPA acceptance, the financial and material conditions of life offered to the Indonesians under the programme were often better than those of today's Japanese young people who 'cannot even think' of having 100,000 yen (around £800 at that time) at their disposal each month. She also jokingly added that having seen the very agreeable (*sugoi kaiteki*; Jpn.) conditions in which the candidates she had met lived, and given the level of pay and financial subsidies towards rent many of them were receiving from their employers, she would not mind 'swapping roles' (*sekigaeru*; Jpn.) and becoming an Indonesian for a while. The conditions of life enjoyed by the EPA Indonesians she had met and/or interviewed seemed to her to surpass the life standards that she, as a professional in her late thirties with several years of experience, was able to afford.

It was also not unusual for the Indonesians to be given sweets or Indonesian spices, to be taken on fully funded trips, for example to Tokyo Disneyland, or to be invited out to dinner by their employers. Although it is a common practice in Japan, just as in other countries, to organise social gatherings for the employees of the same organisation during which individuals can mingle on an interpersonal basis with people in different positions within the organisation's structure, these gatherings are usually organised for everyone in the company or its given section. In the case of the Indonesian workers, they were treated individually and often in secret from the Japanese members of staff. As Lanny's employer once told her, offering her a pair of tickets to FujiQ Highland, an amusement park in Yamanashi Prefecture near Mount Fuji, such personalised provisions were made in the hope that the candidates could be refreshed (*rifuresshu suru*; Jpn.) every now and then so as to be able to do their best (*ganbaru*; Jpn.) at work. That the candidates did not have to pay for such refreshing activities further added to the deal.

Favours and Cooperation

In time, the employers' personal engagement with the Indonesian candidates led to the formation of extra-professional, fairly close relationships between the two parties. For example, after having a minor accident on a bicycle, Iffah felt comfortable enough to approach her employer for help to repair the bike, which he did. In different institutions, a male candidate made it a routine to go shopping with his floor manager, and Lanny's team leader accompanied her to church. On some occasions, favours received by the Indonesian candidates from their employers were of a bigger scale. This was, for example, the case when Iffah's employer borrowed a minivan belonging to the care home in order to collect several household items for the EPA candidates employed in his institution. This happened towards the end of my fieldwork when I was clearing the flat I had been renting. A few months before, Iffah had enquired about what I was going to do with some of the items I had in the flat, including the carpet, chairs, a mini-sofa and a television set. I agreed to give her some of them, but as she lived about two hours away by train, and it would have been a very complicated if not impossible undertaking to transport the larger pieces of furniture on a train, I suggested that she could possibly rent a car for one day and take all the things she wanted in one go. She was thinking of abandoning the whole idea because of the difficulty of using the train and the expected cost of hiring a car. However, a day before I was planning to get rid off of all the items, either by having them taken by my local pawnshop owner or by arranging a collection by the local council, she called me to say that her employer would come with her to collect the items. The next day they arrived in the business van accompanied by the employer's wife, Lazim, and two new EPA candidates employed by the institution during the second round of the acceptance programme. The employer helped to carry the heavy items and loaded them into the back of the van. They explained that they would also take some of the things to furnish Lazim's flat, as the employer had agreed to run an errand to his place as well.

Yet another instance of cooperation, in this case between Lanny and her employer, based on their informal relationship, was during the acceptance of the second batch of foreign care worker candidates. The employer was considering whether to bring in Filipino or Indonesian EPA candidates during one of the forthcoming rounds of the acceptance. Unsure what to do, the employer consulted Lanny for her preferences. She was not enthusiastic about a Filipino person joining her at work, but would welcome an Indonesian. As it happened, two of her friends from nursing school in Indonesia were applying for the EPA programme at the time, and Lanny suggested that they could come to work in the same institution as her. Ultimately, the employer agreed to the suggestion. Although the recruitment process was designed to be anonymous, with the names of the candidates concealed under reference numbers, Lanny and her employer managed to circumvent the system. A few months later the friends arrived to Japan and soon started their appointment at the institution together with Lanny. After their arrival, and aware that the three women wanted to move together to a bigger flat, the employer made arrangements for them to move into his brother's house, situated next door to his own. In this way the employer had a degree of warranty of the quality of the new candidates through their association with Lanny, whom he already knew and trusted. Moreover, by accepting Lanny's friends, the employer also attended to her satisfaction and hoped to guarantee that the three women would become engaged workers.

Thus, the employers were not only concerned with adapting the working environment so that the Indonesian candidates found it as easy to navigate as possible, but were also actively and personally engaged in providing comfort, respite, company and financial support to the Indonesian workers. Such attending to the 'mental health' (*mentaru herusu*; Jpn.) of the workers, sometimes through material means, was to enable them to *ganbaru* (Jpn.), do their best, strive at work. Such association between the general well-being of workers and their performance at work has now become common knowledge in almost any sector. However, it remains of particular significance in jobs like care giving, where an important proportion of the required skills is constituted by the workers' mental ability and willingness to engage emotionally (see Constable 2009) in their tasks. For example, Arlie Russell Hochschild shows in her book *The Managed Heart: Commercialization of Human Feeling* how flight attendants were less willing to perform friendliness when they found their working conditions unsatisfactory (Hochschild [1983] 2012). The primacy of individual ability and the willingness to apply 'soft skills' is also stressed by Rhacel Parreñas and Eileen Boris, who, in their *Intimate Labors*, contend that 'emotional labor relies on the manipulation of one's emotions' (2010: 6). This is not to say that the relationships between the Indonesian candidates and their employers were a calculated and conscious exchange of favours. They rather emerged as a result of the employers' efforts to ease their Indonesian charges into the life and work in Japan, which they expected would be difficult to adjust to for the Indonesian workers. The provisions offered by the employers had indeed an encouraging impact on the Indonesians.

However, apart from the positive attitude to work, the candidates also felt obliged to reciprocate the favours and help they had received from the employers.

Feeling the Obligation

The EPA Indonesians often described their relations with the employers in familial terms, representing the employers as their Japanese fathers (as the employers were predominantly men) or grandfathers. In one institution where the employer was only a few years older than the Indonesian candidate, the relations were still very close and the candidate herself described him as her *onīsan*, or elder brother. Such representations suggested that indeed the role the employers took in their relationships with the young Indonesians was of an intimate figure, but one who had the power to instruct and to require obedience. On our trip to Osaka, two female candidates who had been placed in the same institution, run by a married couple, told me that their employers were strict (*kibishii*; Jpn.) when it came to work, and, for example, required them to eat their lunch together with the elderly, despite the women's objections. They added, however, that it was like a strictness of grandparents who expected rules to be followed when necessary but who, outside of the professional relation, would indulge them with an odd invitation to dinner or a trip.

Having received various forms of help and material support, the Indonesians were compelled to reciprocate through good performance at work, taking into consideration not only the list of duties received upon arrival at the institutions, but also how what they did would be perceived by their employers. In Lanny's words, she did not want to feel *malu*, ashamed, were she to be seen by her manager as not doing her best, either in studying the language or in her work at the institution. Such considerations were visible in the candidates' compliance with the arrangements made for them either at work or in matters not directly related to their employment. For example, Lanny wanted to take two days off to visit her Indonesian friends in a different city, but decided against the trip because she did not want to trouble (*merepotkan*; Jpn.) her employer, who she knew would have been involved in the approval of the roster change. Iffah was once asked to take an additional early morning shift on a weekend she was meant to have off. She agreed, because she 'had received plenty of help' (*sudah banyak bantuan yang saya terima*; Jpn.) and saw agreeing to the shift as returning a favour. When Daris, a male candidate, wanted to move flat, he knew his potential move would have to be arranged with the accepting institution since the rental contract was made under the institution's name. Ultimately, he refrained from even attempting to discuss his concerns, because he felt under obligation to accept what had been given to him. Were he to act otherwise, he feared being judged as ungrateful, or as *orang yang tidak tahu berterima kasih* (lit. a person who does not know how to accept love; Ind.). On another occasion, Lanny was not allowed by her team leader to host a boyfriend intending to visit her from Indonesia. The arguments against his visit were twofold. On the one hand, her manager expressed concern for the boyfriend's safety when left alone at the candidate's flat, with the fears being along the lines of 'What if he gets electrocuted, or what if there is a gas explosion – who is going to be responsible for that?' (as related to me by Lanny). On the other hand, the manager openly admitted that she was apprehensive of the idea because she saw the visit as potentially leading to the candidate becoming pregnant. To a certain extent the fears of the team leader were comprehensible by Lanny herself, but nevertheless she felt that neither she nor her boyfriend were being treated seriously (sarcastically asking me on the phone whether the team leader imagined that the boyfriend would be going around the flat sticking his fingers into electric wall sockets), and found it difficult to accept that the team leader's opposition could effectively lead to the cancellation of the boyfriend's visit. Nevertheless, Lanny felt that she needed to obtain the permission of her manager, and having failed in doing so, she cancelled the visit plans.

Therefore, apart from being a function of offering a comfortable Japanese experience to the Indonesians, and keeping them 'refreshed' so that they could perform well in their duties as care workers, the provisions extending the relationships to a private domain also made it possible for the employers to affect the actions of the candidates at work as well as outside of it. This possibility was important to the extent that, at least initially, the employers did not know much about their Indonesian charges for whom they were made, and felt, responsible. For example, one employer expressed his concern over whom his female Indonesian employee was meeting after work; two women from the second batch were reprimanded for going to a nearby town on their own since, in their manager's words, it could have been dangerous; and Amir and Jasir always had to let their supervisors know if they were planning to travel to a different town. Moreover, to a degree, such extensive and private interactions, which ultimately led to the Indonesians' personalised view of their employment and allowed the employers to monitor the candidates' actions, were also for the employers a means of overcoming the uncertainty stemming from the lack of knowledge about who the Indonesian employees would turn out to be. This was particularly important given the way the recruitment for the EPA scheme was organised.

Impersonal Recruitment Process

Kore dake ja nani mo wakaranai, 'from this only you know nothing', commented Mr Kunihara, the deputy manager of an eldercare institution where Lanny worked. Standing in a hallway next to one of the bedrooms for bedridden elderly, in his hand he was holding several sheets of paper with information about two young Indonesian women who were due to take up employment in the suburban eldercare home in a few months' time. They applied to enter a professional training programme during the second intake organised under the provisions of the EPA between Indonesia and Japan.

As explained earlier, the recruitment for this nationwide programme was administered in Japan by JICWELS, the quasi-governmental organisation acting on behalf of the Japanese MHLW. The recruitment process for the EPA acceptance was based on automated matching, wherein the institutions were asked to select their preferred candidates from a list compiled by JICWELS. Simultaneously, the candidates were choosing from a parallel list of accepting institutions. When the two choices overlapped, the matching was done, and the candidates were assigned and sent to the institutions. If the matching was not achieved in the first round, the process was repeated up to three times until the preferences of the institutions and the candidates coincided. This meant that unless the employers sent representatives to participate in the interviews held in Indonesia by JICWELS, they were unable to meet any of the Indonesian candidates prior to signing contracts. Even if institutional representatives did participate in the interviews, there was still no guarantee that the individuals to whom they talked would actually be those who arrived to work in their institutions. Equally, the language issue aside, the future trainee did not have a chance to directly enquire about the details of his or her prospective workplace.

Although the files delivered to Lanny's deputy manager contained education histories and the names of the potential Indonesian employees, this information clearly felt insufficient. In fact, the documents did not seem to convey any information at all, were Mr Kunihara's words to be taken literally. Having to base their choice solely on the Indonesian candidate's education history, the prospective deputy manager and his superior, Mr Nagatani, were clearly missing an important piece of information about who they were about to employ. When, at the beginning of 2010, I conducted a questionnaire survey among selected employers, supervisors and co-workers of Indonesians who had arrived under the EPA programme in the first batch in 2008, in response to my question about what their thoughts had been about working alongside Indonesians before they arrived, several responded that they had been 'worried, because they could not imagine at all (*mattaku sōzō dekinakute*; Jpn.) what kind of people [the Indonesians] would be'. This task of imagining was the more challenging given that neither the co-workers nor the employers had 'met any Indonesian people before and [so] they did not know what they were like (*jikkan ga wakanakatta*; Jpn.)'. In an effort to learn something more that would facilitate this imagination, Mr Nagatani, the manager of the care home, investigated Indonesian *kunigara* (national character; Jpn.) once he had decided to take part in the EPA programme in 2008. His concern with knowing the *kunigara* of people he would be employing was ultimately one of the two main reasons why he decided against accepting Filipino EPA candidates to his institution when such a possibility arose in 2009 (the other reason being Lanny's preference, as mentioned earlier). Mr Nagatani explained that were he to bring in workers from the Philippines he would have to start investigating the *kunigara* of that country as well. It was something he felt too busy to embark on once again, but above all having already spent a year as Lanny's employer, he felt that he knew something about people from that country in a more general sense. As the cooperation seemed to be going well, it afforded him a degree of confidence in employing more Indonesian workers – the confidence resting on imagining any and all Indonesians as similar to his current employee in some important respects.

Yet, the documents Mr Kunihara commented on that day were not conveying sufficient information. Despite the degree of imagined familiarity with what to expect of Indonesian workers, knowing their professional credentials was not enough. Having learnt about the educational system in Indonesia, Mr Kunihara was also able to make certain assumptions about the skill level of the two candidates, but he still found himself at a loss trying to infer what kind of people to expect. A face-to-face encounter such as interviewing, or *mensetsu* (literally, facing each other, coming into contact face-to-face; Jpn.), offers an opportunity for employers and potential employees alike to access the kind of information about each other that does not necessarily transpire through a curriculum vitae or a job description (see also Martin 1995). Individual personal traits, as much as they can be extrapolated during an interview, complement an image of a person in their professional capacity and add up to represent a worker, colleague or employer who may or may not be desirable to work with. While, on the one hand, Mr Kunihara and Mr Nagatani were satisfied with what they imagined Indonesian workers were like, on the other they were left in want of more personalised information. The sweeping assumption about individuals based on their *kunigara* was informative but not sufficient any more. The national character was now populated with individuals characterised by their idiosyncrasies such as those of the current Indonesian employee and her friends with whom both managers had had multiple occasions to meet over the previous year. In a way, the decision about whom to accept became more difficult to make. During the first intake 'an Indonesian worker' was a uniform, sometimes gendered category, which did not allow for much nuanced differentiation. At the time of the second selection process, Mr Kunihara and Mr Nagatani were looking for a particular type of Indonesian worker – one that would not just have the expected *kunigara*, but would also fit into their image of a desirable worker. Unable to discern these personal qualities from the information sheets provided by JICWELS, the managers decided to rely on extrapolation. They opted for hiring schoolmates of their current employee as if her ways of being could be extended to characterise her friends as well.

Negotiations and Monitoring

While the particularly cordial and ultimately preferential treatment the Indonesian EPA candidates received from their employers implicated them in a web of intimate relations allowing the employers a degree of additional control over the candidates, it also made it possible for the Indonesians to manipulate and use these relationships to their own advantage. They had one more leverage point they could use and which the employers were aware of as well. The delegating of the nitty-gritty task of organising the acceptance on the ground to the very institutions where the Indonesians would be coming to work conferred, at least implicitly, responsibility for the well-being of the candidates and the ultimate success of the programme on to the accepting sites.

Organised under the auspices of a governmental scheme arising from an international agreement, the EPA acceptance was a closely monitored one. Not only did the Acceptance Manual offer guidelines, but their implementation was subject to occasional checks. JICWELS itself set up a system of rotational yearly assessment visits. During these visits the candidates and their supervisors were interviewed separately on the working and training conditions and progress, which was also measured by a specially devised test. Moreover, JICWELS provided a telephone helpline that the candidates could call with any issues concerning their working conditions and daily lives alike. The extent to which JICWELS had power to intervene, were there to be any serious violations of the acceptance agreement, was openly debated by the candidates and the employers equally. For example, one of my informants was disappointed with JICWELS's powerlessness when its officials failed to persuade the candidate's employer to move him to better housing. On the other hand, when candidates in another institution informed JICWELS that the wage they were receiving was lower than that shown on their contract, JICWELS's intervention was successful. The possibility of intervention added to the air of public scrutiny of the practical implementation of the acceptance. In fact, when Iffah offered to cover the cost of her Japanese language tutor, her employer rejected the idea on the grounds that unless he or the institution paid for the language training, it would not be acknowledged as complying with the acceptance regulations.

Although none of the employers I talked to saw it as a real potentiality, it was relatively easy for the EPA candidates to terminate their training midterm and return to Indonesia. The conditions laid out in the contract signed between the employers and the candidates specified that the Indonesians could terminate their training should there be any 'unavoidable reasons' (*yamu o enai jiyū ga aru toki*; Jpn.) to do so (JICWELS 2009: 5). The same applied to the employers. At the same time, the contract between JICWELS and the accepting institutions made it a requirement (among others) that the institutions would provide the necessary facilities (ibid.: 57–58) to ensure that the Indonesian candidates acquired the national qualifications. Should the institution be deemed to not be fulfilling this or other obligations, the contract could be voided. Although the candidates were not explicitly made aware of the clause, they knew more or less what the institutions should be providing.

Moreover, thanks to the fact that they got to know each other well during the preparatory language training, the Indonesians exchanged information on the conditions at work on a daily basis and were therefore aware of the differences between the conditions of employment and the degree of support in preparation for the national examination offered by their respective institutions. Much resented by the employers, the exchange of such information between the Indonesians allowed the latter to argue for changes to the conditions they were receiving if these compared unfavourably with those of their EPA friends.

Apart from the issue of whether Japanese tuition was organised and/ or paid for by the institution, other aspects of the Indonesians' lives were also argued in terms of training. For example, living in an old-style wooden building that did not provide much insulation in winter was presented as not conducive to studying at home because it was too cold. Also, working five days a week, it was argued, did not leave enough time and strength for studying. In the institutions I visited, the employers were making efforts, if to various degrees, to create suitable studying conditions for the Indonesians. Seemingly, however, this was not the case everywhere. Only a few months into the employment the first Indonesian nurse candidate returned to Indonesia. The official explanation published by the national newspapers maintained that the decision was due to the poor health of the candidate, caused by the cold climate of the northern part of Japan where she was dispatched. The information circulating between the Indonesian candidates, however, claimed that it was because the person was dissatisfied with the conditions she was offered at work. In the following months, when several other candidates also left Japan, the newspaper articles explained that it was due to a disappointment with the difference between the reality of the training and what they expected based on the information received during recruitment. According to my informal conversation with a JICWELS employee, in at least one of these cases the cost of a return ticket to Indonesia was covered by the institution originally hosting the returning candidate, even though it was not obligatory for them to do so under the provisions of their contract with JICWELS if it had been breached by the candidate. This meant that the accepting institution either made a generous gesture or was judged as not providing satisfactory facilities for the candidate to train towards the national examination. Such voluntary returns of the candidates showed how the Indonesians, although bound by a contract, could in fact relatively easily decide to abandon the EPA scheme, leaving the institutions with an investment offering no prospect of return.

Beside JICWELS's supervision, the plight of the Indonesian candidates was also of interest for many a Japanese researcher and various support organisations. The candidates I was visiting on a rotational basis often had another researcher lined up to conduct an interview, or had just talked to someone else a week before my visit. When, during a language lesson, Amir and Jasir were informed by the institution's secretary that the following week there would be a person coming from a nearby university to interview them, the teacher – also present in the room at the time – commented that the two men were *ninki mono* (Jpn.), popular people. Similarly, the numerous support organisations aiming to assist the Indonesians, the accepting institutions, or both in any problems arising from the scheme frequently sent questionnaires and leaflets with their contact details. The volume of such mail made the employers I knew from my circulatory visits stop opening envelopes that they suspected might contain yet another survey. The mass media also showed sustained interest in the experiences of the Indonesians, something with which I deal in the next chapter. Such external interest not only put the candidates under a spotlight to the extent that they felt as if they were deprived of privacy (*tidak ada pribadi*; Ind.), but exposed the accepting institutions to a similarly controlling popular gaze as well. For example, Irdina's manager told me a story about how, during a visit by a crew from Japan's biggest public broadcasting corporation, the journalists were surprised to see that 'only three' text books had been provided by the institution for the Indonesian candidates. In the manager's opinion, equipping the candidates with studying materials free of charge was already more than they, as an accepting institution, were obliged to do, and so was done as a matter of good will – but it clearly did not appear to be a satisfactory commitment to the journalists.

Such means as the guidelines of the Acceptance Manual, and the exposure of the practical implementation of the programme to scrutiny

Figure 3.2: Media present at an event organised by one of the support organisations. Photo by author.

by JICWELS, the mass media, researchers, and support organisations, conferred the sense of responsibility for the success of the candidates, and therefore the programme as a whole, onto the accepting institutions. The very structure of the acceptance, which presupposed governmental involvement in the training only up to the point when the candidates graduated from the six-month language training, suggested such ceding. Indeed, Iffah's employer once commented that the accepting institutions were like volunteers working on an implementation of a state policy (*kokusaku*; Jpn.). He referred not only to the responsibility placed on the accepting institutions, but also to the lack of financial and structural support to train the candidates – something I return to in the next chapter. Such delegation of responsibility inherent in the implementation of the EPA acceptance, which was sometimes suggested to be a result of the seemingly haphazard preparation of the scheme discussed earlier, had a direct influence on the organisation of the Indonesians' lives at work, and beyond. This responsibility was translated into the candidates' experiences, and ultimately shaped their relationships with their employers.

***

Due to the nature of the provisions of the EPA programme, the Indonesian candidates occupied a precarious position in the accepting institutions. On the one hand, they were required to train in order to obtain the Japanese national qualifications that would allow them to remain and work in Japan after the EPA training period had finished. This meant that their time in various institutions as EPA candidates might have been only an initial stage in their longer careers in the Japanese eldercare sector. For some of them, this was indeed the goal. On the other hand, the permanence of the Indonesians' professional engagement in Japan was uncertain. For example, Iffah and Lazim never envisaged their lives in Japan. They simply used the opportunity presented by the programme to experience something new and to earn additional income. People like Amir and Daris kept their options open. If they managed to pass the examination, they would consider remaining in Japan, depending on the situation at home and at work at the time. Some others, even if originally toying with the idea of remaining in Japan, became discouraged by the inadequate conditions to learn and train the way they had imagined; some of these candidates decided to tag along until the end of the EPA contract, while others resigned and returned to Indonesia.

For the accepting institutions that entered the programme with a vision of training a new workforce, the outcome was therefore uncertain as well. It was impossible to guarantee that even those candidates eager to remain in Japan would be able to do so. What is more, even if they passed the national examination, the candidates were under no obligation to carry on working for the same institution in which they trained under the EPA scheme. It was not guaranteed that they would reach the objective, even for those accepting care homes that had used the EPA programme as a temporary means of dealing with a labour shortage or a high turnover of staff. Unable to change their place of work, the EPA candidates were perceived as more likely to remain in the same institution for the length of the training programme. However, because the Indonesians were not embedded in the Japanese labour market, it did not matter whether they worked in their accepting institution for one year or four. Neither was it important that they received a positive professional assessment of their performance at work. If they were not planning or were unable to remain in Japan, in the worst-case scenario, they would return to Indonesia. Whatever its length, the Japanese experience on their CV would likely be a bonus, regardless of their performance in Japan.

Further still, since the candidates were protected by the governmental scheme and their situation was closely monitored by the media and supporting organisations, sending back a candidate would have been unacceptable, if possible at all. Even when one of the candidates turned out to be pregnant after several months in training, she was not sent back. By conceiving during the training she came near to breaching the terms of her employment, since one of the conditions for participation in the programme for females was not being pregnant. She worked with her pregnancy concealed until one day she was taken to a hospital feeling unwell. Soon after she gave birth to her child, she and her employers reached the consensus that the child would be taken to Indonesia to live with the young mother's family while she finished her contract in Japan.

While charged with the responsibility for successful practical implementation of the EPA programme, in the constellation of circumstances as described above, the accepting institutions did not have many management tools, such as being able to offer or withhold promotion or discharge the workers. Having invested in their arrival and training, the institutions were eager for the Indonesians to contribute their labour for as long as possible, at the same time contributing to the success of the overall acceptance scheme. It is from such a situation that the interpersonal relationships between the Indonesian candidates and their employers emerged.

To an extent, the objectives of the Indonesian candidates and their employers overlapped. While my informants wanted to optimise their Japanese experience, either in terms of professional development, financial gain, or simply quality of life in Japan, the employers needed them to perform their tasks as well as possible – ideally, to pass the national examination and remain to work in their institutions. Therefore, concerned about the well-being of their charges, but also about the candidates' suitability for care work as individuals and as Indonesians of whom they knew little, the employers took on a role of benevolent but strict wardens, parental figures in the Indonesians' representations. Intentionally or not, such informal relations between the employers and Indonesian candidates implicated them in a network of mutual sympathies and commitments which served as a means to manage and manipulate. On the one hand, while the employers were able to get to know their new staff members, and through this familiarity dispose of any (or at least some) uncertainties (which they had had before) about employing non-Japanese, they also placed themselves in a position close enough to influence the actions of the Indonesian candidates, and not solely through the legitimised authority of formal employment relations.

On the other hand, the same informal relationships allowed the Indonesian candidates to exercise what Halvard Vike calls moral control. He proposes that 'the potential for control within a social group sharing a moral universe lies in the multiplicity of their social relations' (Vike 1997: 205). 'Moral control', he continues, 'is hard to maintain if, say, leaders are known to their followers in a specialized and public capacity only. Therefore, the efficiency of moral control depends on drawing on broad fields of relevance in social relations, so that, for instance, private matters may be made relevant in the evaluation of leadership performance' (ibid.). Hence, the close relationships with their employers provided also an arena for the Indonesians where they could reclaim a degree of control over their lives in Japan – for example, when they requested a long holiday break during Lebaran. In this way, the extra-professional intimacy of close interpersonal relationships between the candidates and the employers imparted to both parties a degree of control, and the ability to manage those matters that concerned them most.

Ultimately, however, what propelled the emergence of the more intimate and personalised relationships were particular kinds of imaginations of people from Japan and Indonesia. The expected differences were accounted for in the Acceptance Manual as well as in the special set-ups and preparatory meetings in the accepting institutions and beyond. Such actions were not simply an expression of perceiving the Indonesians as culturally different. They were also acknowledging the Japanese national self-imagining and the kind of living and working environment it was likely to create for non-Japanese workers. This national self-recognition triggered a response, which, although relying on the fairly stereotypical representations of Indonesia and Japan alike, ultimately conveyed significant power to the Indonesian workers. This power lay not only in their ability to negotiate conditions of employment and training, but also in symbolically (but only potentially) representing a new viable future Japan.

Notes

1. The company that volunteered to prepare the offer and facilitate its implementation suggested the iPhone as the handset to be distributed to the Indonesians. The reason for the choice was twofold. Firstly, at the time, this company was the mobile network, popular among the EPA candidates, that had the monopoly for merchandising the iPhone in Japan. Secondly, the initiative was pursued about the time when a new version of the handset was being introduced to the Japanese market, causing the older version to drop in value and popularity, and thus making the company more willing to give it away in anticipation of income coming from the usage of the network by the new customers.
2. According to an interview with the foundation's chief executive, they distributed personal computers to around 60 per cent of the accepting care institutions. However, as a result of cuts that the foundation faced after the budget/spending review in early 2010, they were unable to continue the initiative (TV Tokyo, 4 February 2010. Available from: http://www.tv-tokyo.co.jp/wbs/highlight/o1_243.html).
3. Twenty-four out of twenty-eight respondents to my own questionnaire were single at the time of the survey (beginning of 2010), three were married or in a relationship and one was widowed. Of all these, only three had children at the time.

 4

NATIONAL PREDICAMENTS

> We must commit ourselves to drawing an image of
> future Japan, and deepen the debate
>
> [*Mirai no nihon no sugata o egaku kakugo de giron o fukameru beki da*]
> – *Nikkei*, 10 November 2010

When speaking to my Japanese friends and other newly met people shortly after I arrived in Japan at the end of November 2008 – that is, about three months after the first Indonesian batch of nurse and caregiver candidates arrived at the Narita and Kansai airports – a common reaction to my research theme in Japan was surprise and a kind of amusement at such an unusual and unheard of topic. 'Unheard of' were the Indonesians I came to study. It seemed that the intergovernmental Japan–Indonesia Economic Partnership Agreement (EPA) and the people coming to Japan under its provisions were not in the minds of people not related directly to the programme. This was despite the fact that in the three major newspapers' national editions, *Asahi Shinbun*, *Nihon Keizai Shinbun* and *Yomiuri Shinbun* (henceforth *Asahi*, *Nikkei* and *Yomiuri*, respectively), there were eighteen separate articles published in the three weeks following the Indonesians' arrival in Japan.

The inconspicuousness of the EPA acceptance gave way to a much wider awareness about the new foreign workers. This began to happen when, at the end of January 2009, the first Indonesian care worker candidates graduated from six months of language and professional training, and were to be dispatched as employees to care institutions across Japan. The graduation ceremonies in the training centres attracted considerable media attention on a national and particularly a local level. After that, between the end of January 2009 and the end of December

2010, the three newspapers published, on average, one article a week in their national editions that specifically related to the EPA Indonesians, with some periods seeing mention of them every day. In an addition to a special section (*tokushū*; Jpn.) on various migrant groups in Japan, the cover of *Nikkei Business* on 23 November 2009 featured a photograph of an Indonesian candidate and an elderly woman apparently involved in a conversation in what seemed like an eldercare home. The main caption at the centre of the cover in bold characters read 'Migrants Yes. Shortage of 10 Million Workers is Coming' (*Senmannin no Rōdōbusoku ga Yatte Kuru*). In addition to the material published by the newspapers, numerous items referring to the EPA Indonesians were published on the internet as well. These included various articles, but also sometimes very informal discussions on different fora. As well as several nationwide television programmes referring to the acceptance, there were also various local television stations that took up the EPA candidates and their accepting institutions as a focus of their reports. These were often accessible for online viewing, and posted on YouTube or embedded in Facebook pages by the candidates themselves. Finally, special editions and special feature articles on the EPA Indonesians or the acceptance programme in general appeared in professional care- and health-related publications, such as *Nurse Senka* (Specialisation Nurse), *Care Management*, and *Iryō Rōdō* (Medical Labour). In 2009, a journalist (Idei 2009) published a book devoted to care provided to Japanese by foreign carers both in Japan and outside of its borders, but mainly focusing on the EPA acceptance. Perhaps hardly surprisingly, such sustained media coverage seemed to eventually mark the presence of Indonesian care workers (and nurses) in the minds of a wider Japanese public. From January 2009 on, I no longer encountered bewildered faces when disclosing my research topic. Instead, I would get involved in concerned discussions over the future of the Japanese care system for the elderly, the current and future situation of the Japanese workforce, the situation of the accepting care facilities, and the plight of the Indonesian candidates.

In this chapter, I look at the various discourses that surrounded the EPA acceptance, basing my discussion primarily on the mass media reports on the programme. In the process I aim to explain why this numerically relatively minor group of foreign workers attracted what seemed to be disproportionate media attention. I suggest that the media representations of the EPA candidates and the debates surrounding the acceptance programme were expressions of particular ideologies of a Japanese nation trying to position itself vis-à-vis the projected demographic changes and globalising processes, such as the EPA, which brought about a need for a redefinition of certain representations of contemporary Japanese society.

Changing Japanese Society

In discussing details of the EPA acceptance, a call for reconsideration of the future shape of Japanese society was voiced by Asato Wako, an associate professor in migration studies at Kyoto University. In an interview televised by a Japan Broadcasting Corporation (henceforth NHK) nationwide station in January 2010, Professor Asato said:

> Japan's proportion of elderly has exceeded 20 per cent; from now on, the population will also continue to decrease. In a time of such transition, it is a matter of great exigency to [decide] what social system to build. If we were, for example, to talk about the nurses, it is of course necessary to supplement the lacking human resources by introducing a comprehensive social security system in order to bring back to work the dormant [qualified but not working in the profession] nurses. However, the situation of health services in different regions [of Japan] is varied; therefore, for example, I think we should have an option to bring human resources from abroad as well.

This statement points to a very important aspect of Japanese society's reality and the discourses about its future that constituted a background to the EPA acceptance, and, as I argue below, also contributed to the presentation of the programme in reference to Japanese ideologies of nation.

Population Crisis and the Future Shape of Japanese Society

The continuing low fertility rate in Japan has been responsible for halting the growth of the population, which reached its peak of 127.75 million in 2005 and is predicted to decline to just above 100 million by 2050, and possibly even to less than 50 million by 2100 (Kono 2011: 42). Framed within the context of a declining population and the subsequent labour shortage – the one already experienced by the care institutions as well as the direr version still to come – it was not uncommon in the Japanese national media to come across such expressions as 'the sense of crisis' (*kikikan*; Jpn.) or 'a population crisis' (*jinkō kiki*; Jpn.) as part of the discussions surrounding the EPA programme (Kono 2011).[1] A *Nikkei* article presented the acceptance of foreign workers with a sense of immediacy:

> Which way to choose, and to what level to increase the 1.7 per cent proportion of foreigners in the population are precisely the topics that ought to be discussed as the national strategy. We must not forget that we are now in a position where the debate cannot be postponed any longer. The time when the medical and care services, agriculture, manufacturing industry, [and] research development are definitely going to lack manpower is right in front of us. (Nikkei 2009d)

One way to mitigate the predicted problems arising from the declining labour force was to invite foreigners and to provide conditions for them to more freely enter the Japanese labour market and settle in Japanese society. For some article authors it was not the time any more when Japan was in the position to benevolently let the foreigners in. Rather the time had come for Japan to ask the foreign workers to grant Japan a favour and offer their labour. The EPA Indonesians were indeed sometimes portrayed as such benevolent guests who offered to look after the elderly for whom they were under no obligation to care. Therefore, placed in the context of the Japanese society's future, which, given the demographic changes, was imagined to be substantially different from its present, the concerns over the ultimate outcome of the EPA programme were connected to a wider issue of Japan's strategy for the coming decades. Another facet of this strategy was related to the issue of a growing proportion of elderly in Japanese society.

Silver Society

Shōshi kōrei shakai, 'a society of few children and longevity' (Jpn.), and its variations, such as *shōshi kōrei mondai* and *shōshi kōrei ka,* 'the problem of the declining birth rate' and 'the low fertility and ageing' respectively, had by the time of this research long become widely used terms to describe the condition of Japanese society (see also Coulmas 2007). Events such as the conference organised by the German Institute for Japanese Studies, which took place in June 2009 in Tokyo under the telling title *Imploding Populations: Global and Local Challenges of Demographic Change,* indicated the currency of the issues.[2]

Concomitant with the longevity of the Japanese was the issue of securing care provision for these growing numbers of long-living elderly. While many people in their 'silver years' were enjoying good health (and tapping into their needs and vitality were the so-called silver markets and offers of silver employment), many Japanese elders still needed vital support in their everyday life. Everyone was expecting to need it at some stage of their life. Therefore, the implementation of a system that would guarantee adequate provisions to those who may need to rely on others (read: the state) for well-being in their old age featured in many a discussion I happened to listen to or partake in among the Japanese with whom I worked during my research. Admittedly, the majority of the individuals with whom I shared these conversations were related to the nurse and caregiver acceptance programme. Their interest in and awareness of the looming 'care crisis' might therefore be more pronounced than among the wider Japanese society.

However, the subject was a common theme in the media as well. Alongside speculative deliberations about who would provide eldercare and fill state coffers in about forty to fifty years, it was also common to encounter published reports describing current 'care hell' (*kaigo jigoku*; Jpn.) of care provision at home often by a single family member, dealing with the growing problem of 'elderly to elderly care' (*rōrō kaigo*; Jpn.) among aged couples, 'care exhaustion' (*kaigo tsukare*; Jpn.), and, most disturbingly, 'care suicides' (*kaigo jisatsu*; Jpn.) committed by family members turned carers, 'care murders' (*kaigo satsu-jin*; Jpn.) of incapacitated parents, and 'double suicides' (*kaigo shinjū*; Jpn.) of elderly couples who could not face the burden of caring for each other. Even if the general statements about the problems of an ageing society might not have conveyed a clear idea what these would be, the vivid descriptions of individual struggles and of people pushed to commit drastic acts most likely brought the problems closer to the wider population as well. During the electoral campaign of 2009, all parties' manifestos declared a commitment to introducing improvements in the long-term care provision system and/or improvement of the working conditions in the sector – another indicator of mainstreaming the problem of the aged society and of the awareness that 'silver democracy', in which the majority of votes would be in the hands of the elderly, was arriving (see also Coulmas 2007).

The ageing society and the anticipated shortage of people able to contribute their labour to the Japanese economy and, not least, to support the care provision for the growing numbers of retired elderly carried an image of a society structured in new ways. Most evidently, the difference in the population size of the young and the aged generations was expected to become even more disproportionate, the national economy was expected to have to be scaled down, and robots were imagined to become a more common appearance, filling positions that lacked manpower in public spaces and at home. Conversely, Japan could also become a home for more foreigners.

EPA Candidates Supplying Japanese Labour Force

The arrival of the EPA Indonesian workers fed directly into such debates over the appropriate means to tackle the various projected problems coming with Japan's ageing society and the declining population. Long at the forefront of public debate were the questions of who was going to provide financially for the expanding numbers of elderly in need of support and, with the falling fertility rate, who in the 'shrinking society' was going to contribute to the national treasury to secure the tax base necessary to sustain Japan's economic prosperity and guarantee its citizens the standard of living to which they had become accustomed. Depending on the proposed solutions, the vision of the future Japanese society varied, as presented in the Introduction. In one incarnation, Japanese society, albeit less numerous, remained self-sufficient – that is, not reliant on foreign workers. The other vision presented a Japanese future as unavoidably opened

Figure 4.1: Cartoon published by *Fukushi Shinbun* [Welfare Newspaper] in 2009. The banner reads: 'Symposium on falling birth rate countermeasures'. © 2009 Fukushishimbun Inc.

to significant numbers of migrant workers in order to sustain the country's existence. The EPA Indonesian caregiver candidates arrived to work in a sector where these various concerns over Japan's future converged. Therefore, their arrival under a scheme that offered a possibility (however uncertain) for the foreign workers to remain in Japan permanently was taken to represent a step in the direction of opening Japan to foreign labour. *Nikkei* (2008) made this link directly by writing that 'the EPA has the potential to provide a breakthrough in initiating a change in the closed Japanese labour market'. As such, the EPA acceptance, although numerically insignificant, triggered debates over what the future shape of the Japanese society should be, and how, and whether, foreigners could be included in it.

In this context of Japan's changing demographics and the forecast difficulties the country might face in securing a sufficient labour force within its own borders, the EPA Indonesians were referred to as *kichōna jinzai, senryoku, kichōna senryoku* and *kuni senryoku*, or 'precious, valuable human resources', 'strategic potential', 'precious strategic potential', and 'national strategy', respectively, which was not to be wasted for the sake of Japan's future (for example, Yomiuri 2008; Asahi 2009f; Nikkei 2009b, 2010a). In the light of the perceivably 'half-baked' (*chūtohanpa*; Jpn.) acceptance programme, which was in many an opinion fated to send the candidates back to their country, an article in Asahi (2009j) pessimistically predicted: 'If things carry on like this, pretty much everyone will fail [the exam] and return to their country, which will put into question the whole meaning of the EPA [acceptance]'. It was therefore common to read in the national newspapers the calls for the *kuni*, the country, or the *seifu*, the government, to take responsibility for the acceptance. Without the guidance and perpetually called for financial support, it was the accepting institutions and hospitals that were charged with the task of realising what was perceived to be a national policy, or *kokusaku*. The articles often used such terms as *genba marunage*, or 'dumping it on the [accepting] sites' (for example, Asahi 2009h and 2009i), *shisetsu makase*, or 'leaving it to the institutions' (for example, Nikkei 2009c), or *genba ni ichinin sarete iru*, 'left entirely to the [accepting] sites' (Asahi 2009h), and *hottarakasu*, meaning 'to neglect' (Asahi 2009j). The general gist of the articles was that the government once again had not tackled the foreign workers issue with full force. The media represented it as a demonstration of a lack of responsibility (*musekinin*; Jpn.) on the side of the central government for dealing with the issues on which Japan's future hinged, and the EPA acceptance itself as a litmus test for Japan as a country open to immigration.

Test Case

Although not necessarily always in the same words, the idea of the EPA acceptance as being a 'breakthrough' in labour migration regulations and a 'test case' or 'model case' for the future, larger-scale acceptance of foreign workers indeed often appeared in the articles published by the *Asahi*, *Nikkei* and *Yomiuri* between 2008 and 2010. Even if at the time it was limited to those institutions having the capacity to support the training of foreign workers, the EPA acceptance was to provide the 'know-how', and if implemented smoothly in the care sector, some hoped it could be expanded to other sectors as well – for example, Fukuma Tsutomu, a chief secretary of the Japanese Council of Senior Citizens Welfare Services in NHK Debate held in October 2006 (NHK 2006).

In March 2009, during a conference organised by the Japan Association for Migration Policy Studies at Waseda University, Furuya Tokurō, who took part in the EPA negotiations on behalf of the Japanese Ministry of Foreign Affairs (MoFA), was reported to comment: '[A]t the same time as the issue [acceptance of foreign workers] has been attracting national attention, this [EPA] acceptance is considered to be a pilot case foretelling the shape of the future acceptance of foreign workers' (Furuya 2009). The idea of testing in preparation for the larger-scale intake of foreign workers in the future, presented as unavoidable, was combined with the hopes for the 'settlement' of the EPA candidates in Japan. This showed that at least part of the discourse produced by the official sources, here a pro-migrant workers MoFA, was presenting the EPA as something more than a clause in an economic agreement. On the day following the approval of the EPA with Indonesia by the Japanese higher house of parliament, the House of Councillors, the *Nikkei* newspaper published an article presenting the forthcoming acceptance in the context of the foreign population in Japan and the foreseen problems they might encounter. The last lines of the first paragraph read:

> From now on the labour shortage in nursing and care will become even direr due to the low birth rates and the ageing of society. It is often pointed out that the future of social security is contingent on the success or failure of the labour open country – the acceptance of the Indonesian nurses and whether they will start to settle (*teichaku*) is the touchstone (*shikinseki*). (Nikkei 2008)[3]

This perception dominated among the accepting institutions and hospitals as well. Expressed through the notion of *teichaku*, meaning 'becoming established, fixed down', or settled, it reflected the objectives and hopes of the accepting institutions for the Indonesian EPA candidates to become a permanent addition to their workforce.

The perceived need to test foreigners' acceptance in view of a future wider opening of the country implied two things. Firstly, as pointed out above, it suggested that, contrary to the officially approved goal, the EPA acceptance was perceived in terms of Japan's internal labour market issues. Secondly, the need for a test run, and its possible failure, rested on an assumption that working and settling in Japan might not be an easily achievable goal. The settlement of non-Japanese required some testing for their compatibility with the Japanese social milieu to find out who would fit in, how to help them to fit in, whether they would be perceived as fitting in, and also, importantly, whether the new arrivals would find Japan enticing enough to consider it an option to settle there at all. Such deliberations pointed to the idea that apart from the procedural adjustments, such as the organisation of training, there would need to take place less tangible changes in order to welcome the foreigners not only to the labour market but to the society as well. The concern was with the ability of foreigners to fully participate in the Japanese social fabric, not least due to the internal dynamics of Japanese society.

Therefore, the importance of the EPA acceptance did not rest in its numerical scope. It was rather the programme's timing and location within the particular sector that had long been an object of popular interest. However, as already suggested, it is not sufficient to consider this demographic and labour-oriented context to account for why this particular workers' group should become a centrepiece in debating Japan's immigration policies. The Japanese ideology of homogeneity, combined with the collapsing of such notions as society, nation and ethnicity, as pointed to in the Introduction, also contributed to the EPA acceptance's media popularity and its framing within the discourses of Japan's future as a nation.

Kaikoku, an Open Country

A 2006 article discussing the EPA between Japan and the Philippines referred to the deal as a 'new step towards a country open to labour' (Asahi 2006). In the first five short paragraphs the article briefly commented on the general provisions of the agreement and mentioned several points still to be agreed upon by the negotiators. The remaining eleven paragraphs concentrated on the clause within the agreement that regulated the acceptance of foreign carers and nurses. According to the author of the article, the commercial arrangements to be implemented between the two countries were welcome developments in Japan's international trade relations, but the acceptance of carers and nurses was 'epoch making' (*gakiteki na*; Jpn.) (ibid.). On another occasion the acceptance was an issue of 'utmost interest' (*saidai no shōten*; Jpn.) (Asahi 2004).

What new epoch was proclaimed to be in the making was expressed through the compound *kaikoku*, literally meaning an 'open country'. On the occasion of the Indonesian workers' arrival, it was the second most often used expression in the articles related to the EPA acceptance published between 2004 and 2008 in the national editions of the *Asahi*, *Yomiuri* and *Nikkei* newspapers. Coming second only after 'Indonesia', used either as a denominator of a country or as a part of the nationality indicator, the *kaikoku* was sometimes used with a preceding qualifying *rōdō*, meaning 'labour', or *jinzai*, 'human resources',[4] to form the expressions 'labour open country' or 'country open to labour', and 'country open to human resources', respectively.

Kaikoku, an 'open country', is an antonym of *sakoku*, a 'closed country' or a 'country in isolation'. Originally, the latter term was used to describe the isolationist policy of the Tokugawa shogunate ruling over feudal Japan in the Edo era between 1600 and 1868. After a period of relatively abundant relations with peoples from outside the Japanese archipelago, shortly after gaining control over other clans, the first of the shoguns, Tokugawa Iemitsu, introduced *sakoku*, or isolation policy (the term used at the time was *kaikin*, meaning 'sea restrictions'). The policy remained in force until 1853, when the arrival of 'the Black Ships' under Commodore Perry at the Japanese islands 'reopened' Japan and brought it back into the international political scene. Even if the extent to which Japan of the Tokugawa era was a 'closed country' is debatable and the origins of the term as coined by the Japanese as a self-description is questioned (see Lie 2001: 22–26), the very idea of Japan as having a history and perhaps a tradition of being closed or as remaining in a self-imposed isolation remained alive, and found its expression in the homogeneity discourses.

Despite the official statements on the purpose of the EPA acceptance programme, which was presented by the Japanese government as a Japanese contribution to training Indonesian care and nursing specialists, framing of the EPA programme to refer to an increase in human movement across the country's borders suggested an interpretation of the EPA acceptance as representing a shift in Japanese migration policies. Just as at the end of the Tokugawa period Japan saw an increase in foreign presence on the isles, so was to be the function of the EPA acceptance. Such interpretations of the EPA programme (i.e. as an opening up to international flows of people) were evidently based on self-reflective representations of Japan as 'Japanese only'. These representations were at the base of arguments supporting the 'opening' as well as of those against it.

Boring Homogeneity

Sakanaka Hidenori, the head of the Japan Immigration Policy Institute and a former director of the Tokyo Immigration Bureau, was concerned with the political and social qualities of the Japanese society under the current immigration policy, and has been one of the vocal proponents of redesigning it. In summer 2009 he shared with me, somewhat jokingly, his view that Japanese society as it was, with a limited number of non-Japanese within it, was simply 'boring' (*tsumaranai*; Jpn.). Referring to the EPA acceptance, which, in Mr Sakanaka's opinion, should be but the first step to a more general acceptance of foreign workers, he added that with the acceptance of more foreigners there would be more people with new, fresh ideas revitalising society.

Similarly, during our interview, a manager, and a son of an owner of a care home participating in the EPA acceptance, laid out a vision of having people of multiple nationalities working in his institution. He had accepted one Indonesian worker during the first intake, and continued to accept others during every following effectuation of the EPA acceptance programme. At the time of the interview, he had already accepted Filipino workers from the first batch and Indonesians from both intakes, and was planning on accepting the EPA Vietnamese as well, were the agreement between Japan and Vietnam to go through. Despite anticipating it to be more challenging than having people arriving from only one country, he entertained the idea that such diversity would not only increase the vitality of the Japanese staff, who through interactions with foreigners would have a chance to experience something new, but also positively affect the well-being of the elderly living in his facility, precisely because it would not be 'just Japanese' (*nihonjin bakkari*; Jpn.), and would therefore be less monotonous. 'It is so enjoyable to have a foreigner around' (*gaikoku no kata ga irassharu to totemo tanoshii desu*; Jpn.), commented an elderly woman residing in another accepting institution when I asked her to reflect on the candidates' performance at work.

That being a foreigner could be a very compelling factor in its own right became palpable when I was trying to obtain permission to observe one of my Indonesian friends at his workplace. After being introduced to the head consultant of the institution, over the following two weeks I was invited to a series of meetings attended by increasingly 'important' people. After explaining the content of my research, I had to justify my request for not just a one-off visit but a series of regular visits over the coming months. I felt that I had gained an understanding when the head of personnel answered the question directed at me, saying that an extended observation should allow me to notice changes over time, which was not far from what I would have said. Finally, during our last meeting, I was informed that an executive director of the institution had decided to allow me access to the ward where my friend was employed. According to his words, conveyed to me by the head consultant, who later became my main contact person there, my presence was expected to be interesting and beneficial for the residents, who would have a chance to see and interact with a white person (*hakujin*; Jpn.). A foreigner in an institution for the elderly was seen as an attraction, introducing an element of rarely encountered national (ethnic, cultural) otherness, an entertaining novelty to the residents' monotonous lives.

The Japanese homogeneity, otherwise valued positively as a source of societal cohesion and uniqueness, and indirectly as the reason for Japan's economic success, in the context of the EPA acceptance was represented as something that needed to be mitigated. The homogeneity was, therefore, not just a source of harmony, familiarity, and praised predictability in which it was possible to achieve 'communication of unity' (Lebra 1976: 115). It was also a source of monotony, even dullness. Japan's stringent immigration regulations were seen as isolating the nation from foreigners and their invigorating influence. Pointing to the unusualness of such a situation, in reaction to an NHK radio programme featuring a telephone interview with one of the EPA Indonesian care workers, a listener pondered:

> In Japan, where a dwindling birth rate and an ageing society are steadily progressing, if we import only goods but not people, Japan as a country will not be able to survive. Shouldn't the Japanese, too, learn more about their partners' languages and customs? There exist in the world multi-ethnic states. Only Japan's insular as ever [invocation] "because they are foreigners" is a puzzle. (NHK 2009)

Against the idealised image of Japan as mono-ethnic, the NHK listener proposed an alternative view of his country, where cultural and linguistic exchanges could be a norm. Such a proposition reimagined the Japanese nation as not necessarily bounded by shared language and customs. Moreover, it proposed disconnecting the idea of Japanese society and the state from the ethnically defined nation. A similar undertone was implicit in the statements suggesting the internationalisation of the Japanese language.

An employer overseeing the acceptance of two Indonesian female care workers from the second batch told me during an interview in January 2010 that for him it did not really matter whether someone was Japanese or not. He asked, 'What does it mean to be a Japanese?', and clarified his approach by saying, 'If only you can speak the language you should be allowed to live and work here'. For him the language was the qualifying factor for a person to be accepted as a member of the society and as a co-worker, or an employee in this particular case. This did not mean, however, that getting over this hurdle was to be easy. He appreciated the long way his two Indonesian charges still had ahead of them to become independent members of his working team, and of the wider society as well.

Mitigating the perceived difficulty of the Japanese language was therefore one of the means to make Japan into a more hospitable place for foreigners and potential future co-residents, if not co-nationals. Two newspaper texts suggested that the Japanese language should no longer be considered a language exclusively for the Japanese people. In June 2010, *Asahi* newspaper published an interview with a former chairman of The Society for Japanese Linguistics, Nomura Masa'aki. The chairman argued against a notion contained in a report recently submitted to the Ministry of Education, which proposed increasing the number of Sino-Japanese characters designated for everyday use (*jōyō kanji*). In the chairman's understanding, an excessive number of obligatory Sino-Chinese characters was not only a significant barrier to everyday functioning for individuals with impaired vision but, being impossible to memorise, threatened the very survival of the Japanese language. Moreover, he stated that:

> The Japanese language is no longer the property of the Japanese people only. There have already arrived in Japan candidates for carers and nurses from Indonesia and the Philippines, but they struggle at work as well as with the national examination due to the Sino-Japanese characters. Undoubtedly, from now on there will be more and more foreigners coming to Japan. In the world of the internet where the English language holds an imperialistic power, for the Japanese language to survive it is essential that we decrease the number of Sino-Japanese characters to make it easy to use and learn for the foreigners. (Asahi 2010)[5]

A similar point was made by a 76-year-old man teaching the Japanese language to Indonesian technical trainees, who sympathised with the EPA candidates expected to gain command of the language within three to four years while working full time. According to his letter to the *Asahi* newspaper, he felt for the trainees as he admitted that the different modalities of the language, such as the women–men variants, dialects, and polite forms, were plentiful enough to confuse even him as a Japanese. It went without saying that if the Indonesians were to work in Japan they should have a grasp of the language sufficient not to hinder their performance at work. However, he saw a need to 'start treating the beautiful Japanese language, which is so rich and diverse, not as a national language, but rather as [one to be learnt as] a second language, that is, an international language' (Asahi 2009g). While by the reference to its difficulty the representation of the Japanese language does not challenge the notion of its uniqueness, the above propositions suggest opening up to foreigners one of the emblematic elements of the Japanese nation. Such 'internationalisation' of the language was to be one of the necessary, but beneficial, changes of the internationalised (globalised) Japan where it was possible to imagine a coexistence with such 'hybrids' as non-Japanese people speaking Japanese, and with larger numbers of non-Japanese residents in general.

Invigorating Internationalisation

Similar ideas were presented by the Japanese media, which situated the EPA acceptance within the discourses of diversity, glossed as *tayōsei*, and multiculturalism, or literally multicultural coexistence, *tabunka kyōsei*. The advent of both, which came to the accepting institutions with the EPA programme, was to lead to revitalisation of the atmosphere in the accepting care homes. For example, it was expected that the foreign employees would revitalise the working atmosphere of the institutions by introducing some difference and hence variety to the predominantly, and often solely, Japanese working environment. One of the articles read:

> The institution said that they accepted [the Indonesians] hoping for intermingling, socialisation (*jinzai kōryū*) with the staff. Despite bearing the cost of 600,000 yen [around 4,500 pounds sterling] for the half-year training after the arrival in Japan, ... the director of the care home said: "Rather than being motivated by the shortage of hands to work, our primary aim is to introduce diversity (*tayōsei*) into the workplace". (Asahi 2009f)

The revitalisation or invigoration (*kasseika* and *kappatsuka*; Jpn.) of the workplace expected to come with the foreign employees also figured as the second most common reason (on a par with *kokusai kōken*, or 'international contribution', and *kokusai kōryū*, or 'international exchange, mingling'), for accepting the EPA Indonesians to care institutions in the already mentioned survey conducted towards the end of 2009 by the grass-roots support group I cooperated with. In a broader perspective, the foreign workers were presented as indispensable for Japan's ability to sustain 'the society's vitality' (*shakai no katsuryoku*; Jpn.) (Asahi 2006). Another article saw the internationalisation as inevitable:

> Green Homeland [a care home] as a consigned institution engaged in training and promotion of employment has been unaffected by the labour shortage of the recent years. The ... institution's director explains her aim in accepting the Indonesian candidates: "While supporting foreigners aspiring to become carers we contribute to international cooperation/aid (*kokusai kōken*), simultaneously we can cultivate an international way of thinking, international feel (*kokusai kankaku*) among our Japanese members of staff, and we can learn from each other ... [W]e were fortunate to have received skilled workers thanks to which the staff morale rose and the workplace livened up; these things are difficult to translate into a monetary value. It [the acceptance] is also an advance investment towards the internationalisation era that will definitely come". (Yomiuri 2009d)

In these article fragments the EPA acceptance was not seen solely in terms of training Indonesian care specialists in line with the official goals of the programme. Rather, while the Indonesian workers were depicted as already contributing to improving the working environment of the accepting institutions by their sheer presence, the praising of the opportunity for international 'mingling' and for fostering the 'international feel' among the Japanese pointed towards the future. Such exposure to non-Japanese workers, effected by the EPA programme, was to prepare the Japanese for living in a diversified, internationalised Japanese society that would 'definitely come'. Such discourses clearly suggested a vision of Japan and Japanese society as being at or approaching a threshold between the imagined 'open' future and the closed, 'Japanese-only' present (and past).

As indicated in the Introduction, the majority of the accepting institutions claimed to have accepted the EPA Indonesian workers in order to mitigate the labour shortage, either one already experienced or one expected in the near future. In the mediated representations, the EPA scheme was simultaneously perceived in terms of labour market needs and of Japanese ideas of a homogeneous nation. If it were not for the assumed present homogeneity of the Japanese, the Indonesian workers would not have been posed to introduce difference, revitalise workplaces, or provide an introduction for Japanese workers to internationalised interactions. There would have been no need to rethink the approach to the native language or indeed to open up the country and take responsibility for how such a policy was being implemented. Perhaps, the Indonesians would not have been represented in such a positive light either. The following sections show how the Indonesian workers were imagined as agents of such revitalising internationalisation. They also illustrate the ways in which the Indonesians were imagined as compatible with the social milieux of the Japanese eldercare institutions. However, before moving to the images of the candidates as they appeared in the Japanese mass media, I pause on the source of these images and discuss how they came to be influenced by the Indonesians themselves.

Production of EPA Indonesian Mediated Images

In his analysis of television programmes representing Brazilian *Nikkeijin* in the early 1990s, Tsuda Takeyuki (2003b) discusses the extent to which the Japanese media were engaged in reproduction of the establishment views and what conditions made it possible for them to take an adversarial position to them. Tsuda suggests that in Japan the mode of acquiring information through *kisha kurabu* (journalists' club; Jpn.) convened by governmental departments and other institutions tended to restrict the material disseminated by the media to that reflecting the official stance. However, as he also notes, there were certain areas on which information could not be obtained through such dominant channels. One of these areas was immigration. The lack of official information forced journalists to conduct independent research in order to produce materials on immigrant lives. In fact, as Tsuda further notes, at the time of his research numerous documentaries were produced criticising the Japanese government for inadequacies in the way Japan was receiving foreigners.

Because initially there was indeed a lack of official sources of information on the lives of the EPA candidates, throughout my time in Japan the EPA Indonesians were frequently visited by various journalists. Such direct collection of information undeniably affected the image constructed by media representations. They were predominately sympathetic towards the Indonesians and critical of the government. One of the reasons why these images were positive was the friendly, intimate relationships which the Indonesian candidates developed with their employers and with some of their co-workers and the elderly. It is possibly sensible to assume that those accepting institutions where the relationships between the Indonesians and the staff and/or employers were not running as smoothly for whatever reason would be less inclined to accept a request for a journalist visit. What is more, the candidates were aware of what kind of stories the Japanese journalists were expecting to hear, and sometimes adjusted their comments to these perceived expectations. As Amir once told me, referring to his latest interview, he simply said what they wanted to hear – that is, that it was difficult, that he was trying, and that he wanted to work in Japan in the future, while in fact he was still undecided and was planning to build a house in Indonesia for himself and his newly wedded wife.

Another factor that had a bearing on the kind of images conveyed in the Japanese newspapers and other reports had to do with the EPA Indonesians' embeddedness in a network of relations that sometimes extended back to their time at the training centre. For example, some of the teachers from the centre remained actively engaged, not only in the private lives of the candidates. I would also meet them at different gatherings organised by support groups, or at conferences where the EPA issue was being debated. Similarly, those who had volunteered to become host families or *kaiwa* partners (conversation partners; Jpn.) to the Indonesians during their language training remained involved, maintaining phone contact, sometimes sending letters and even visiting their 'adopted' children, but also participating in various support organisations. As already noted, these organisations lobbied for improvements to the EPA programme, and through their personal contacts with the Indonesians their information was directly based on the narratives produced by the candidates – not solely on their own personal experiences but, thanks to the continuing contact between the candidates, on an accumulation of others' histories too.

My informants' connectedness with the individuals from the training centre and among themselves was further accompanied by their contacts with the officials from the Indonesian embassy as well as from the Japanese political scene. In May 2009 the Japanese Council of Senior Citizens Welfare Services organised a *happyōkai* (Jpn.), a presentation day, during which the EPA caregiver candidates of the associated institutions presented their experiences to date. Many of them, including Amir and Jasir who wrote a joint presentation, decided to use the opportunity to appeal for improvements to the programme. This was particularly significant since one of the main individuals in the organisation hosting the event was an *amakudari* (Jpn.), a former senior bureaucrat, who maintained personal connections to powerful figures within the central administration. The same meeting was attended by representatives of the Indonesian embassy, one of the minister-counsellors and his secretary, and an Indonesian news agency reporter currently based in Tokyo. During the reception that followed the formal presentation part, the candidates freely mingled with all the guests present, and took the opportunity to introduce themselves to the minister-counsellor and to take one or two photographs together. A month later, in June 2009, an official launch (attended by many media representatives) of a newly formed support organisation, which aimed at supporting both the candidates (care workers as well as nurses) and their accepting institutions, took place in the Shibuya district of Tokyo. Among the invited guest speakers were representatives of the Indonesian embassy. After they had addressed the audience the representatives joined the candidates in a small room booked for them to eat lunch (provided by the support organisation) and to store their belongings. In the cosy atmosphere of the room, the candidates engaged in friendly, open conversation with the officials discussing their experiences, expectations and problems. These problems were to be later conveyed to the Japanese counterparts of the Indonesian officials.

Therefore, although it was not within the competence of any of the mentioned organisations or individuals to introduce any changes to the programme, they provided channels through which to disseminate the Indonesians' views publicly in a manner that guaranteed their being listened to, as well as having their statements recorded by the national mass media. The agenda presented by the Indonesians could therefore be passed on through Japanese official channels and used in the lobbying to reform the foreign care workers acceptance system. This agenda was also the source of the EPA Indonesians' representations dominant in the Japanese newspapers during the period of this research.

EPA Candidates' Media Representations

Alongside the explicit debates of a new, diverse Japanese society, there were a great number of media-produced descriptions that presented the EPA Indonesian candidates in a positive, often enthusiastic way. In fact, I did not come across any account of the acceptance that would in any way put the candidates in a negative light. Any criticism was always levelled at the organisation of the acceptance programme, usually stressing the hardship it caused for the Indonesians. Negative reactions of the elderly towards the Indonesian workers were also only rarely reported in the media. Rather, through building up their stories from personalised reporting about individuals in specific accepting institutions, the newspaper articles and television and radio programmes gave a friendly 'face' to the practical implementation of the governmental agreement and to the workers who arrived. Unlike images of a generalised portrait of foreigners in Japan, these new workers were not engaging in illicit activities or heightening crime rates. Instead, they were smiling. *Egao*, or 'smiling face(s)', was one of the most commonly used words in the descriptions of the Indonesians' demeanour after their arrival in Japan. 'Care in a foreign country – supported by *smiling faces*' (Asahi 2009b, my emphasis), and '"I'll stick it out with work and studying" – *smiling faces* and confusion – Indonesian carer candidates one month into appointment' (Asahi 2009d, my emphasis) are just two examples of article titles using the noun. In the short scenes described in the texts depicting the EPA Indonesians at work, they were usually interacting with the elderly, pushing their wheelchairs, or feeding them – always with a smile on their faces (*egao*), affectionate, kind (*yasashii*), cheerful (*akarui*), and/or polite (*teinei*). Beside the text one could often see a photograph conveying the heart-warming atmosphere of the moment described.

An article titled 'The Spirit of Care – Having Crossed the Border' published in the *Yomiuri* (2009a)[6] reported: 'In an elderly care institution, Indonesians [names of candidates], smiling, nestle close to the elderly who are enjoying their *osechi ryōri*'[7]; the same newspaper a little over a month later described a scene whereby, 'in an elderly care institution, Indonesians from the island of Java who arrived in Japan to obtain carer qualifications, … somewhat shyly danced "*Ohara Bushi*"[8] in a garden bathed in sunlight as though spring had arrived. Around them

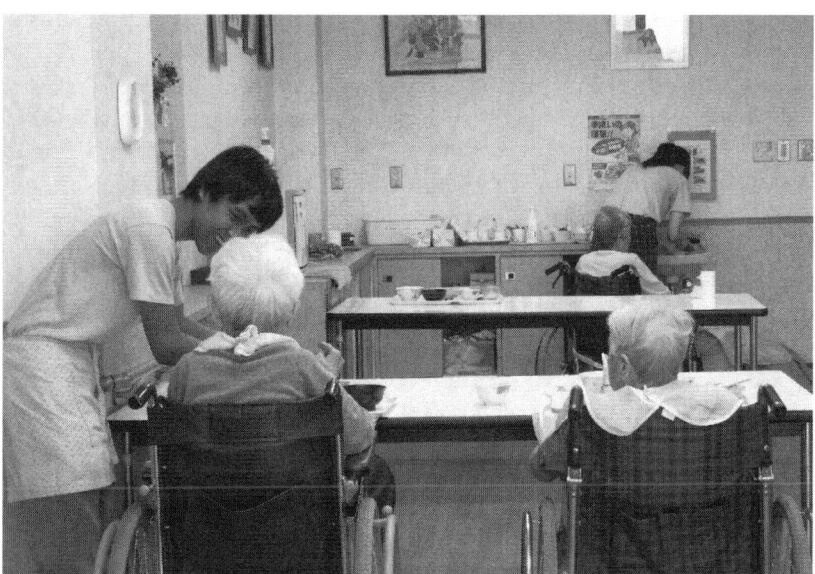

Figure 4.2: After a meal with the elderly. Photo by author.

the smiling faces of the elderly ... one person in a wheelchair was even following their movements with both hands', while a caption to one of the accompanying pictures showing an elderly resident with one of the candidates in the middle of some verbal exchange, read: 'Speaking affectionately to the elderly in Japanese, with a warm look in their eyes' (Yomiuri 2009b). On another occasion, it was reported that a 'cheerful voice and a smile on the face ... softens the expressions of the patients. "He's very attentive", the elderly think of him very highly' (Yomiuri 2009c).

Similar accounts were produced by readers and listeners of the media reporting on the EPA Indonesians' situation at work. The following is the final section of a letter from a 71-year-old male reader whose mother lived in a care institution that had accepted two female Indonesians:

> "Ms Nagatani, let's wash hands", they said to my 99-year-old mother whose name they so quickly memorised. Those affectionate smiling faces, [that] natural cheerfulness – I'm sure the trainees have a lot of problems, but I hope they will keep cheering up the Japanese elderly. (Asahi 2009c)

Such affectionate attitudes were also expressed by presenters as well as listeners of an NHK Radio programme, 'Will They Settle? Foreigners in Care and Nursing', broadcast on 10 November 2009. The discussion revolved around the problems with the organisation of the EPA programme, but the presenters had also arranged a live phone conversation with an Indonesian caregiver candidate living now in one of the northern, and therefore considered cold, prefectures of Japan's main island. The candidate answered the questions about her work and the cold weather in simple sentences, sometimes losing grammatical fluency, but often laughing, and claimed that even though it was difficult for her to communicate in Japanese at the moment, she would 'do her best' (*ganbarimasu*; Jpn.). Once the conversation was over, those present in the studio commented on her good Japanese and perseverance despite having to work in such unfamiliar conditions, not only in a foreign country, but also in a climate to which she was not accustomed. Later, one of the presenters posted a commentary on the programme on the internet. It read:

> That voice, considering the unfamiliar everyday environment and [her] work, so unimaginably cheerful, frank and strong, brimful of positive attitude, made me spontaneously encourage her to 'keep up the good work'; but it was not only me, I have received emails as well. (NHK 2009)

The author of one of these emailed messages, a woman in her sixties, praised the candidate:

This Indonesian young lady is splendid, isn't she? I'm sure her cheerful and vigorous responsiveness makes the atmosphere around her brighten up as if flowers blossomed. My mother is also receiving care in an institution, and she relaxes whenever there is a cheerful member of staff around. (NHK 2009)

On a different occasion, quoted in a newspaper article, a colleague of two female candidates admitted:

Before they took up their positions, I was worried whether or not they would be able to follow shift reports, but I was worrying unnecessarily. If anything, their cheerful and hard-working attitude has been acting as a stimulus. The institution has become better. (Nikkei 2009a)

Such highly praised conduct of the Indonesians was reported to have affected not only the elderly Japanese residents of the institutions but the candidates' co-workers as well. According to a director of an elder-care institution where two Indonesian candidates were working:

It seems that, through their [the EPA candidates] frank, polite and respectful approach towards the elderly, we, the Japanese are being reminded of what we began to forget (Yomiuri 2009b),

because, although

the government sees it [the EPA acceptance] not as a means to reduce the labour shortages, but as an element in an economic exchange … it has a great impact on the care sites. For the Japanese staff working alongside the candidates, it seems to be an occasion to reconsider what working in care means. (Yomiuri 2009d)

Meanwhile, a team leader of five male nurse candidates conceded:

They are hard working but are able to remain attentive. They have something that we Japanese have lost and hence provide a stimulus. (Yomiuri 2009c)

A similar thought was expressed by a Japanese colleague of two young Indonesian women who, exempted from the initial language training, took up their appointment earlier than the majority of the EPA carer candidates:

But I needn't have worried. They pray outside of working hours, do not arrive late [for work], and so on. They grasp things quickly, and soon became an asset. I was glad to see that, appeased by their friendly, smiling faces and affectionate tone, one resident, who used to be angry on a daily basis, stopped complaining. They have a strong sense of respect for the elderly, always trying to think from the position of the other person. It made me reflect on myself – in the busyness of things, I tend to lose this compassion. (Yomiuri 2009d)

Moreover, the relations between the 'attentive and considerate' Indonesian workers and the elderly who received their care were often presented in the paradigm of family relations. A resident receiving care from two female Indonesian candidates was reported to say: 'I was worried about the language, etc., but now I do not feel any inconvenience. It feels as if I am being looked after by my grandchildren' (Nikkei 2009a). A direct link between care for the residents and care for one's family members was also drawn by quoting the words of a male candidate who was looking after his grandmother before departing for Japan: 'I will look after the residents just as I did after my grandmother' (Asahi 2009a).

The individualised representations of the Indonesian care workers as providing affectionate care to the Japanese elderly therefore built an image of the Indonesians as more familiar. Moreover, through the references to the cared-for residents enjoying and appreciating the presence of the foreign workers, the Indonesians were constructed as idealised substitutes for familial carers. Perhaps more evidently, this was effected through the narratives of the Japanese co-workers and supervisors who, in the Indonesians' affectionate comportment, saw a reflection of qualities that, as they claimed, had in fact been characteristic of the Japanese. Through such narratives they created an image of the Indonesian carers as possible to identify with. In a later section I expand in more detail on the function fulfilled by such endorsing representations of the EPA candidates, while here I turn to the other side of the debate, one that argued against the desirability of Indonesian care workers, and foreigners in general.

Homogeneity, Comfort and Security

At the beginning of my first research visit to Ajisai, Jasir's and Amir's manager marvelled about the courage of the two young men who took up the challenge of living and working in a foreign country, the language and customs of which they had little knowledge. She reminisced on her own younger years when she was deciding on her career direction, and claimed that she did not even consider taking the challenge (*chōsen shinai*; Jpn.) of going abroad. Even given an opportunity similar to the EPA acceptance, she would most likely not have taken the risk of abandoning the familiar living environment (*najimi aru seikatsu kankyō*; Jpn.) because she was Japanese, who are of an 'insular country' (*shima-guni*; Jpn.). On another occasion, Kenta, a young male colleague of Iffah, my Indonesian female informant based in Blue Bara special nursing home in central Japan, could not imagine himself, as he put it, plunging (*tobikomu*; Jpn.) into a foreign country like Iffah had, and living there for longer than a week or so of holidays. His reason was that he had been brought up in the same 'insular country', where things Japanese were all one needed to know. He expected life overseas to feel uncomfortable (*fuben*; Jpn.), with many bothersome aspects to it (*mendōkusai*; Jpn.), and therefore tiring (*tsukaresō*; Jpn.). This did not mean that he had no will or desire to experience non-Japanese cultures or to interact with non-Japanese people. Kenta would often quiz me about different aspects of life in Europe, his questions ranging from education systems to the types of car driven on European streets. However interesting the details of life overseas (*kaigai*; Jpn.) were, the perceived complications and resulting discomfort made leading life there appear to Kenta as unsuitable for him.

Although representing reflections on the possibility of migration rather than actual experiences, these two examples imply how Kenta and the manager imagined their relationship to foreign countries. Described in reference to the same Japanese expression, *shimaguni*, 'insular country', the reflections convey the idea of Japan as a country in isolation from others, which is then translated into the particular sensitivity of people living there. Although the phrase *shimaguni konjō*, 'insular country's guts, nature or spirit', can be an expression of admiration for Japanese perseverance and cooperation in the face of various disasters (see Lie 2001), both natural and of human making, when it was used during my fieldwork with the 'guts' part dropped, it referred to a different inclination. In this incarnation it often conveyed a slightly regretful and perhaps fatalistic justification of the Japanese being 'what they were', their lack of knowledge, and the (expected) uneasiness of dealing with unfamiliar cultures. The two accounts are not meant, however, to represent the Japanese as being particularly indisposed to living in foreign countries or to interacting with people seen as coming from different cultural backgrounds. They are presented here to highlight the expected lack of comfort of living in an unfamiliar environment or encountering unfamiliar individuals, which may be equally applicable to other nationalities as well. Oliver (2011) describes similar perceptions of (dis)comfort experienced by some British retirement migrants to southern Spain.

In many representations of foreigners in Japan, the discursive homogeneity achieved through the shared inherited essence served as a guarantor of harmonious coexistence. The representations of foreigners as posing a danger to public security and the dissemination of information about rising crime rates among the non-Japanese populations in

Japan were not anything new or unique (Tsuda 2003b). The opponents of relaxing Japanese immigration policy, or those who argued for approaching the issue with caution (*shinchō*; Jpn.), would point to those European countries that were presented as 'failed' examples of immigration, where the inflow of foreigners had led to a variety of social problems and sometimes to violent confrontations with the local population and/or authorities. For example, in a 2009 *Nikkei* article, Saeki Hirobumi, the chairman of a multinational electronics corporation and a proponent of the 'unnecessary immigrants theory',[9] was reported to say:

> I often used to travel with work to foreign countries, and had many opportunities to listen to people from the developed European countries that had accepted many immigrants, such as the United Kingdom, Germany and France. They would all tell me that 'it was a mistake to accept immigrants. Japan should not accept [them]'. I cannot understand the efforts to simply accept immigrants and not learning from the so many examples when it failed. (Nikkei 2009b)

That they were singled out as suspicious in the midst of the predominantly Japanese society seemed to be confirmed in the eyes of the EPA Indonesians by the fact that they were often subjected to searches by the police, especially at the busier train stations. It was an experience common to Daris in particular, to the extent that when he came to pick up some household goods I was giving away on my departure from Japan, he felt apprehensive about taking a set of kitchen knives to carry in his backpack. To get to his apartment, he had to change trains at one of the larger train stations in the area where he had been subjected to police searches numerous times before. He feared that if the police were to find the knives on him, he would be in deep trouble. Luckily, having decided to take the knives after all, this time he managed to get home without being apprehended. When I relayed the story to Jasir and Amir they laughed and commented that with a face like Daris's this (i.e. being stopped by the police so often) was not a mystery – it was obviously because 'he had the face of a terrorist'. At the same time, they recalled being stopped by the police while cycling back from work one day, suspected of having stolen the bicycles. The bikes were registered with the Ajisai care home in which they worked, but the explanation they gave to the police officers was not sufficient. The case was not resolved until the police contacted the office in the care home where they could receive confirmation that the Indonesians indeed worked there and were entitled to use the bicycles. What was significant here for Jasir and Amir was not so much the fact that the confirmation by Ajisai was required, but that they had been stopped purely, as they saw it, on the basis of their non-Japanese appearance, which implied that they might have been up to something illicit in the eyes of the Japanese police officers.

The requirement for me to have Japanese guarantors countersign my own rental agreement had a similar air to it. When my delegated agent was calling the landlords of flats matching my criteria, the inevitable detail that had to be mentioned was that I was not Japanese. The information would usually be preceded by 'oh, and there is one more thing you should know' kind of an introduction, followed by responses to the questions, which I could sometimes overhear, assuring the landlord that I was a white Westerner, a researcher, and that there should be no problems with me as a tenant. Several such calls ended with the landlord deciding not to take a chance with a foreigner, and my candidature as a tenant was rejected. Although at the beginning the agent was trying to soften the blunt rejections when conveying the information to me, when he noticed that I was closely following the conversations and smirking to myself whenever I could sense the unfavourable direction of his conversations, he would simply say *gaikokujin dakara*, because you're a foreigner, after he had put the handset down. When we finally managed to agree several viewings, he openly said to me that I was lucky not being a Chinese, as it would have been even more difficult to find a place to live. He expounded on the causes, explaining that in the past there had been many Chinese who would not pay their bills, or rent, and move out of the property leaving the landlords with their dues to pay and possibly some damage to the property as well. Since then, he continued, people were afraid to accept foreign (*gaikokujin*) tenants. Once the rental had been agreed, it was still not enough for me to sign the required forms, have my passport copied together with a document stating my affiliation with Waseda University, a well-known and well-regarded university in Japan, and a letter confirming my (Japanese government–funded) scholarship. I also needed to obtain signatures and stamps (*hanko*) of two Japanese guarantors who had to provide full information on their employment status, their income and the yearly profit of the companies they worked for. I was warned that, as a foreigner, depending on the landlord and/or agency managing my chosen flat, I may have to acquire three or four such signatures; but, as I was told in the end, the prestige attached to the places of employment and the salaries of my two friends who agreed to vouch for me saved me the trouble. The normality and permissiveness granted to such statements and actions aimed either at a particular group or foreigners in general, the outright banning of foreigners from bars and clubs (sometimes lifted if a foreigner is in the company of a Japanese person), and other means of systemic differentiation and exclusion of the foreigner have fed into the imagination of Japan, which was to remain Japanese and for Japanese only, and therefore comfortable and safe. In the context of care provision, the presence of foreigners amidst and in close proximity to the Japanese bodies was also presented as a less than welcome possibility.

Foreigners in Care

During the press conference for The Foreign Correspondents' Club of Japan held on 3 August 2010, Nakamura Hirohiko, a director of an accepting institution and a former chairman of the Japanese Council of Senior Citizens Welfare Service, paralleled the opposition to accepting foreign workers under the EPA to the imaginations of Japan as a closed country of the Edo period. During a Q&A session, to a question on whether the Japanese nurse associations were not opposed to the EPA programme, Nakamura replied:

> This is an embarrassing story, but… The first to proceed with the negotiations were the Philippines. Really, regardless of the request made by the Philippines, the nursing circles wanted to set the number [of accepted workers] at 10, 20 people – this was the nursing organisation. They did not want to allow foreign hands to touch Japanese patients; this was… a really unthinkable… [voice from behind the camera: *chairman, simply, they were against*] …They were very much against, it was just like the way of thinking of Tokugawa Iemitsu [laughter from the audience] … who did *sakoku*, that is [directed at the interpreter as if clarifying the analogy; audience laughs and the same voice from behind the camera says: *he did put it succinctly*].

Nakamura's reference to *sakoku* – the already mentioned national closed-door policy implemented in Tokugawa-era Japan (1603–1868) and initiated by the first shogun of the dynasty, Iemitsu – was a deliberate attack on the often xenophobic reactions towards foreigners' presence in Japan, and the idea that Japan should remain as free from foreign population influences as possible. His comment on the undesirability of the foreign touch on Japanese bodies made in response to a question which was, rather, intended to elicit information about labour-market-related objections, reveals the usually unvoiced concerns over the bodily proximity of the foreigners to Japanese bodies. The objection, allegedly made by one of the nursing organisations, points to the particular sensitivity of the EPA acceptance given that its provisions placed foreigners in a setting where they were working directly on Japanese bodies, not on machines.

Apart from the sheer physicality of contact, those opposed to inviting foreigners to work as care providers presented their objections in terms of the quality of care. The concerns primarily revolved around the foreign workers' ability to communicate in Japanese. The insufficient mastery of the language could pose dangers to the elderly (and hospital patients in the case of foreign nurses), but was also a likely obstacle to sustaining the psychological component of care. For In Toshie, the chairman of the Japan Home Helpers Association who took part in a debate over the acceptance of foreign care and medical workers, broadcast by the NHK television channel in October 2006,

> the question is whether it really would be possible to maintain the quality, were we to expand the acceptance. Care is a difficult task for the Japanese themselves. It requires the exquisite ability to read the subtleties of the elderly's heart and to sense or infer their needs. This would be very difficult for foreigners coming from a different culture. (NHK 2006)

The lack of an intimate knowledge of the Japanese culture was to preclude the foreign carers from providing satisfactory care to the elderly, because as non-Japanese they would not be able to learn it or to sufficiently identify with the cared-for residents. Moreover, the foreigners' ability to provide adequate care to the Japanese was also thought to be precluded by their coming from outside the relations of national reciprocity.

In the same debate, In Toshie was also of the opinion that 'we Japanese, grateful to our seniors for their efforts, such as during the War, are able to provide them with care of a far greater quality than foreigners' (ibid.). The statement can be read with two meanings. Firstly, it assumes that Japanese carers, either medical or caregiver, are inherently better equipped to care for their fellow countrymen than those who do not share this commonality. Secondly, the association of the quality of care with one's loyalty to the elders based on an assumed relation of 'obligation and duty in the intergenerational pact' (Simoni and Trifiletti 2004) suggests that this loyalty might (could) not be expected from those who were not Japanese nationals. In either case, the quality of care is linked directly to one's national belonging and an unspecified ability to relate to one's co-nationals on the basis of this belonging. As non-Japanese, the EPA workers were excluded from such national 'mateship' – the 'egalitarian principle of natural sociality and reciprocity between equals' (Kapferer [1988] 2012: 158) – that would implicate them in nation-specific intergenerational reciprocity on par with the

Japanese. Being Japanese implied a bond between the cared-for and the carers that endowed certain rights, but also imposed obligations. In In's opinion, foreigners could not be presumed to respond to the intergenerational obligations existing among the Japanese.[10]

In a similar vein, Nakamura Hirohiko and Wahyudin, one of the EPA Indonesians who was one of the panellists during the press conference for The Foreign Correspondents' Club of Japan, alluded to the reluctance of the accepting institutions to allow the Indonesian caregiver candidates to perform tasks directly on the Japanese elderly's bodies. Wahyudin, at the time employed in a care home belonging to the consortium run by Mr Nakamura, expressed his confusion over the system, which allowed any Japanese individual without qualifications to perform the exact same tasks as certified carers, but prevented foreigners from doing so even if they were in possession of a nursing qualification, just as the first batch of EPA Indonesians were. This was what puzzled my friends as well. The qualification required of the Indonesian caregivers-to-be was possessed by only around 30 per cent of the Japanese care personnel in 2009. The majority of Japanese care workers held the non-obligatory entry level qualification for a helper.[11] Meanwhile, it was required of the Indonesian trainees that they pass the Japanese national caregiver examination in order to be granted the right to remain and work in Japan beyond the four-year period specified by the agreement. Moreover, many of the Japanese employees who newly entered the institutions in which the Indonesian candidates worked had neither undergone education in care provision or any related area, nor possessed any relevant work experience, and yet they were allowed to perform bodily care tasks much sooner than the Indonesian candidates. This research was taking place in 2009 and the beginning of 2010, when the economic downturn was pushing many people employed in the Japanese car industry out of jobs. A significant portion of these people turned to care work, as this sector had long been suffering from a labour shortage, and apparently the job seemed fairly easy to learn. In two institutions that became my primary sites for research, there were several new employees who admitted to being assembly line operators turned care workers. Despite no previous encounters with care work, they were performing direct care tasks on the elderly bodies soon after their employment began, much to the amazement and disillusionment of my informants who were excluded from such tasks. It was thus possible to view this preference to delegate bodily care tasks to non- or less-experienced Japanese rather than to qualified non-Japanese as a demonstration of crediting with greater trust, or at least trusting sooner, a Japanese person than a non-Japanese one. Such, at least, was the interpretation of the situation by the Indonesian EPA workers.

In 2005, a nurse born and bred in Japan and with seventeen years of professional experience under her belt heard the Japanese Supreme Court upholding a 1994 decision of the Tokyo Metropolitan Government prohibiting her from taking an examination that would qualify her to be promoted to a managerial position, despite her professional credentials. She was a *Zainichi* ('permanent resident') Korean. The ruling referenced the Japanese nationality clause as a condition for becoming a civil servant in Japan (see McNeill 2005 for a more detailed description of the case).[12] Commenting on the ruling, the Tokyo governor, Ishihara Shintarō, was quoted as saying: 'What if a decision about the life or death of a critically ill patient has to be made. How can we trust a foreign nurse?' (McNeill 2005). Never mind that technically such a decision would have to be made by a doctor, not a nurse, and leaving aside the highly problematic classification of Korean permanent residents as foreigners in Japan,[13] the message of the comment was that the Japanese cannot trust foreigners.

Distrust based on one's ascription to a perceivably non-Japanese category directly affected the experiences of a *Zainichi* Korean nurse aspiring to move her career beyond direct nursing tasks. The positioning of the EPA Indonesians as less suitable to care for the elderly because they were not Japanese was based on similar ideas related to trust and reciprocity. People are not always guided in their actions by calculated assumptions or trust in the compensation for their contributions to society; neither are they inclined to think of their own actions in terms of such an altruistic contribution. However, trust in reciprocal benefits underpins the majority, if not all, of the social relations and transactions in the society. From relying on a doctor's diagnosis or the state paying out one's pension when the time arrives to the expectation that the meal served in a restaurant has not been poisoned, the relations are based implicitly on trust and expected reciprocity. That the decisions made by the *Zainichi* nurse were not to be trusted was based on the perception of her as an outsider to the Japanese national community of reciprocal obligations, as was the case with the Indonesian EPA workers. The lack of confidence in foreign workers to provide Japanese elderly with adequate care (and, conversely, the seemingly unwavering trust in Japanese to be able to do so on the sole basis of being Japanese), seemed to rest in the inability to know the Indonesians as people with whom the Japanese could identify, because they were imagined outside of the national community (Anderson 1983).

The question arises of how trust, and therefore reciprocity, comes to be presumed of those considered to be co-nationals. This is where the essentialising notions and stereotypical representations support the distinction. Both the Japanese and the Indonesian workers operated on such notions arguing for their mutual dissimilarity and a consequent inability to know what the other experienced or intended. On one occasion, Iffah had to summon the help of her former Japanese language teacher, Ms Ito, to persuade Iffah's employer to consider replacing her current tutor with someone more suitable. After a long discussion in which Ms Ito played a crucial role, Iffah's employer conceded to the change. He admitted that the most difficult thing to deal with in this situation would be *giri* (obligation; Jpn.), because he had found the tutor through personal connections. He had relied on a favour from his father's friend, and now he found it problematic to dismiss the tutor without disrespecting the obligation such an arrangement incurred. Assuming that Iffah and I, who were present during the discussion as well, would not understand his situation, he turned to Ms Ito and summed up that 'unless you are a Japanese, you won't get it' (*nihonjin ja nai to wakaranai*; Jpn.). The privileging of the opinions expressed by a Japanese person over those of a non-Japanese, or assuming an inability to grasp the intricacies of the Japanese reality of life and/or interpersonal relations, was based on the idea that in order to achieve these goals one needed to be Japanese, and that the differences characteristic of foreigners would preclude them from doing so. Such perceptions were possible because of the essentialising ideas of Japanese homogeneity, which not only imply cultural familiarity but also presuppose tacit knowledge indispensable to interpret the Japanese social reality based on individual similarities, and available to any and all Japanese, but not to others.

Georg Simmel (1950: 318) writes that 'the person who knows completely need not trust; while the person who knows nothing can, on no rational grounds, afford even confidence'. Erik Ringmar, in his discussion of the connection between nationalism and intimacy, presents both nationalism and democracy as built on the same premise of intimacy between members of a given population. He writes: '[I]f intimacy is the standard by which public life is to be measured, then intimacy is possible only between some. There can be no "we" among strangers since it is difficult to identify with people very different from ourselves' (Ringmar 1998: 545). The ability to imagine others as sharing certain characteristics, such as beliefs, values and culture, creates also, as already argued by Benedict Anderson (1983), a sense of unity among people who might have never met. Such familiarity, or intimacy, is therefore presumed, or taken as inherent, among co-nationals and based on, as Erik Ringmar notes, the imagination of the others as being similar to the imagining individual. Considering himself to be Japanese, Iffah's employer made explicit his assumption that Ms Ito, equally Japanese in his eyes in contrast to Iffah and me, would share his understanding and knowledge of social convenances thought to be typically Japanese. Similarly, for the chairman of the Japan Home Helpers Association, for the Tokyo governor and seemingly for the employers in the institutions where Japanese workers were trusted with attending to the elderly bodies well ahead of the qualified Indonesian workers, being Japanese implied knowledge and trustworthiness that was not as readily granted to non-Japanese. Yet, despite and because of such sentiments, the mass media painted an image that represented the EPA Indonesians as individuals who were not only possible to identify with and to relate to in an effective and mutually intelligible way, but also as making a positive, necessary and welcome contribution to the accepting care homes, and to Japanese society more broadly. The internationalised *kaikoku*, or open country, that Japan was to become was to do away with the homogeneity discourse allowing for inclusion of non-Japanese as viable members of the Japanese society.

Internationalisation Once More – The Third Opening of Japan?

The beginning of the 1990s in Japan witnessed a debate between the proponents and opponents of 'opening the country' to foreign workers, similar to the one surrounding the EPA acceptance. Lie (2001: 20–21) suggests that the earlier emergence of the debate was a function of the growing visibility of foreign workers, particularly Iranians, who, due to the lack of other information outlets, gathered in public spaces, such as the cities' major parks, to exchange information about work opportunities (Morita 2003: 161–62). Goodman et al. (2003: 3) note that the debate was also linked to the fact that in 1993 Japan's migrant population was recorded to have increased 62 per cent since 1983. This proliferation of references in the Japanese media to Japan as an 'open country' akin to the end of the isolationist policy of the Tokugawa era, Lie (2001: 6; Chapter 1) calls somewhat ironically, the second opening of Japan. The irony lies in his contention that Japan was never really a closed country, either under the Tokugawa rule, or immediately before the 1990s. It could not, therefore, be 'opened'. The silencing of the colonial period when the nascent Japanese nation-state accepted millions of non-Japanese, notably Koreans, and the later confining to the closet of the existing minorities merely served as ideological tools for creating the image of a mono-ethnic, and therefore closed to foreign people and influences, nation-state identifiable with the dominant group of the Japanese. In reality, Lie argues, 'the myth of mono-ethnic Japan is fundamentally a post–World War II construct' (2001: 141). Academic representations of Japan have long accepted and argued for such a view (for example, Denoon et al. 1996; Weiner 1997; Douglass and Roberts 2000; Goodman et al. 2003; Graburn and Ertl 2008; Willis and Murphy-Shigematsu 2008).

Another parallel between the earlier debates and the current one is the invocation of the internationalisation and diversification of Japanese society. As Chris Burgess ([2004] 2012) argues, the use of such terms as *kokusaika* (internationalisation), *kyōsei* (coexistence, symbiosis), and *tabunka* (multicultural) in Japan, despite their face-value connotations, served in fact to reaffirm the notions of Japanese national homogeneity through the control of others by including them within reaffirmed boundaries between the Japanese and the others who were locked into particular kinds of difference. As a result there was more pressure on Japanese to become 'more Japanese' and on foreign residents to become 'more ethnic' (ibid.). This indeed seemed to be the case with the EPA Indonesians who, unlike the Japanese, were, for example, always smiling. Such results of official multiculturalism – dividing and reasserting difference – have been widely criticised and are behind the declarations of the 'death of multiculturalism' in Western industrialised countries (Kundani 2002; for an alternative view, see Kymlicka 2012).

However, seeing the overly positive representations of the EPA Indonesians in the media and the projections of multiculturalism as merely ideological discourses serving the dominant national ideology would be as negligent as taking them at face value. As we have seen in the previous chapters, the Indonesian candidates forged a variety of meaningful relationships with the co-workers, elderly residents, and employers, which cut across rigid cultural differentiations inherent in the idea of so-called 'hard multiculturalism'. Such experiences became the basis for the media representations, which, I suggest, can be seen as a form of criticism, or rueful self-recognition (Herzfeld 1997), and a function of imagining an alternative reality achieved by distancing oneself from the dominant ideologies.

Slavoj Žižek, in his introduction to *Mapping Ideology*, discusses propositions of *Neues Forum* groups in former East Germany which, at the time of the disintegration of the Communist regime, argued for a 'third way' for East Germany, which would be neither capitalism nor the already existing socialism. Although Žižek deems the propositions 'illusory', he acknowledges that they were the only ones that did not obliterate the social antagonisms inherent in the capitalist (or socialist, for that matter) system – antagonisms that were subdued under the dominant, and ultimately realised, project of including East Germany in the capitalist world (Žižek 1994: 7). Žižek concludes that we should look out for the 'narratives of possible but failed alternative histories [which] point towards the system's antagonistic character, and thus "estrange" us to the self-evidence of its established identity' (ibid.). Against the voices denying the possibility of mutual identification and trust between the Japanese host society and the Indonesian workers, the narratives of a possible, if not failed, satisfying coexistence – with the Indonesian workers and other foreigners more broadly – served as a tool to distance the actual representations from the official (and operating at the level of folk theories) ideology. Posed as representing the popular perspective through the use of individual voices, these media narratives projected a novel image of a workplace where Japanese and foreigners could successfully co-create wholesome working relations. The concerns over how and whether the Indonesians would adapt, whether they would decide to stay on, and whether and how Japan, for its part, could adapt to their needs all attested to the existence of the dominant homogeneity ideologies, but at the same time questioned their legitimacy.

Presenting the reaction of a nursing organisation as embarrassing in his statement quoted above, Nakamura Hirohiko echoed voices that, concerned with the success of the EPA acceptance, feared that the programme would fail (the success of the scheme being measured by the ability of the Indonesians to acquire Japanese qualifications by the end of their on-the-job training, and by their consequent settlement, or at least long-term residence and work in Japan). On the one hand, the failure was presented in terms of the Japanese state being unable or unwilling to establish a sustainable immigration system allowing foreign workers such as the EPA candidates to more freely take advantage of the opportunities in the Japanese labour market. An EPA-like system was not only 'impudent' towards the candidates (*kōhoshatachi ni shitsurei*; Jpn.), but also an 'internationally embarrassing' matter (*kokusaiteki ni mite hazukashii hanashi*; Jpn.). The international gaze looking at Japan's way of dealing with foreign workers was a recurring theme, particularly in the conversations among the members of the support group with whom I worked. To return the Indonesian candidates back to Indonesia if they did not pass the Japanese national examination was to contribute to the worsening of Japan's international image, or the 'feelings about Japan' (Asahi 2009e). On the other hand, the concern was whether Japan as a whole would prove hospitable and adaptable enough to provide the Indonesians with an environment in which they would feel welcome and be willing to settle. Either way, were the EPA programme to fail, it would be an 'embarrassment' on an international scale, giving away Japanese uneasiness and ambivalence about welcoming foreigners in their country, either on a systemic or social level. Nakamura's introduction of his tale as 'embarrassing' was an expression of collective acknowledgement, or rueful recognition, of the Japanese predicament underlying the established national identity.

Sakanaka Hidenori, the already introduced head of the Japan Immigration Policy Institute, noted a change in the attitudes towards foreigners in Japan. As if to substantiate the basis for his optimism, towards the end of my visit to his office in July 2009, Mr Sakanaka presented me with newspaper clippings discussing an opinion poll on the attitudes towards receiving medical and care services from foreigners, which had been published by the *Sankei Newspaper* five days before our meeting. The results showed that out of 910 respondents (629 men and 281 women) 58 per cent were in favour of the acceptance of foreigners into medical and care sectors, 44 per cent responded that they would not feel uneasy or anxious if cared for by a foreigner, and 52 per cent agreed that the present acceptance should be extended beyond the current two countries (Indonesia and the Philippines). Despite the majority of the respondents admitting to expecting discomfort if cared for by a foreigner, and nearly half not supporting the idea of expanding the acceptance, Mr Sakanaka found the results very pleasing, as he saw them as indicative of attitudes towards foreigners in Japan undergoing changes in the direction he had been advocating. As a comparison with past attitudes, he recalled that not so long ago many people were even against accepting foreigners to Japan as tourists. He added that the results would probably have been even more 'pro-foreigners' had the survey been conducted by another newspaper, as the *Sankei Newspaper* was rather conservative – as were, presumably, its readers.

Although Mr Sakanaka saw the EPA programme as a harbinger of change, he appreciated the limited nature of the acceptance that did not promise any great systemic transformations any time soon. He remained, however, optimistic about the meaning and ultimate function the EPA acceptance would play in shaping Japanese attitudes towards foreigners. He saw such small, as if uncertain, steps as a typically Japanese 'revolution' (*kakumei*; Jpn.) that was at the same time progressive and conservative. 'Even in [Meiji] *ishin* there is an "*i*"', he said, referring to the Meiji Restoration which marked the end of the Japanese feudal era of the already discussed closed-country, *sakoku*, policy. The Sino-Japanese character '*i*' in the Japanese term for 'restoration', *ishin*, means 'rope, tie', but also 'to maintain, to keep', suggesting perseverance despite the coming of the new, indicated by the other character forming the term for restoration, *shin*, meaning 'new'.

***

The seemingly disproportionate interest of the Japanese media in the EPA acceptance and the predominantly positive representations of the Indonesian candidates were an expression of and a commentary on the anxieties born from the contemporary condition of Japan as a nation. Faced with the prospect of a growing number of foreigners settling in Japan as a result of its demographic changes, and facilitated, but also caused, by Japan's international engagements (such as the EPA), the Japanese had to revisit the ideological underpinnings constructing their society. The EPA acceptance, which brought non-Japanese to work on Japanese bodies, placed them at the heart of ideological conflations of race, culture and nation, and therefore forced a rebranding of foreigners from dangerous unknowns to goodhearted, familiar individuals with whom one could connect and identify. This new brand of foreigner was then disseminated through the mass media. Therefore, rather than dismiss the positive images as simply reinforcing the ideas of national uniqueness, I believe that we should see them as examples of reassessment and as an exercise in re-imagining a different definition of a Japanese society. If not the third opening of Japan, at least the EPA acceptance can be seen as one additional push towards the continuous reconceptualisation of Japan as a country and a nation partaking in global engagements that inevitably influence the social imaginations feeding the construction of national intimacies.

Notes

1. Refer to Goodman and Harper 2008a for alternative views on Japan's demographic situation.
2. See Coulmas and Lützeler 2011 for a publication based on the conference; see also Goodman and Harper 2008b.
3. I am referring here to the text layout as it appears in the Portable Document Format (pdf) obtained from the electronic databases. Despite differences stemming, for example, from a horizontal orientation of the text as opposed

to the vertical of the original, the division of the text into parts seemed to reflect the organisation of the original articles.

4. This latter example comes from later articles, Nikkei 2009a and 2009e, where the term is used in the bodies of the text.

5. Ultimately, the number of daily-use Sino-Japanese characters was increased in November 2010.

6. This article describes the situation in a care home that received two Indonesian candidates who were exempted from the introductory Japanese language course and so took up their positions as candidates ahead of everyone else. Therefore, the newspaper could report on a situation in the institution before the main group of the candidates had completed their language training.

7. Japanese New Year food in which each ingredient and dish has a symbolic meaning.

8. A rhythmic dance performed to a traditional melody from the Kagoshima Prefecture.

9. See his book: *Imin fuyō ron: shōshika, jinkō genshō nani ga warui?*, or 'Argument for Unnecessary Migrants: What's Wrong with Low Fertility and Population Decline?', Sankei Shinbun Publishing, 2010.

10. This paragraph has previously been published in Świtek 2014.

11. See Note 2, Chapter 2.

12. The condition that 'Japanese nationality is required for civil servants who participate in the exercise of public power or in public decision making' is stipulated in the Second Periodic Report by the Government of Japan under Articles 16 and 17 of the International Covenant on Economic, Social and Cultural Rights. Japanese Ministry of Foreign Affairs. Available from: http://www.mofa.go.jp/policy/human/econo_rep2/general.html.

13. It is an issue that has anew attracted attention in summer 2014 with the ruling by Japan's Supreme Court stating that Japan's permanent residents are not entitled to welfare payouts, even if they have paid taxes their whole lives.

 Conclusion

RELUCTANT INTIMACIES

> Intimacy is not being absorbed by the other, but knowing his or her
> characteristics and making available one's own.
>
> – Anthony Giddens, *The Transformation of Intimacy*

The Japanese Ministry of Health, Labour and Welfare calculate that, up to the 2014 Economic Partnership Agreement (EPA) intakes, there have been 1,235 Indonesians (481 nurse and 754 caregiver candidates), 1,004 Filipino (337 nurse and 667 caregiver candidates) and 138 Vietnamese (21 nurse and 117 caregiver candidates) who have arrived in Japan under the bilateral agreements between Japan and the three countries (MHLW 2014). According to a short article published by the *Yomiuri* newspaper in mid-2014 (Yomiuri 2014), out of 402 nurse and caregiver candidates both from Indonesia and the Philippines who had passed their respective national examinations in Japan, 82 (68 Indonesians and 14 Filipinos) have returned to their home countries.[1] The news about first returns of some who had managed to pass the examinations, re-portedly came as a surprise to the policy makers. However, to those observing the Indonesians' (and perhaps the Filipinos') experiences in Japan, such decisions were far less unexpected. Both systemic and so-cial changes are still needed to encourage non-Japanese to arrive and remain in Japan.

Both Jasir and Amir passed the examination, but decided to return to Indonesia. Already that night in August 2009 when Jasir was reflecting on his first year as an EPA caregiver candidate, a year spent confined to performing housekeeping tasks rather than engaging in bodily care of the elderly, he seemed to have resolved to abandon any plans of re-maining in Japan for the sake of finding a job in Indonesia. He wanted a job where there would be 'no boss' to direct his actions and to deny him his value and usefulness as a human being. The fourth of eight siblings,

Jasir was thinking of disburdening his parents from running a fresh rise (*beres*; Ind.) shop. As already mentioned, from the first year in Japan, he had already begun discussing with his mother where to buy more space for a larger family enterprise that he would contribute to from his earnings in Japan, and which he would potentially take over. The business, he said, was not easy because there was a lot of competition, but since the demand for rice in Indonesia was unlikely to fall, Jasir was optimistic that he would be able to establish himself as an independent and successful shop owner.

At the time of his comments during our cycle through the rice fields, Amir was still unsure whether he would like to stay in Japan beyond the initial four years guaranteed under the EPA scheme. He continued thinking of building a house in Indonesia. Ultimately, he returned there in 2012 even though he had passed the Japanese national caregiver examination that granted him the right to remain and work in Japan. A son of a village leader, Amir had experienced what it meant to matter. Working as a caregiver in Japan was not that much of a problem in and of itself (although, as we have seen, it came with its own stigma and hardships), it was a job and one in which interpersonal relationships could be very rewarding. What bothered Amir, as it did Jasir, was the subsumption of himself as a viable person under the blanket of linguistic incomprehension, cultural differentiation and political-economic categorisations as 'migrant', or 'foreign worker' (*gaikokujin rōdōsha*; Jpn.), which obstructed his recognition as an individual. Like other candidates, he wanted to be *dihargai*, appreciated.

Lanny, Iffah and Lazim have also gone back. Although they did not pass the national examination, they are capitalising on their experience in Japan. While Lanny and Iffah are continuing their careers in care-related jobs (Iffah is lecturing at one of the health academies in Indonesia while Lanny is working as a nurse), Lazim took a position in one of the fifteen hundred Japanese companies operating in Indonesia. He is but one of about two hundred former EPA Indonesians who are believed to have been using their linguistic skills and work experience gained in Japan to initiate a career within Japanese businesses operating in Indonesia.

Daris is one of the 167 Indonesian caregiver candidates (up to 2013) who has succeeded in passing the national examination (MHLW 2013), but unlike Amir and Jasir decided to remain in Japan. After qualifying as a caregiver, he moved to a different institution in the same city where he now lives with his wife and a newborn baby. The life is easier, communication more effective, work less confusing, and his circle of friends larger and more mixed. Yet, for the most part he socialises with other

Indonesians, most of them Muslim as they are still the people with whom he feels most at ease. He is actively engaged in organising networking and mutual support activities for the continuously expanding number of EPA candidates, both nurses and caregivers. When I talked to him at the beginning of 2016, the plan was to remain in Japan given the educational opportunities it has to offer to his child.

Irdina also passed the examination. Following her initial plan, she has brought her family to Japan. She says she is happy now, and with the family living together, a circle of Japanese and Indonesian friends and a job where she has become more independent, this does not come as a surprise. When I visited her in September 2013, she seemed pleased with her life and optimistic about the future. Nonetheless, when relaying a story from work, Irdina noted that it is still difficult for her to get over certain limitations as an Indonesian. She concluded that *ternyata, di sini tidak boleh pintar* (Ind.), or apparently you are not allowed to be clever here. The differentiation between the Japanese and Indonesian staff and the extent of trust in the latter's judgement continues to influence Irdina's experiences.

The arguments throughout this book have revolved around the idea of intimacy. Intimacy has been evoked as a representation of a national community as well as a mode of interpersonal relationship. A perceived lack of intimacy, notably on a cultural level, has been shown to bring about conflicts, fears, frustrations, and negative stereotyping. As indeed has long been argued for Japan, so too in the case of the Indonesian workers' acceptance under the EPA, the construction of the foreigners' otherness was influenced by the potent intuitive theories that conflate the local notions of nationhood with the ideas of race, ethnicity and culture. These essentialising ideas, acting as discursive means for the exclusion of those deemed non-intimate, have been shown to guide the Japanese (but also the Indonesians) in their mutual encounters on a personal as well as on a national level.

As I was working on this book, a link to a TED Talk by Paul Bloom, a professor of psychology and cognitive science at Yale University, arrived in my mailbox. It appeared very timely. Bloom proposed that:

> Our ability to stereotype people is not some arbitrary quirk of mind, but rather it's a specific instance of a more general process, which is that we have experience with things, with people in the world that fall into categories, and we can use our experience to make generalisations about novel instances of these categories … [N]ow, we might be wrong … but for the most part we are good at this, for the most part we make good guesses both in a social domain and a non-social domain. And if we

weren't able to do so, if we weren't able to make guesses about new instances that we encounter, we wouldn't survive. (Bloom 2014)

What Bloom was arguing for was seeing stereotypisation as an activity that is quite common and not necessarily negatively charged, ill-intended or resulting in negative consequences. Rather, it is but one of the cognitive tools to organise and navigate the environing world. In everyday interactions with other people, or in the ways we engage with animals, objects and places, individuals are, as Anthony Giddens argued, 'knowledgeable *agents* who are capable of accounting for their action: they are neither "cultural dopes" nor mere "supports" of social relations, but are skilful actors who know a great deal about the world in which they act' (Thompson 1989: 58, emphasis in original). Such knowledgeability (Giddens 1979, 1984), however bounded, of the social milieu allows people to predict and interpret with a great degree of accuracy their surroundings, an ability that consequently informs their own conduct and facilitates avoidance of undesirable situations.[2] In this sense of a script informing action, culture, or Michael Herzfeld's more processual 'cultural engagement' (1997: 3), is the embodied knowledge obtained through repetition, which can be consciously or unconsciously applied and utilised in pursuing everyday life. It provides people with 'the continuity and reliability of familiar enactions [that] contribute to a sense of security "grounded in [the] experiences of predictable routines in time and space"' (Edensor 2002: 88, quoting Silverstone 1994). In this sense, one not only stereotypes and depersonalises those perceived as different (as we have seen, for example, in the lack of recognition of Indonesians and the elderly as comprehending human beings; see also Tajfel 1981, 1984), but we also stereotype those who are familiar and with whom we identify.[3] Merely trying to deconstruct or simply dismiss such stereotypes as false and overly simplifying runs a risk of omitting one significant impetus behind how people relate to one another.

Sarah Mahler in her book *Culture as Comfort* argues that through socialisation we learn a certain cultural order in which we 'find comfort … because, subconsciously, it makes most social interactions predictable' (Mahler 2013: 31). 'Learning culture', Mahler writes, 'is how repeated activities in everyday life – routines or, in anthropological terms, rituals … create *culturally specific* social contexts of predictability' (ibid.: 22, emphasis in original). Although he does not explicitly link the familiarity with the working of the environing world to comfort, Pierre Bourdieu, too, in explaining how cultural milieux offer a degree of certainty in social interactions, alludes to the preference for the known. He writes:

the dispositions durably inculcated by objective conditions (which science apprehends through statistical regularities as the probabilities objectively attached to a group or class) engender aspirations and practices objectively compatible with those objective requirements; the most improbable practices are excluded, either totally without examination, as *unthinkable*, or at the cost of the *double negation* which inclines agents to make a virtue of necessity, that is, to refuse what is anyway refused and to love the inevitable. (Bourdieu 1977: 77, emphases in original)

I read 'love of the inevitable' as an expression of preference for and comfort felt in experiencing the familiar. One young Indonesian woman commented on the differences she experienced between working in Japan and Indonesia: 'It differs a lot. Perhaps because the country and culture differ. When working in Japan, there are many things that differ – for example, communication and culture, which sometimes causes slight problems. Maybe if I worked in Indonesia, I would have felt safer and more comfortable, because it would have been my own country'. Such comfort is made possible thanks to the folk theories – stereotypical imaginations that render some situations, groups and individuals recognisable and/or similar to oneself. In the case of the Indonesian–Japanese encounters, the ideas of likeness that delineate who can and cannot be trusted were based on a conflation of cultural and racial imaginings, often collapsing physical – that is, bodily – and cultural representations. The EPA Indonesians were seen (and saw themselves) as dissimilar to the Japanese on all accounts, and therefore it was possible to infer their 'untrustworthiness' from this dissimilarity. In order for the likeness to have any rhetorical force (Herzfeld 1997: 56) in constructing the imagined national community that excludes the unfamiliar, it has to appear natural – that is, not constructed. Such a naturalising function is served by stereotyping and essentialist representations that have real effects on people's everyday actions and interactions.

However, as I hope has become clear from the accounts throughout the chapters, inside the Japanese eldercare homes that accepted the Indonesian care workers, such essentialising conceptualisations became complicated by (but also served as catalysts for) the development of intimate relationships on different levels of experience. These relationships allowed for attributes other than cultural to become the basis for mutual identifications that could then serve as alternative reference points in everyday interactions. Such reconfiguration of encounters, from being seen primarily in terms of cultural affinities (as was evident in the Indonesians' constructing an image of a head-driven Japanese, in the preparations of the eldercare homes for the candidates' arrival, in the reactions of some of the elderly to their presence, or indeed in the media discourses invoking 'diversity' and 'multicultural coexistence'), into encounters between individuals who are culturally different but, on other levels, possible to identify with, exposed the existence of a double register according to which the application of the established divisions between *us* and *them* became less straightforward. This double register resulted in the fluctuating mutual recognition of the Indonesian and Japanese viability as colleagues, friends and co-residents.

Such practical identifications stemmed from the nature of the tasks in which the Indonesians were involved in the care homes. Through crossing boundaries of the cared-for bodies, the Indonesian workers crossed boundaries between themselves and the Japanese carers on an individual, rather than a cultural, basis. These and other bodily engagements, such as in sport, overrode the saliency of cultural identifications and distinctions. The underlying non-verbal knowledge of the other person created through shared practices allowed for a greater affinity and an ever-expanding capacity for comprehension. The commonality of positioning within the hierarchy of a larger-scale organisation, be it an eldercare institution or a country, could also become a source of extra-cultural identification beyond any folk theorisation. This was, for example, visible in the alliances between the Indonesian workers and the elderly residents who shared their marginality in relation to those 'of power' within the institutions – that is, the Japanese staff who oversaw the lives of the elderly and who usually supervised the Indonesians. An identification was also found in the mutual self-recognition between the Indonesians and Japanese of a shared plight as care workers within the value system of a wider society. The care workers, through the direct, intimate nature of their involvement in the body-work of eldercare, shared in the knowledge of the practices placed 'beyond the limits of official discourse' (Twigg 2000a: 400). Perhaps not exactly class consciousness, but through being implicated in the transgressions of the bodily and social taboos associated with dirt and the limits of human bodies (Twigg 2000a) as a part of their everyday routines, the Indonesian and Japanese eldercare workers come to share a 'solidarity of the workgroup' (ibid.: 402) that was also based on their perceived as stigmatised, if rhetorically valued (Anderson 2010: 66), profession.

Such alliances should not be underestimated. It has been recognised that the so-called 'new elite' of professional world travellers find that they have more in common with each other – that is, with those who lead a similar lifestyle and perhaps have the same profession – than with their co-nationals. At the lower-earning echelons of societies the international movement of people has more often been represented in oppositional, or conflictual, terms. While indeed jobs and income might be less stable in lower-paying positions and among so-called manual, or low-skilled, workers and therefore more likely to lead to disgruntlement over economic rights and privileges, this does not have to imply a lack of possibility for workers to identify with each other across the national divisions often translated into, and sometimes stimulated by, cultural stereotypes. Such a possibility of identification was realised in the accepting eldercare homes.

At the same time, at the level of public discourse as reflected in the Japanese mainstream newspapers and a selected number of other media's reports on the EPA acceptance, the popular representation of the Japanese nation-state as culturally homogeneous (although not questioned on the grounds of its ideological nature) came to be reimagined in 'multicultural', 'internationalised' and 'diversified' terms. Such discursive reconstitution was apparent in the narratives of 'boring homogeneity' and 'revitalising diversity', in the propositions to 'internationalise the Japanese language', and in the representations of the Indonesian workers as compatible with the Japanese ideas of eldercare workers, and as possible to identify with.

This is not to say that the idea of the Japanese nation-state as culturally uniform has been done away with. The associations of foreigners with danger, social discord and perhaps even disgust (as in the opposition to the foreign hands touching Japanese bodies) were still powerful. The notion of a closed Japan has indeed been reflected in the very way the EPA acceptance came to be and in the schism between the governmental departments over the issue. The terms of the Indonesian workers' acceptance maintained a certain representational balance. This was achieved not only by allowing small numbers to train in Japan and presenting the scheme as an international assistance programme, but also by demanding that the candidates all be qualified nurses in the first round, and graduates in any specialisation at a high education level in the consecutive rounds. Presented as Indonesian 'elite' (*erīto*; Jpn.) and as *yūshū*, that is, 'excellent' or 'superior' (Jpn.), the EPA candidates were not simply unskilled and training to become professionals in Indonesia, and not really migrants, either. Through such means the EPA scheme fitted within the popularly recognised paradigm of Japan as a non-immigration country. As Bridget Anderson argued, 'states must be seen to prioritise the interests of the "nation" and "the people" in ways that go beyond simply a response to the demands of capital, [especially given that] "national interest" is bound up with "national identity"'(Anderson 2014: 31). The introduction of a small number of highly educated and to-be-qualified migrant workers who were to return to Indonesia in exchange for beneficial economic provisions, on paper, would not 'upset the country's mythical ethnic homogeneity' (Cornelius 1994: 396).

However, as we have seen, the presence of migrant workers in Japan has gained an additional dimension. It has come to be posed at the centre of the debates over the future definition of the Japanese nation-state in the face of ongoing demographic changes. Because the EPA Indonesian workers arrived in Japan to provide care for the elderly, they had to be assigned a status different to that of other migrants who were engaged in such activities as automobile production (rather than social re-production), or fishery. The difference in status, and the treatment the Indonesians received in Japan, consisted in their positioning as rather influential guests with a potential to turn into permanent dwellers, and therefore into members of the Japanese society, if not necessarily of the Japanese nation. Importantly, unlike those foreigners who worked, for example, in Japanese heavy industry, the EPA workers came to Japan to look after people. The Japanese government, while trying to maintain control over the intake of the EPA candidates, also took the responsibility for the outcome of the programme. When people arrive in another country and apply for jobs as individuals, the role of the state/government as a guardian of success and merit for the employers and employees alike is pushed to the background. In the case of the EPA, the state's role was very much exposed, and therefore expected to be fulfilled. Given the discourses of population crisis, and the ambivalent message that the EPA scheme's provisions sent about the 'opening' of Japan, the fulfilment of the government's role came to be seen in terms of the Indonesians' settlement in Japan. In a way, a policy aiming at containment of foreignness created accidental heroes (or martyrs) of Japan's continously-debated future.

Such positioning of the EPA acceptance affected the development of cordial relationships between the Indonesian candidates and their employers. Although partially predicated on the perceptions of cultural otherness, they also eventually came to be primarily a function of a professional engagement rather than a cultural negotiation. The difficulty of studying towards the examination set as one of the conditions of the EPA acceptance, the efforts to try and avert the anticipated failure to pass it, the shared frustration over the inability to count and be counted as workers equal to the Japanese personnel, the questioning of the very requirement to obtain the Japanese qualifications, the solitude of deployment, and other 'problems' stemming from the organisation of the acceptance created the shared feeling of being in it together. This brought the employers and the Indonesian candidates closer to each other, more than would have been possible were the Indonesian workers to have arrived unsolicited under widely available care worker visas (were such existent in Japan). Even if for different reasons, the Indonesian workers and their Japanese employers were involved in the same endeavour. Effectively, Japan's official attention to the national interest as articulated by Bridget Anderson (2014), cited above, prepared the ground for alliances that were to stand in opposition to these officially sanctioned representations.

As Lauren Berlant writes, 'intimacy builds worlds' (2000: 2). If multiculturalism is not to represent societies divided by sharply defined cultural enclaves, and integration is not to stand for flat-out assimilation, then there is a need for a platform on which people otherwise conceiving of themselves as different can identify. As was apparent in the experiences of the Indonesian EPA workers, their Japanese colleagues, the cared-for elderly, and the employers, bodily and interpersonal intimacies achieved through shared experiences and outlooks can become such a platform. Cultural non-intimates, therefore, do not need to 'absorb' one another, just as Anthony Giddens (1992: 94) suggests (although his thoughts refer specifically to a romantic relationship) in the quotation opening this Conclusion. Rather, they should acquire knowledge of one another. In Japan such knowledge-conveying platforms are formed particularly where, as was the case with the EPA candidates, foreigners are seeded in small numbers in local communities (see also Burgess 2008). There they have greater opportunities for person-to-person interactions and, therefore, for forging various intimacies on which to build mutual understanding and tolerance. As Nelson Graburn and John Ertl (2008: 23) suggest, in such specific settings cultural markers of identity may be increasingly less deterministic in constructing the social scapes of these settings. In fact, many of the ethnographic instances relayed in this book deal with something akin to what Kathleen Stewart (2007) has presented as 'ordinary affects'. For example, Stewart outlines a situation when, about to leave a roadside restaurant, two bikers explain that they have hit a deer and ask if she could help them look for bike parts on the road. This simple event engaged not only Stewart and the two bikers, but drew in the other clientele who had all been keeping to themselves up to this point. Just as in the roadside restaurant, where the initial approach by the bikers opened up 'a "we" of sorts in the room, charging the social with lines of potential' (ibid.: 11), so did the arrival of the Indonesian workers and their involvement in eldercare create a similar kind of conditions to break the surface tension of mutual recognition, making it possible for complete strangers to imagine each other as people with whom it was possible to engage. Such intimate imagination made it possible to see the other as being similar to oneself in particular respects, thus acknowledging their viability as a person in relation to the self.

There are now questions as to the legitimacy of the still-powerful discourses of homogeneity as constructing the Japanese reality that increasingly do not reflect the everyday experiences of the people at whom they are directed. Moreover, these discourses are perceived as potentially harmful to the future of the Japanese nation-state. In part, the basis for such questioning lies in direct personal experience, such as that made possible by the EPA acceptance. In his own work among factory workers, Michael Burawoy (1979: 18) proposes that ideology becomes 'a material force once it has gripped the masses', and he also points out that 'ideology is … not something manipulated at will by agencies of socialization – schools, family, church, and so on – in the interests of a dominant class. On the contrary, these institutions elaborate and systematize lived experience and only in this way become centers of ideological dissemination' (ibid.: 17). Despite their small numbers, the images of intimate encounters between the EPA Indonesian eldercare workers and their colleagues, the elderly residents and the employers reached the wider society through the mass media representations. The discourses reluctantly, and sometimes quite boldly, questioned the ideas of Japanese nationhood within the current political–economic and, arguably, demographic globalising processes. The eldercare institutions served as conduits for the dissemination of new viable visions of the Japanese society that, if sustained, could eventually open up the often-disabling and depersonalising imaginations of foreigners in Japan to wider scrutiny and recognise the already existent real-life diverse constellations of relationships.

Notes

1. The total numbers of EPA Indonesian and Filipino candidates who have arrived in Japan stated by the article do not correspond to the sums I calculated based on the tables published by the MHLW. Since no exact source is quoted by the article, I use the data I found on the publicly available MHLW website (MHLW 2014).
2. See Oliver and O'Reilly 2010 for an account of the sustained importance of readily intelligible behavioural clues for the organisation of one's social life amongst British lifestyle migrants in Spain; see also Turner 1999.
3. Such was also an argument on self-categorisation developed by social psychologist John C. Turner – see, for example, Turner 1999.

Bibliography

Allison, Anne. 1994. *Nightwork: Sexuality, Pleasure, and Corporate Masculinity in a Tokyo Hostess Club*. Chicago: University of Chicago Press.

Anderson, Benedict. 1983. *Imagined Communities: Reflections on the Origin and Spread of Nationalism*. London and New York: Verso.

Anderson, Bridget. 2000. *Doing the Dirty Work?: The Global Politics of Domestic Labour*. London and New York: Zed Books.

———. 2010. 'Mobilizing Migrants, Making Citizens: Migrant Domestic Workers as Political Agents', *Ethnic and Racial Studies* 33(1): 60–74.

———. 2011. 'Us and Them, or One of the Family? Migrant Domestic Workers in Private Households', *Making Connections: Migration, Gender and Care Labour in Transnational Context Conference, Oxford, 14-15 April 2011*. Oxford: Centre on Migration, Policy and Society.

———. 2014. 'Nation Building: Domestic Labour and Immigration Controls in the UK', in *Migration and Care Labour. Theory, Policy and Politics*, edited by Bridget Anderson and Isabel Shutes. Migration, Diasporas and Citizenship Series. Basingstoke: Palgrave MacMillan, pp. 31–48.

Ando, Haruhiko, and Etsuko Hasegawa. 1970. 'Drinking Patterns and Attitudes of Alcoholics and Nonalcoholics in Japan', *Quarterly Journal of Studies on Alcohol* 31(1-A): 153–61.

Asahi Shinbun. 2004. 'FTA Sōki Teiketsu, Hidaitōryō ni Yōbō' [A Request to the Philippine President for an Early Conclusion of FTA], 4 November.

———. 2006. 'Nippi Kyōtei Rōdō Kaikoku e Arata na Ippo' [Japan–Philippine Agreement: A New Step towards a Labour Open Country], 26 September.

———. 2009a. 'Indoneshiajin Kaigofukushishi Kōho, Kennai de 4 Nin Shūro "Sobo to Dōyō ni Kaigo" (Chiba)' [4 Indonesian Caregiver Candidates in the Prefecture 'Caring like after Grandmother'], 31 January.

———. 2009b. 'Ikoku Kaigo, Egao ga Sasae. Indoneshiajin Kaigofukushishi/ Kangoshi Kōhosha' [Care in a Foreign Country, Supported by Smiling Faces: Indonesian Caregiver and Nurse Candidates], 22 February.

———. 2009c. 'Yasashiku Akarui Ihō no Kenshūsei' [Kind and Cheerful Foreign Trainees]. *Koe* [Voice] *Column*, 13 March.

———. 2009d. '"Hataraku to Benkyō, Ganbaru" Egao to Tomadoi, Indoneshiajin Kaigoshi Kōho, Chakunin Ikkagetsu' ['I Do My Best to Work and Study' – Smiling Faces and Confusion – Indonesian Caregiver Candidates One Month into Employment], 27 March.

———. 2009e. 'EPA Kenshūsei. Nihon Teichaku e Hādoru Sagete' [EPA Trainees. Lower the Hurdle for Settling in Japan], Opinion Column, 2 April.

———. 2009f. 'Indoneshiajin Kaigofukushishi Kōhosha, Shisetsu no Kichō na Senryoku ni: Shokugyō Sankagetsu' [Indonesian Caregiver Candidates Becoming a Precious Strategy for Institutions: Three Months into Employment], 28 April.

———. 2009g. 'Oshieru Tachiba de Nihongo o Toraenaosu' [Re-evaluating Japanese Language from the Teaching Perspective], 23 July.

———. 2009h. 'Genba Marunage Shidōhō, Karikyuramu, Kijun Nashi' [Wholesale Delegation to the Accepting Sites. No Methods of Instruction, No Curriculum, No Standard], 2 November.

———. 2009i. 'Nayamu Byōin Jihi de Nihongo Kyōzai, Senjūshokuin mo Kango Kaigo Setsumeikai' [Troubled Hospitals. Japanese Language Materials and Specialised Staff at Their Own Expense. Nursing and Care Work Briefing Session], 26 November.

———. 2009j. 'Gaikokujin Kangoshi no Shiken Kaizen Teigen e. Shimin Dantai ga Osaka Suita de Shūkai' [Towards a Proposal to Improve the Examination for Foreign Nurses. Citizens Group Meets in Suita, Osaka], 29 November.

———. 2010. 'Jōyōkanji o Fuyasu na. Nihongo ga Horobiru. Zennihongo Gakkai Kaichō, Nomura Masa'aki' [Don't Increase the Number of Sino-Japanese Characters in Regular Use. Japanese Language Will Perish]. Former chairman of The Society for Japanese Linguistics, Nomura Masa'aki, 26 June.

Ashforth, Blake E., and Glen E. Kreiner. 1999. '"How Can You Do It?": Dirty Work and the Challenge of Constructing a Positive Identity', *Academy of Management Review* 24(3): 413–34.

Atsumi, Reiko. 1979. 'Tsukiai: Obligatory Personal Relationships of Japanese White-Collar Employees', *Human Organisation* 38(1): 63–70.

Befu, Harumi. 1971. *Japan: An Anthropological Introduction*. San Francisco: Chandler.

———. 1974. 'An Ethnography of Dinner Entertainment in Japan', *Arctic Anthropology* 11 (Supplement: Festschrift Issue in Honor of Chester S. Chard): 196–203.

———. 2001. *Hegemony of Homogeneity: An Anthropological Analysis of Nihonjinron*. Melbourne and Portland, OR: Trans Pacific Press.

Berlant, Lauren (ed.). 2000. *Intimacy*. Chicago and London: University of Chicago Press.

Bestor, Theodore C. 1989. *Neighbourhood Tokyo*. Studies of the East Asian Institute. Stanford, CA: Stanford University Press.

———. 2004. *Tsukiji: The Fish Market at the Centre of the World*. Berkeley and London: University of California Press.

Bethel, Diana Lynn. 1992a. 'Life on Obasuteyama, Or, Inside a Japanese Institution for the Elderly', in *Japanese Social Organisation*, edited by Takie Sugiyama Lebra. Honolulu: University of Hawaii Press, pp. 109–34.

———. 1992b. 'Alienation and Reconnection in a Home for the Elderly', in *Re-Made in Japan: Everyday Life and Consumer Taste in a Changing Society*, edited by Joseph J. Tobin. New Haven, CT and London: Yale University Press, pp. 126–42.

Bettio, Francesca, Annamaria Simonazzi and Paola Villa. 2006. 'The "Care Drain" in the Mediterranean: Notes on the Italian Experience Change in Care Regimes and Female Migration', *Journal of European Social Policy* 16(3): 271–85.

Bloom, Paul. 2014. 'Can Prejudice Ever Be a Good Thing?' TEDSalon New York, January. Available from: http://www.ted.com/talks/paul_bloom_can_prejudice_ever_be_a_good_thing?language=en [25 February 2015].

Bolton, Sharon C. 2005. 'Women's Work, Dirty Work: The Gynaecology Nurse as "Other"', *Gender, Work and Organization* 12(2): 169–86.

Borovoy, Amy. 2005. *The Too-Good Wife: Alcohol, Codependency, and the Politics of Nurturance in Postwar Japan*. Berkeley: University of California Press.

Bourdieu, Pierre. 1977. *Outline of the Theory of Practice*. Cambridge: Cambridge University Press.

Boyer, Pascal. 1996. 'What Makes Anthropomorphism Natural: Intuitive Ontology and Cultural Representations', *Journal of the Royal Anthropological Institute* 2(1): 83–97.

Brettell, Caroline B. 2003. *Anthropology and Migration: Essays on Transnationalism, Ethnicity, and Identity*. Walnut Creek, CA, Lanham, MD, New York and Oxford: Alta Mira Press.

Brubaker, Rogers. 2002. 'Ethnicity without Groups', *Archives Européennes de Sociologie* XLIII(2): 163–89.

Burawoy, Michael. 1979. *Manufacturing Consent: Changes in the Labor Process under Monopoly Capitalism*. Chicago and London: University of Chicago Press.

Burgess, Chris. 2008. '(Re)Constructing Boundaries: International Marriage Migrants in Yamagata as Agents of Multiculturalism', in *Multiculturalism in the New Japan: Crossing the Boundaries Within*, edited by Nelson H.H. Graburn, John Ertl and R. Kenji Tierney. New York and Oxford: Berghahn Books, pp. 63–81.

———. (2004) 2012. 'Maintaining Identities: Discourses of Homogeneity in a Rapidly Globalizing Japan', *Electronic Journal of Contemporary Japanese Studies*.

Candea, Matei. 2010. '"I Fell in Love with Carlos the Meerkat": Engagement and Detachment in Human–Animal Relations', *American Ethnologist* 37(2): 241–58.

Cangiano, Alessio, et al. 2009. *Migrant Care Workers in Ageing Societies: Research Findings in the United Kingdom*. Report. Oxford: Centre on Migration, Policy and Society.

Carvalho, Daniela de. 2003. 'Nikkei Communities in Japan', in *Global Japan: The Experiences of Japan's New Immigrants and Overseas Communities*, edited by Roger Goodman et al. London and New York: RoutledgeCurzon, pp. 195–208.

Chapman, David. 2008. *Zainichi Korean Identity and Ethnicity*. New York: Routledge.

Chin, Christine B.N. 1997. 'Walls of Silence and Late Twentieth-Century Representations of the Foreign Female Domestic Worker: The Case of Filipina and Indonesian Female Servants in Malaysia', *International Migration Review* 31(2): 353–85.

Christensen, Paul A. 2014. *Japan, Alcoholism, and Masculinity: Suffering Sobriety in Tokyo*. Lanham, MD: Lexington Books.

Clark, Scott. 1994. *Japan: A View from the Bath*. Honolulu: University of Hawaii Press.

Clifford, James. 1986. 'Introduction: Partial Truths', in *Writing Culture: The Poetics and Politics of Ethnography*, edited by James Clifford and George E. Marcus. Berkeley, Los Angeles and London: University of California Press, pp. 1–26.

Clough, Roger. 1981. *Old Age Homes*. London, Boston and Sydney: George Allen & Unwin.

Constable, Nicole. 2009. 'The Commodification of Intimacy: Marriage, Sex, and Reproductive Labour', *Annual Review of Anthropology* 38: 49–64.

Cornelius, Wayne A. 1994. 'Japan: The Illusion of Immigration Control', in *Controlling Immigration: A Global Perspective*, edited by Wayne A. Cornelius, Philip L. Martin and James Frank Hollifield. Stanford, CA: Stanford University Press, pp. 375–410.

Coulmas, Florian. 2007. *Population Decline and Ageing in Japan: The Social Consequences*. New York: Routledge.

Coulmas, Florian, and Ralph Lützeler (eds). 2011. *Imploding Populations in Japan and Germany: A Comparison*. International Comparative Studies Series. Leiden and Boston: Brill.

Croll, Elisabeth J. 2008. 'The Intergenerational Contract in the Changing Asian Family', in *Ageing in Asia*, edited by Roger Goodman and Sarah Harper. London and New York: Routledge Taylor & Francis Group, pp. 100–18.

Dahle, Rannveig. 2005. 'Men, Bodies and Nursing', in *Gender, Bodies and Work*, edited by David Morgan, Berit Brandth and Elin Kvande. Aldershot and Burlington, VT: Ashgate Publishing, pp. 127–38.

Denoon, Donald, et al. (eds). 1996. *Multicultural Japan: Palaeolithic to Postmodern*. Cambridge: Cambridge University Press.

Diamond, Timothy. 1992. *Making Grey Gold: Narratives of Nursing Home Care*. Women in Culture and Society. Chicago and London: University of Chicago Press.

Dijk, Teun A. van. 2006. 'Discourse and Manipulation', *Discourse and Society* 17(3): 359–83.

Douglas, Mary. 1966. *Purity and Danger: An Analysis of the Concepts of Pollution and Taboo*. London and New York: Routledge.

——— (ed.). 1987. *Constructive Drinking: Perspectives on Drink from Anthropology*. Cambridge: Cambridge University Press.

Douglass, Mike, and Glenda S. Roberts (eds). 2000. *Japan and Global Migration: Foreign Workers and the Advent of a Multicultural Society*. London and New York: Routledge.

Dunlop, Margaret J. 1986. 'Is a Science of Caring Possible?', *Journal of Advanced Nursing* 11(6): 661–70.

Dyer, S., L. McDowell and A. Batnitzky. 2008. 'Emotional Labour/Body Work: The Caring Labours of Migrants in the UK's National Health Service', *Geoforum* 39(6): 2030–38.

Eagleton, Terry. 2000. *The Idea of Culture*. Oxford: Blackwell.

Eco, Umberto. 1976. *A Theory of Semiotics*. Bloomington: Indiana University Press.

Edensor, Tim. 2002. *National Identity, Popular Culture and Everyday Life*. Oxford and New York: Berg.

Edwards, Walter Drew. 1989. *Modern Japan Through Its Weddings: Gender, Person, and Society in Ritual Portrayal*. Stanford, CA: Stanford University Press.

Ehrenreich, Barbara, and Arlie Russell Hochschild (eds). 2002. *Global Woman: Nannies, Maids, and Sex Workers in the New Economy*. New York: Owl Books.

Embree, John F. (1939) 1946. *Suye Mura: A Japanese Village*. London: Kegan Paul.

England, Kim, and Bernadette Stiell. 1997. '"They Think You're as Stupid as Your English Is": Constructing Foreign Domestic Workers in Toronto', *Environment and Planning A* 29(2): 195–215.

Faier, Lieba. 2009. *Intimate Encounters: Filipina Women Remaking Rural Japan*. Berkeley, Los Angeles and London: University of California Press.

Finch, Janet, and Dulcie Groves (eds). 1983. *A Labour of Love: Women, Work and Caring*. London, Boston and Melbourne: Routledge & Kegan Paul.

Fine, Michael, and Caroline Glendinning. 2005. 'Dependence, Independence or Inter-Dependence? Revisiting the Concepts of "Care" and "Dependency"', *Ageing and Society* 25(4): 601–21.

Fisher, Lucy T., and Miliann Kang. 2013. 'Reinventing Dirty Work: Immigrant Women in Nursing Homes', in *Immigrant Women Workers in the Neoliberal Age: Interdisciplinary Perspectives on an Underrepresented Labor Force*, edited by Anna Flores-González et al. Urbana, Chicago and Springfield: University of Illinois Press, pp. 164–85.

Flowers, Petrice R. 2012. 'From Kokusaika to Tabunka Kyōsei', *Critical Asian Studies* 44(4): 515–42.

Folbre, Nancy, and Julie A. Nelson. 2000. 'For Love or Money – or Both?', *Journal of Economic Perspectives* 14(4): 123–40.

Foner, Nancy. 1994. *The Caregiving Dilemma: Work in an American Nursing Home*. Berkeley, Los Angeles and London: University of California Press.

Fox, Nick J. 1999. *Beyond Health: Postmodernism and Embodiment*. London: Free Association Books.

Friebe, Jens. 2011. 'Care for the Elderly and Demographic Change: Ageing and Migrant Nurses in the German State of North Rhine-Westphalia', in *Imploding Populations in Japan and Germany: A Comparison*, edited by Florian Coulmas and Ralph Lützeler. Leiden and Boston: Brill, pp. 347–60.

Fukihara, Yutaka. 2009. 'Nihon e no Kanshin to Nihongo Gakushū. Indoneshia ni Okeru Nihongo Kyōiku no Kadai' [Interest in Japan and Japanese Language Learning: The Issue of Japanese Language Education in Indonesia], in *Nihon no Indoneshiajin Shakai. Kokusai Idō to Kyōsei no Kadai* [Indonesian Community in Japan: Questions of International Mobility and Coexistence], ed. Mika Okushima. Tokyo: Akashi Shoten, pp. 69–84.

Fukushi Shinbun. 2008. 'Indoneshia Kangoshi Kōho, Kaigofukushishi Kōho Ukeire Kikan Ichiran' [List of Institutions Accepting Indonesian Nurse and Cargiver Candidates], 18 August.

Furuya, Tokurō. 2009. 'EPA (Keizai Renkei Kyōtei) ni Okeru Shizenjin no Idō Kōshō' [Negotiations Regarding Movement of Natural Persons under EPA (Economic Partnership Agreement)]. Abstract. In *Spring Conference 2009*.

Imin Seisaku Gakkai [Japan Association for Migrant Policy Studies]. Tokyo: Waseda University.

Gelman, Susan A., and Cristine H. Legare. 2011. 'Concepts and Folk Theories', *Annual Review of Anthropology* 40: 379–98.

Giddens, Anthony. 1979. *Central Problems in Social Theory: Action, Structure and Contradiction in Social Analysis*. London: Macmillan / Berkeley: University of California Press.

———. 1992. *The Transformation of Intimacy: Sexuality, Love and Eroticism in Modern Societies*. Cambridge: Polity.

———. (1984) 2011. *The Constitution of Society: Outline of the Theory of Structuration*. Cambridge: Polity.

Gil-White, Francisco J. 2001. 'Are Ethnic Groups Biological "Species" to the Human Brain? Essentialism in Our Cognition of Some Social Categories', *Current Anthropology* 42(4): 515–53.

Glenn, Evelyn Nakano. 1992. 'From Servitude to Service Work: The Historical Continuities of Women's Paid and Unpaid Reproductive Labor', *Signs: Journal of Women in Culture and Society* 18(1): 1–44.

Goffman, Erving. 1961. *Asylums: Essays on the Social Situations of Mental Patients and Other Inmates*. Oxford: Anchor.

Goodman, Roger. 1990. *Japan's 'International Youth': The Emergence of a New Class of Schoolchildren*. Oxford: Clarendon Press.

———. 2008. 'Afterword: Marginals, Minorities and Migrants – Studying the Japanese Borderlands in Contemporary Japan', in *Transcultural Japan: At the Borderlands of Race, Gender and Identity*, edited by David Blake Willis and Stephen Murphy-Shigematsu. London and New York: Routledge Taylor & Francis Group, pp. 325–33.

Goodman, Roger, and Sarah Harper. 2008a. 'Introduction: Asia's Position in the New Global Demography', in *Ageing in Asia*. London and New York: Routledge Taylor & Francis Group, pp. 1–13.

——— (eds). 2008b. *Ageing in Asia*. London and New York: Routledge Taylor & Francis Group.

Goodman, Roger, et al. (eds). 2003. *Global Japan: The Experiences of Japan's New Immigrants and Overseas Communities*. London and New York: RoutledgeCurzon.

Gottlieb, Nanette (ed.). 2012. *Language and Citizenship in Japan*. New York: Routledge.

Graburn, Nelson H.H., and John Ertl. 2008. 'Introduction: Internal Boundaries and Models of Multiculturalism in Contemporary Japan', in *Multiculturalism in the New Japan: Crossing the Boundaries Within*, Asian Anthropologies Vol. 6, edited by Nelson H.H. Graburn, John Ertl and R. Kenji Tierney. New York and Oxford: Berghahn Books, pp. 1–31.

Graburn, Nelson H.H., John Ertl and R. Kenji Tierney (eds). 2008. *Multiculturalism in the New Japan: Crossing the Boundaries Within*. Asian Anthropologies. Vol. 6. New York and Oxford: Berghahn Books.

Graham, Hilary. 1983. 'Caring: Labour of Love', in *A Labour of Love: Women, Work and Caring*, edited by Janet Finch and Dulcie Groves. London: Routledge, pp. 13–30.

――――. 1991. 'The Concept of Caring in Feminist Research: The Case of Domestic Service', *Sociology* 25(1): 61–78.

Gubrium, Jaber F. 1975. *Living and Dying at Murray Manor*. London and New York: St. Martin's Press.

――――. 1995. *Speaking of Life: Horizons of Meaning for Nursing Home Residents*. New York: Aldine de Gruyter.

Hannerz, Ulf. 2003. 'Being There… and There… and There! Reflections on Multi-Site Ethnography', *Ethnography* 4(2): 201–16.

Haswidi, Andi. 2007. 'EPA Offers Opportunities and Challenges', *The Jakarta Post*, 20 August.

Henderson, J. Neil. 1995. 'The Culture of Care in a Nursing Home: Effects of a Medicalized Model of Long-Term Care', in *The Culture of Long-Term Care: Nursing Home Ethnography*, edited by J. Neil Henderson and Maria D. Vesperi. Westport, CT and London: Bergin & Garvey, pp. 37–54.

Hendry, Joy. 1994. 'Drinking and Gender in Japan', in *Gender, Drink and Drugs*, edited by Maryon McDonald. Oxford and New York: Berg, pp. 175–90.

――――. 1995. *Wrapping Culture: Politeness, Presentation, and Power in Japan and Other Societies*. Oxford Studies in the Anthropology of Cultural Forms. Oxford: Oxford University Press.

Henry, Jules. 1963. *Culture Against Man*. New York: Vintage.

Herzfeld, Michael. 1997. *Cultural Intimacy: Social Poetics in the Nation-State*. New York and London: Routledge.

Hester, Jeffry T. 2008. 'Datsu Zainichi-Ron: An Emerging Discourse on Belonging among Ethnic Koreans in Japan', in *Multiculturalism in the New Japan: Crossing the Boundaries Within*, edited by Nelson H.H. Graburn, John Ertl and R. Kenji Tierney. Asian Anthropologies. Vol. 6. New York and Oxford: Berghahn Books, pp. 139–50.

Higler, M. Inez. 1971. *Together with the Ainu: A Vanishing People*. Norman: University of Oklahoma Press.

Hochschild, Arlie Russell. 2001. 'Global Care Chains and Emotional Surplus Value', in *On the Edge: Living with Global Capitalism*, edited by Anthony Giddens and Will Hutton. London: Vintage, pp. 130–46.

――――. (1983) 2012. *The Managed Heart: Commercialization of Human Feeling*. Berkeley, Los Angeles and London: University of California Press.

Huang, Shirlena, Brenda S. Yeoh and Mika Toyota. 2012. 'Caring for the Elderly: The Embodied Labour of Migrant Care Workers in Singapore', *Global Networks* 12(2): 195–215.

Hughes, Everett Cherrington. 1962. 'Good People and Dirty Work', *Social Problems* 10(1): 3–11.

Idei, Yasuhiro. 2009. *Chōju Taikoku no Kyokō. Gaikokujin Kaigofukushishi no Genba o Ou* [The Fiction of the Great Nation of Longevity: Following the Reality of Foreign Caregivers]. Tokyo: Shinchosha.

IPSS (National Institute of Population and Social Security Research). 2012. 'Population Projections for Japan (January 2012): 2011 to 2060'. Appendix: Auxiliary Projections 2061 to 2110. National Institute of Population and Social Security Research. Available from: http://www.ipss.go.jp/site-ad/index_english/esuikei/ppfj2012.pdf [6 January 2014].

Isaksen, Lise Widding. 2002. 'Toward a Sociology of (Gendered) Disgust: Images of Bodily Decay and the Social Organisation of Care Work', *Journal of Family Issues* 23(7): 791–811.

———. 2005. 'Gender and Care: The Role of Cultural Ideas of Dirt and Disgust', in *Gender, Bodies and Work*, edited by David Morgan, Berit Brandth and Elin Kvande. Aldershot and Burlington, VT: Ashgate, pp. 115–26.

Japan Economic Research Institute [Nihon Keizai Chōsa Kyōgikai]. 2008. 'Gaikokujin Rōdōsha Ukeire Seisaku no Kadai to Hōkō. Atarashii Ukeire Shisutemu o Teian Suru' [The Issue and Direction of the Foreign Workers' Acceptance Policy – Proposing a New Acceptance System]. Research Report 2008-1. Tokyo: Japan Economic Research Institute.

Jervis, Lori L. 2001. 'The Pollution of Incontinence and the Dirty Work of Caregiving in a U.S. Nursing Home', *Medical Anthropology Quarterly New Series* 15(1): 84–99.

JICWELS (Japan International Corporation of Welfare Services). 2008. 'Indoneshiajin Kangoshi Kaigofukushishi Jinzai Manejimento Tebiki' [The Indonesian Nurse and Caregiver Human Resources Management Manual]. Tokyo: JICWELS.

———. 2009. 'Indoneshiajin Kangoshi Kaigofukushishi Ukeire Wakugumi. Koyō Keiyaku Teiketsu kara Shisetsunai Kenshū Koyō Kanri made no Tebiki (Kaigofukushishi Kōsu)' [Indonesian Nurse and Caregiver Acceptance Framework. From Employment Contract to Training and Employment Supervision in Institutions Manual (Caregiver Course)]. Tokyo: JICWELS.

Kang, Sangjung. 2003. 'Ethnic Minority Citizenship and the Japanese Constitution', in *Constitution and Human Rights in a Global Age: An Asia Pacific Perspective (Conference Papers)*, edited by Tessa Morris-Suzuki. Canberra: Australian National University, pp. 103–8.

Kapferer, Bruce. (1988) 2012. *Legends of People, Myths of State: Violence, Intolerance, and Political Culture in Sri Lanka and Australia*. New and Revised Edition. Smithsonian Series in Ethnographic Inquiry. Washington, DC: Smithsonian Institute Press.

Kawaguchi, Yoshichika, Yuko O. Hirano and Shun Ōno. 2008. 'Nihon Zenkoku no Byōin ni Okeru Gaikokujin Kangoshi Ukeire ni kan suru Chōsa (Dai Ippō). Kekka no Gaiyō' [A Nationwide Survey on Acceptance of Foreign Nurses in Japan's Hospitals (1): An Outline of the Results], in *Kyūshū Daigaku Ajia Sōgō Seisaku Sentā Kiyō* 3: 53–58.

Kayser-Jones, Jeanie Schmit. 1990. *Old, Alone, and Neglected: Care of the Aged in Scotland and the United States*. Comparative Studies of Health Systems and Medical Care. Berkeley: University of California Press.

Ko, Mika. 2009. *Japanese Cinema and Otherness: Nationalism, Multiculturalism and the Problem of Japaneseness*. Sheffield Centre for Japanese Studies/Routledge Series. London: Routledge.

Kono, Shigemi. 2011. 'Confronting the Demographic Trilemma of Low Fertility, Ageing and Depopulation', in *Imploding Populations in Japan and Germany: A Comparison*, edited by Florian Coulmas and Ralph Lützeler. Leiden and Boston: Brill, pp. 35–53.

Kreiner, Glen E., Blake E. Ashforth and David M. Sluss. 2006. 'Identity Dynamics in Occupational Dirty Work: Integrating Social Identity and System Justification Perspectives', *Organization Science* 17(5): 619–36.

Kundani, Arun. 2002. 'The Death of Multiculturalism', *Race and Class* 43(4): 67–72.

Kymlicka, Will. 2012. *Multiculturalism: Success, Failure, and the Future.* Washington, DC: Migration Policy Institute.

Laird, Carobeth. 1979. *Limbo: A Memoir about Life in a Nursing Home by a Survivor.* Novato, CA: Chandler & Sharp.

Lawler, Jocalyn. 1991. *Behind the Screens: Nursing, Somology and the Problem of the Body.* Melbourne: Churchill Livingstone.

———. 1997. *The Body in Nursing: A Collection of Views.* Melbourne: Churchill Livingstone.

Lawton, Julia. 1998. 'Contemporary Hospice Care: The Sequestration of the Unbounded Body and "Dirty Dying"', *Sociology of Health and Illness* 20(2): 121–43.

Lebra, Takie Sugiyama. 1976. *Japanese Patterns of Behavior.* Honolulu: University of Hawaii Press.

———. 2004. *The Japanese Self in Cultural Logic.* Honolulu: University of Hawaii Press.

Lee-Treweek, Geraldine. 1996. 'Emotional Labour, Order and Emotional Power in Care Assistant Work', in *Health and the Sociology of Emotions*, edited by Veronica James and Jonathan Gabe. Sociology of Health and Illness Monographs. Oxford: Wiley-Blackwell, pp. 115–32.

———. 1997. 'Women, Resistance and Care: An Ethnographic Study of Nursing Auxiliary Work', *Work, Employment and Society* 11(1): 47–63.

Liebelt, Claudia. 2011. *Caring for the 'Holy Land': Filipina Domestic Workers in Israel.* New York and Oxford: Berghahn Books.

Lie, John. 2000. 'The Discourse of Japaneseness', in *Japan and Global Migration: Foreign Workers and the Advent of a Multicultural Society*, edited by Mike Douglass and Glenda S. Roberts. London and New York: Routledge Taylor & Francis Group, pp. 70–90.

———. 2001. *Multiethnic Japan.* Cambridge, MA and London: Harvard University Press.

Lindquist, Johan A. 2009. *The Anxieties of Mobility: Migration and Tourism in the Indonesian Borderlands.* Honolulu: University of Hawaii Press.

Linger, Daniel Touro. 2001. *No One Home: Brazilian Selves Remade in Japan.* Stanford, CA: Stanford University Press.

Litwin, Howard, and Claudine Attias-Donfut. 2009. 'The Inter-Relationship between Formal and Informal Care: A Study in France and Israel', *Ageing and Society* 29(1): 71–91.

Lopez, Mario. 2012. 'Reconstituting the Affective Labour of Filipinos as Care Workers in Japan', *Global Networks* 12(2): 252–68.

Lovebond, Anna. 2003. 'Positioning the Product: Indonesian Migrant Women Workers in Contemporary Taiwan', *Southeast Asia Research Centre Working Papers*, Series 43.

Lutz, Helma (ed.). 2008. *Migration and Domestic Work: A European Perspective on a Global Theme.* Aldershot: Ashgate.

Lyon, Dawn. 2010. 'Intersections and Boundaries of Work and Non-Work: The Case of Eldercare in Comparative European Perspective', *European Societies* 12(2): 163–85.

Mahler, Sarah J. 1995. *American Dreaming: Immigrant Life on the Margins.* Princeton, NJ and Chichester: Princeton University Press.

———. 2013. *Culture as Comfort: Many Things You Know About Culture (But Might Not Realize).* Upper Saddle River, NJ: Prentice Hall.

Mandel, Ruth. 2008. *Cosmopolitan Anxieties: Turkish Challenges to Citizenship and Belonging in Germany.* Durham, NC and London: Duke University Press.

Martin, Ernst. 1995. 'Communication in Asian Job Interviews', in *Communicating Organisational Change: A Management Perspective,* edited by Donald Peter Cushman and Sarah Sanderson King. SUNY Series in International Management. Albany, NY: State University of New York Press, pp. 275–310.

Mason, Lynn D. 1995. 'Ethnography and the Nursing Home Ombudsman', in *The Culture of Long-Term Care: Nursing Home Ethnography,* edited by J. Neil Henderson and Maria D. Vesperi. Westport, CT and London: Bergin & Garvey, pp. 71–91.

Massey, Douglas S., et al. 1993. 'Theories of International Migration: A Review and Appraisal', *Population and Development Review* 19: 431–66.

McConnell, David L. 2000. *Importing Diversity: Inside Japan's JET Program.* Berkeley, Los Angeles and London: University of California Press.

McNeill, David. 2005. '"I Just Want to Make Japan a Better Place to Live": Korean National Blocked from Promotion by Tokyo Government Vows to Fight On', *The Asia-Pacific Journal: Japan Focus.*

MHLW (Ministry of Health, Labour and Welfare). 2003. '2015 Nen no Kōreisha Kaigo: Kōreisha no Songen o Sasaeru Kea no Kakuritsu ni Mukete' [Eldercare in 2015: Towards Establishing Care Supporting Dignity of the Elderly]. Available from: http://www.mhlw.go.jp/topics/kaigo/kentou/15k-ourei/3.html#1 [11 November 2013].

———. 2010. 'Indoneshiajin Kaigofukushishi Kōhosha Ukeire Jittai Chōsa no Kekka ni Tsuite' [Survey Results on the Current Status of the Indonesian Caregiver Candidates' Acceptance]. Available from: http://www.mhlw.go.jp/stf/houdou/2r985200000054my.html [5 April 2012].

———. 2013. 'Nyūkoku Nendobetsu Kōhosha no Ruiseki Gōkakuritsu' [Accumulative Pass Rate by Year or Arrival]. Media Release. Available from: http://www.mhlw.go.jp/file/04-Houdouhappyou-12004000-Shakaiengokyo-ku-Shakai-Fukushikibanka/0000041987.pdf [14 January 2015].

———. 2014. 'Indoneshia, Firipin, Betonamu kara no Gaikokujin Kangoshi, Kaigo Kōhosha no Ukeire ni Tsuite' [About the Acceptance of the Nurse and Caregiver Candidates from Indonesia, the Philippines and Vietnam]. Available from: http://www.mhlw.go.jp/stf/seisakunitsuite/bunya/koyou_roudou/koyou/gaikokujin/other22/index.html [14 January 2015].

Milligan, Christine. 2003. 'Location or Dis-Location? Towards a Conceptualization of People and Place in the Care-Giving Experience', *Social & Cultural Geography* 4(4): 455–70.

Moeran, Brian. 1998. 'One over the Seven: Sake Drinking in a Japanese Pottery Community', in *Interpreting Japanese Society: Anthropological Approaches,* edited by Joy Hendry. London: Routledge, pp. 243–58.

————. 2005. 'Drinking Country: Flows of Exchange in a Japanese Valley', in *Drinking Cultures: Alcohol and Identity*, edited by Thomas M. Wilson. New York: Berg, pp. 25–42.

Momsen, Janet Henshall. 1999. *Gender, Migration and Domestic Work*. London: Routledge.

Mori, Junko. 2006. 'The Workings of the Japanese Token Hee in Informing Sequences: An Analysis of Sequential Context, Turn Shape, and Prosody', *Journal of Pragmatics* 38(8): 1175–205.

Mori, Kathryn, and Carolyn Scearce. 2010. 'Robot Nation and the Declining Japanese Population'. ProQuest Discovery Guides. Available from: http://www.csa.com/discoveryguides/robots/review.pdf [25 March 2014].

Morita, Toyoko. 2003. 'Iranian Immigrant Workers in Japan and their Networks', in *Global Japan: The Experiences of Japan's New Immigrants and Overseas Communities*, edited by Roger Goodman et al. London: Routledge, pp. 159–64.

Morris-Suzuki, Tessa. 1998. *Re-Inventing Japan: Time, Space, Nation*. Armonk, NY: M.E. Sharpe.

————. 2006. 'Invisible Immigrants: Undocumented Migration and Border Controls in Early Postwar Japan', *The Asia-Pacific Journal: Japan Focus*.

NHK (Japan Broadcasting Corporation). 2006. 'Nihon no Kango to Kaigo Genba ni Gaikokujin o Ukeireru Beki Ka' [Should Foreigners be Accepted to Japanese Nursing and Care Sites?]. Available from: http://www.nhk.or.jp/bsdebate/0610/data.html [17 November 2009].

————. 2009. 'Teichaku Suru Ka? Gaikokujin no Kaigo/Kango' [Will They Settle? Foreigners' Care and Nursing]. Available from: http://www.nhk.or.jp/hitokoto/archives/archives2009/200911/archives20091110.html [23 November 2009].

Nikkei (Nihon Keizai Shinbun). 2008. 'Rōdō Sakoku Dakkyaku e Ippo: Kango/Kaigo Bunya Jinzai Ukeire' [A Step towards Escaping from a Labour Closed Country: Acceptance of Human Resources in Nursing and Care], 17 May.

————. 2009a. 'Indoneshiajin Kaigoshi "Shinpai Muyō": Shigotoburi Junchō – Riyōsha to Hazumu Kōryū' ['No Need to Worry' about Indonesian Care Workers: Work Going Well – Lively Interaction with Service Users], 23 January.

————. 2009b. 'Indoneshiajin Kaigoshi no Tamago, EPA de Shokugyō Ikkagetsu "Kichō na Senryoku" Funtōchū' [Indonesian Care Workers in the Making, 'Precious Strategy' Struggle One Month into Employment under EPA], 9 March.

————. 2009c. 'Kangoshi e no Michi, Gaikokujin, Kabe ni Chokumen – Taisaku wa Shisetsu Makase, Keitōteki Ikusei ga Hitsuyō' [A Road to Nursing, Foreigners Facing a Wall – Measures Left to the Institutions, Systematic Cultivation Is Needed], 27 September.

————. 2009d. 'Kokka Senryaku o Tou Jinkō Kiki. Sakete Tōrenu Imin Seisaku' [Population Crisis Questioning National Strategy. Unavoidable Immigration Policy], 28 September.

————. 2009e. 'Nikkei Burajirujin Kaigo Genba e, Kōreisha Kangei, Kadai wa Gogakuryoku, Fukyō de Seizōgyō kara Tenshoku' [Nikkei Brazilians

Turn to Care Work. The Elderly are Welcoming. The Problem, Language Proficiency, Changing Jobs due to Recession], 19 October.

——. 2010a. 'Gaikokujin Kōdo Jinzai, Ukeire Sokushin. Shutsunyū Kanri Kihon Keikaku' [Promotion of Acceptance of High-Grade Foreign Human Resources. Basic Plan for Immigration Control], 30 June.

——. 2010b. 'TPP Sanka e Jinzai Sakoku ya Kisei mo Minaose' [Reconsider Human Resources Closed Country and Regulations. Towards Participation in TPP], 10 November.

Nishikawa, Makiko, and Kazuko Tanaka. 2007. 'Are Care Workers Knowledge Workers?', in *Gendering the Knowledge Economy: Comparative Perspectives*, edited by Sylvia Walby et al. London: Palgrave Macmillan, pp. 207–27.

Nissōnet, Kabushiki Gaisha. 2008. 'News Release'. Available from: http://www.nissonet.co.jp/pdf/news_080924.pdf [25 February 2010].

Oguma, Eiji. 2002. *A Genealogy of 'Japanese' Self-Images*. Melbourne: Trans Pacific Press.

Okushima, Mika (ed.). 2009. *Nihon no Indoneshiajin Shakai. Kokusai Idō to Kyōsei no Kadai* [Indonesian Community in Japan: Questions of International Mobility and Coexistence]. Tokyo: Akashi Shoten.

Oliver, Caroline. 2008. *Retirement Migration: Paradoxes of Ageing*. London and New York: Routledge.

——. 2011. 'Pastures New or Old? Migration, Narrative and Change', *Anthropologica* 53(1): 67–77.

Oliver, Caroline, and Karen O'Reilly. 2010. 'A Bourdieusian Analysis of Class and Migration: Habitus and the Individualising Process', *Sociology* 44(1): 49–66.

Onishi, Akiko. 2008. '"Becoming a Better Muslim": Identity Narratives of Muslim Foreign Workers in Japan', in *Transcultural Japan: At the Borderlands of Race, Gender and Identity*, edited by David Blake Willis and Stephen Murphy-Shigematsu. London and New York: Routledge Taylor & Francis Group, pp. 217–36.

Parreñas, Rhacel Salazar. 2001. *Servants of Globalisation*. Stanford, CA: Stanford University Press.

——. 2011. *Illicit Flirtations: Labor, Migration, and Sex Trafficking in Tokyo*. Stanford, CA: Stanford University Press.

Parreñas, Rhacel, and Eileen Boris. 2010. *Intimate Labors: Cultures, Technologies, and the Politics of Care*. Stanford, CA: Stanford University Press.

Parsons, Talcott. 1951. *The Social System*. England: Routledge & Kegan Paul.

Phizacklea, Annie, and Bridget Anderson. 1997. *Migrant Domestic Workers: A European Perspective*. Brussels: Equal Opportunities Unit, European Commission.

Polanyi, Karl. 2001. *The Great Transformation: The Political and Economic Origins of Our Time*. Boston: Beacon Press.

Puwar, Nirmal. 2004. *Space Invaders: Race, Gender and Bodies Out of Place*. Oxford and New York: Berg.

Qureshi, Hazel. 1996. 'Obligations and Support within Families', in *The New Generational Contract: Intergenerational Relations, Old Age and Welfare*, edited by Alan Walker. London and Bristol, PA: University College London Press, pp. 101–20.

Ringmar, Erik. 1998. 'The Idiocy of Intimacy', *The British Journal of Sociology* 49(4): 534–49.

Roberson, James E. 1998. *Japanese Working Class Lives: An Ethnographic Study of Factory Workers*. London and New York: Routledge.

Roberts, Glenda S. 1994. *Staying On The Line: Blue-Collar Women in Contemporary Japan*. Honolulu: University of Hawaii Press.

Roth, Joshua Hotaka. 2002. *Brokered Homeland: Japanese Brazilian Migrants in Japan*. The Anthropology of Contemporary Issues. Ithaca, NY and London: Cornell University Press.

Rudnyckyj, Radomir. 2004. 'Technologies of Servitude: Governmentality and Indonesian Transnational Labour Migration', *Anthropological Quarterly* 77(3): 407–34.

Russ, Ann Julienne. 2005. 'Love's Labor Paid For: Gift and Commodity at the Threshold of Death', *Cultural Anthropology* 20: 128–55.

Sahlins, Marshall. 2005. *Culture in Practice. Selected Essays*. New York: Zone Books.

Sakanaka, Hidenori. 2005. *Nyūkan Senki* [Immigration Battle Diary]. Tokyo: Kodansha. Also available in abridged translation as: *The Future of Japan's Immigration Policy: A Battle Diary*. Japan Focus. http://www.japanfocus. org/-sakanaka-hidenori/2396 [25 March 2014].

Sassen, Saskia. 1984. 'Notes on the Incorporation of Third World Women into Wage Labour through Immigration and Offshore Production', *International Migration Review* 18(4): 1144–67.

Satō, Noriko, Takako Shirai and Takako Terashima. 2011. *Kaigo no Kiso* [The Fundamentals of Care]. Fukushi Jimu Kanri Ginō Kentei Tekisuto 3 [Welfare Management Test Textbook 3]. Tokyo: Iryō Hisho Kyōiku Zenkoku Kyōgikai [National Council of Medical Secretaries Education], Kenpakusha. Available from: http://www.kenpakusha.co.jp/np/isbn/9784767937151/ [20 August 2012].

Savishinsky, Joel S. 1991. *The Ends of Time: Life and Work in a Nursing Home*. New York, Westport, CT and London: Bergin & Garvey.

Schmidt, Mary Gwynne. 1990. *Negotiating a Good Old Age: Challenges of Residential Living in Late Life*. San Francisco, CA: Jossey Bass.

Shield, Renée Rose. 1988. *Uneasy Endings: Daily Life in an American Nursing Home*. Ithaca, NY and London: Cornell University Press.

Silverstone, Roger. 1994. *Television in Everyday Life*. London: Routledge.

Simmel, Georg. 1950. *The Sociology of Georg Simmel*. Compiled and translated by Kurt Wolff. Glencoe, IL: Free Press.

Simoni, Simonetta, and Rossana Trifiletti. 2004. 'Caregiving in Transition in Southern Europe: Neither Complete Altruists nor Free-Riders', *Social Policy and Administration* 38(6): 678–705.

Smith, Stephen Richard. 1988. 'Drinking and Sobriety in Japan'. PhD dissertation. New York: Columbia University.

Sokolovsky, Jay (ed.). 1987. *Growing Old in Different Societies: Cross-Cultural Perspectives*. Littleton, MA: Copley.

Somera, Rene D. 1995. *Bordered Aging: Ethnography of Daily Life in a Filipino Home for the Aged*. Manila: De La Salle University Press.

Spivak, Gayatri Chakravorty. 1987. 'Subaltern Studies: Deconstructing Historiography', in *In Other Worlds. Essays in Cultural Politics*. London and New York: Routledge, pp. 270–304.

Stacey, Clare L. 2005. 'Finding Dignity in Dirty Work: The Constraints and Rewards of Low-Wage Home Care Labour', *Sociology of Health and Illness* 27(6): 831–54.

Stewart, Kathleen. 2007. *Ordinary Affects*. Durham, NC: Duke University Press.

Stott, David Adam. 2008. 'The Japan–Indonesia Economic Partnership: Agreement between Equals?', *The Asia-Pacific Journal: Japan Focus*.

Świtek, Beata. 2014. 'Representing the Alternative: Demographic Change, Migrant Eldercare Workers, and National Imagination in Japan', *Contemporary Japan. Journal of the German Institute for Japanese Studies Tokyo* 26(2): 263–80.

Tahhan, Diana Adis. 2010. 'Blurring the Boundaries between Bodies: Skinship and Bodily Intimacy in Japan', *Japanese Studies* 30(2): 215–30.

Tajfel, Henri. 1970. 'Experiments in Intergroup Discrimination', *Scientific American* 223(5): 96–102.

―――. 1981. *Human Groups and Social Categories: Studies in Social Psychology*. Cambridge: Cambridge University Press.

―――. 1984. 'Intergroup Relations, Social Myths and Social Justice in Social Psychology', in *The Social Dimension*, edited by Henri Tajfel. Vol. 2. European Developments in Social Psychology. Cambridge: Cambridge University Press, pp. 695–715.

Tegtmeyer Pak, Katherine. 2000. 'Foreigners are Local Citizens, Too: Local Governments Respond to International Migration in Japan', in *Japan and Global Migration: Foreign Workers and the Advent of a Multicultural Society*, edited by Mike Douglass and Glenda S. Roberts. London and New York: Routledge Taylor & Francis Group, pp. 244–74.

Thompson, John B. 1989. 'The Theory of Structuration', in *Social Theory of Modern Societies: Anthony Giddens and His Critics*, edited by David Held and John B. Thompson. Cambridge, New York, Port Chester, Melbourne and Sydney: Cambridge University Press, pp. 56–76.

Tisdale, Sallie. 1987. *Harvest Moon: Portrait of a Nursing Home*. New York: Henry Holt & Company.

Tronto, Joan C. 1993. *Moral Boundaries: A Political Argument for an Ethic of Care*. New Haven, CT and London: Routledge.

―――. 2001. 'An Ethics of Care', in *Ethics in Community-Based Elder Care*, edited by Martha B. Holstein and Phyllis B. Mitzen. New York: Springer, pp. 60–68.

Tsuda, Takeyuki. 2003a. *Strangers in the Ethnic Homeland: Japanese Brazilian Return Migration in Transnational Perspective*. New York: Columbia University Press.

―――. 2003b. 'Domesticating the Immigrant Other: Japanese Media Images of Nikkeijin Return Migrants', *Ethnology* 42(4): 289–305.

Turner, John C. 1999. 'Some Current Issues in Research on Social Identity and Self-Categorisation Theories', in *Social Identity: Context, Commitment, Content*, edited by Naomi Ellemers, Russell Spears and Bertjan Doosje. Oxford: Wiley-Blackwell, pp. 6–34.

Twigg, Julia. 1999. 'The Spatial Ordering of Care: Public and Private in Bathing Support at Home', *Sociology of Health and Illness* 21(4): 381–400.
———. 2000a. 'Carework as a Form of Bodywork', *Ageing and Society* 20: 389–411.
———. 2000b. *Bathing: The Body and Community Care*. London: Routledge.
Ungerson, Clare. 2004. 'Whose Empowerment and Independence?', *Ageing and Society* 24: 189–212.
United Nations. 2013. 'World Population Prospects: The 2012 Revision. Key Findings and Advance Tables'. ESA/P/WP.227. New York: United Nations Department of Economic and Social Affairs Population Division. Available from: http://esa.un.org/wpp/Documentation/pdf/WPP2012_%20 KEY%20FINDINGS.pdf [11 November 2013].
Vesperi, Maria D. 1987. 'The Reluctant Consumer: Nursing Home Residents in the Post-Bergman Era', in *Growing Old in Different Societies: Cross-Cultural Perspectives*, edited by Jay Sokolovsky. Littleton, MA: Copley, pp. 225–37.
———. 1995. 'Nursing Home Research Comes of Age: Towards an Ethnological Perspective on Long-Term Care', in *The Culture of Long-Term Care. Nursing Home Ethnography*, edited by J. Neil Henderson and Maria D. Vesperi. Westport, CT and London: Bergin & Garvey, pp. 7–21.
Vike, Halvard. 1997. 'Reform and Resistance: A Norwegian Illustration', in *Anthropology of Policy: Critical Perspectives on Governance and Power*, edited by Cris Shore and Susan Wright. European Association of Social Anthropologists. London and New York: Routledge, pp. 195–216.
Vogt, Gabriele. 2006. 'Doors Wide Shut? The Current Discourse on Labour Migration to Japan'. Working Paper 06/3. Deutsches Institut für Japanstudien.
———. 2007. 'Close Doors, Open Doors, Doors Wide Shut? Migration Politics in Japan', *Japan Aktuell* 5: 3–30.
———. 2011. 'The Political Economy of Health-Care Migration: A Japanese Perspective', in *Imploding Populations in Japan and Germany: A Comparison*, edited by Florian Coulmas and Ralph Lützeler. Leiden and Boston: Brill, pp. 323–46.
Vogt, Gabriele, and Phoebe Holdgrün. 2012. 'Gender and Ethnicity in Japan's Health-Care Labor Market', *ASIEN* 124: 69–94.
Vogt, Gabriele, and Glenda S. Roberts (eds). 2011. *Migration and Integration: Japan in Comparative Perspective*. Tokyo: Deutsches Institut für Japanstudien.
Vos, George De, and Hiroshi Wagatsuma (eds). 1967. *Japan's Invisible Race: Caste in Culture and Personality*. London: Cambridge University Press.
WAN-IFRA (World Association of Newspapers and News Publishers). 2009. *The Power of Print. Strategy Report* 8(5). Available from: http://pressacademy. org/sites/default/files/resources_pdf/The%20Power%20of%20Print.pdf [31 March 2014].
Watson, Wilbur H., and Robert J. Maxwell (eds). 1977. *Human Ageing and Dying: A Study in Sociocultural Gerontology*. New York: St. Martin's Press.
Weiner, Michael (ed.). 1997. *Japan's Minorities: The Illusion of Homogeneity*. Sheffield Centre for Japanese Studies/Routledge Series. London and New York: Routledge.

Wetherall, William. 2008. 'The Racialization of Japan', in *Transcultural Japan: At the Borderlands of Race, Gender and Identity*, edited by David Blake Willis and Stephen Murphy-Shigematsu. London and New York: Routledge Taylor & Francis Group, pp. 264–81.

Williams, Fiona. 2001. 'In and Beyond New Labour: Towards a New Political Ethics of Care', *Critical Social Policy* 21(4): 467–93.

Williams, Fiona, and Anna Gavanas. 2008. 'The Intersection of Child Care Regimes and Migration Regimes: A Three-Country Study', in *Migration and Domestic Work: A European Perspective on a Global Theme*, edited by Helma Lutz. Aldershot: Ashgate, pp. 13–27.

Williams, Raymond. 1976. *Keywords: A Vocabulary of Culture and Society*. London: Croom Helm.

Willis, David Blake, and Stephen Murphy-Shigematsu (eds). 2008. *Transcultural Japan: At the Borderlands of Race, Gender and Identity*. London and New York: Routledge Taylor & Francis Group.

Wolkowitz, Carol. 2006. *Bodies at Work*. London, Thousand Oaks, CA and New Delhi: Sage.

Wu, Yongmei. 2004. *The Care of the Elderly in Japan*. London and New York: RoutledgeCurzon.

Yamamoto, Beverley Anne. 2010. 'International Marriage in Japan: An Exploration of Intimacy, Family and Parenthood', in *The 18th Biennial Conference of the Asian Studies Association of Australia in Adelaide, 5–8 July 2010*. Adelaide: University of Adelaide.

Yamanaka, Keiko. 1996. 'Return Migration of Japanese-Brazilians to Japan: The Nikkeijin as Ethnic Minority and Political Construct', *Diaspora: A Journal of Transnational Studies* 5(1): 65–97.

Yamawaki, Keizō, Chikako Kashiwazaki and Atsushi Kondō. 2002. 'Shakai Tōgō Seisaku no Kōchiku ni Mukete' [Towards Construction of Social Integration Policy]. *Meiji Daigaku Shakai Kagaku Kenkyūjo*, no. J-2002-1.

Yeates, Nicola. 2004. 'Global Care Chains: Critical Reflections and Lines of Enquiry', *International Feminist Journal of Politics* 6(3): 369–91.

Yomiuri Shinbun. 2008. 'Gaikokujin Kangoshi. Taisetsu na Jinzai Toshite Sodatetai' [Foreign Nurses. We Want to Develop Them as an Important Human Resource], 3 August.

———. 2009a. 'Kea no Kokoro, Kokkyō Koe' [The Spirit of Care, Having Crossed the Border], 7 January.

———. 2009b. 'Ikoku de Manabu Kaigo' [Learning How to Provide Care in a Foreign Country], 17 February.

———. 2009c. 'Indoneshiajin Kangoshi Kōho ni Aseri, Chakunin Ikkagetsu, Kokka Shiken ni Kotoba no Kabe' [Anxiety among Indonesian Nurse Candidates. One Month since Deployment, Linguistic Barrier to the National Examination], 15 March.

———. 2009d. '"Sasaetai" Gaikokujin Kaigofukushishi Kōhosha: "Kyōdō" de Shigoto Mitsumenaosu' ['We Want to Support' Foreign Caregiver Candidates: Reconsidering Work by 'Co-working'], 24 May.

———. 2014. 'Gaikokujin no Kaigofukushishi, Sudeni ni 2 Wari ga Kikoku' [Already 20 per cent of Foreign Nurses and Caregivers Have Returned to their Countries]. *Yomiuri Online*, 27 June. Available from: http://www.yo-midr.yomiuri.co.jp/page.jsp?id=100937 [14 January 2015].

Yoshino, Kosaku. 1992. *Cultural Nationalism in Contemporary Japan*. London and New York: Routledge Taylor & Francis Group.

Yulisman, Linda. 2015. 'Indonesia Asks Japan to Review Partnership Agreements', *The Jakarta Post*, Business, 17 January. Available from: http://www.thejakartapost.com/news/2015/01/17/indonesia-asks-japan-review-partnership-agreements.html [17 January 2015].

Zelizer, Viviana A. 2000. 'The Purchase of Intimacy', *Law and Social Inquiry* 25(3): 817–48.

———. 2005. *The Purchase of Intimacy*. Princeton, NJ and Oxford: Princeton University Press.

Žižek, Slavoj. 1994. 'Introduction: The Spectre of Ideology', in *Mapping Ideology*, edited by Slavoj Žižek. London and New York: Verso, pp. 1–33.

Index